ROYAL COURTS
OF
FASHION

NORMAN HARTNELL

ROYAL COURTS
OF
FASHION

CASSELL · LONDON

CASSELL & COMPANY LTD
35 Red Lion Square, London WC1
Sydney, Auckland
Toronto, Johannesburg

© Norman Hartnell 1971

First published 1971

I.S.B.N. 0 304 93830 0

Printed by The Camelot Press Ltd,
London and Southampton
F.671

CONTENTS

ILLUSTRATIONS

PORTRAITS IN BLACK AND WHITE

following page 36

Mary Cornwallis wearing exquisite Elizabethan 'blackwork'. George Gower (*Manchester City Art Galleries*)
Henry VIII in gorgeous apparel. Holbein School (*Walker Art Gallery, Liverpool*)
Diana Cecil, Countess of Oxford. Attributed to William Larkin (*The Executors of the Estate of the late Countess of Suffolk and Berkshire*)
Two of Queen Elizabeth's magnificent dresses. (*Left*) Detail of Armada portrait. (*Right*) Nicholas Hilliard (*Private Collection*)
(*Below, right*) An unknown girl of 1569 dressed in high fashion. British School (*Tate Gallery*) (*Below, left*) Henry, Prince of Wales. Unknown artist (*Copyright reserved*)
Mary Throckmorton, Lady Scudamore, 1614. Attributed to Gheeraerts (*National Portrait Gallery*)
Lady Jane Grey in heavy brocades. Master John, *c.* 1545 (*National Portrait Gallery*)
The Duke of Buckingham and his family. After Honthorst (*National Portrait Gallery*)
Queen Henrietta Maria. Van Dyck (*Copyright reserved*)
Dorothy St. John, Lady Cary. Attributed to William Larkin (*The Executors of the Estate of the late Countess of Suffolk and Berkshire*)
Prince Rupert. Studio of Van Dyck, *c.* 1637 (*National Portrait Gallery*)
Charles I. Daniel Mytens, *c.* 1623 (*National Portrait Gallery*)
Charles II in Garter Robes. J. M. Wright (*National Portrait Gallery*)
Catherine of Braganza. Dirk Stoop (*National Portrait Gallery*)
Mary of Modena in male riding habit. Simon Verelst (*Copyright reserved*)

following page 68

Catherine de Medici. Tintoretto (*Mansell Collection*)
The boy-king Louis XIII. Unknown artist (*Mansell Collection*)
Madame de Châtillon, *c.* 1630. Attributed to Ferdinand Elle (*Copyright reserved*)
Henry III and Louise de Mercoeur attend a water fête at Fontainebleau. Tapestry (*Mansell Collection*)

Marie de Medici (*Mansell Collection*)

The pretty twin sisters Henriette de Blois and Mlle de Nantes. Philippe Vignon (*Mansell Collection*)

Maria Theresa, Empress of Austria. Attributed to Beaubrun (*Mansell Collection*)

Louis XIV with some of his family. Largillière (*Mansell Collection*)

The Sun King ablaze in all his glory. Rigaud (*Mansell Collection*)

Madame de Sevigné. Roger Viollet (*Mansell Collection*)

Madame de Maintenon with her young niece. Ferdinand Elle (*Mansell Collection*)

Mary Bentinck, Countess of Essex. Kneller (*Copyright reserved*)

Queen Anne. M. Dahl (*National Portrait Gallery*)

The Princess of Orange. William Wissing, *c.* 1685 (*Copyright reserved*)

Matthew Prior, *c.* 1705. Simon Belle (*The Master and Fellows of St John's College, Cambridge*)

Mary Isabella, Duchess of Rutland. After Reynolds (*The Duke of Rutland*)

Anne, Princess Royal. Amigoni, *c.* 1734 (*Copyright reserved*)

following page 116

Princess Louisa and Princess Caroline, granddaughters of George II. Francis Cotes (*Copyright reserved*)

George I in Garter Robes. Studio of Kneller (*National Portrait Gallery*)

Marie Antoinette dressed as a country girl. Joseph Caraud (*Mansell Collection*)

Marie Leszczyńska, Polish wife of Louis XV. A.S. Belle (*Alinari/Mansell*)

The Queen's Lady-in-Waiting, 1776. Moreau le Jeune (*Photo Flammarion*)

A lady of the Court of Louis XVI. (*Photo Flammarion*)

Le Comte de Vaudreuil in clothes of subtle colours. Drouais, *c.* 1758 (*National Gallery*)

Madame Roland. J. Goupil (*Mansell Collection*)

Napoleon's sister, Marie Pauline Borghese. Robert Lefevre (*Mansell Collection*)

The Archduchess Maria-Louisa of Austria. Pauline Auzou (*Mansell Collection*)

A sketch of the *Incroyables* and the *Merveilleuses* (*Mansell Collection*)

Madame Récamier. Gérard (*Mansell Collection*)

Napoleon's sister, Marie Murat, Queen of Naples. Vigée-Lebrun (*Mansell Collection*)
Isabella, Marchioness of Hertford. Reynolds, *c.* 1781 (*Leeds City Art Galleries*)
Queen Charlotte, *c.* 1779. Benjamin West (*Copyright reserved*)

following page 148

Martha, Countess of Elgin. Allan Ramsay (*By courtesy of Lord Bruce*)
The Duchess of Argyll when Lady Lorne. Drouais, *c.* 1763 (*By courtesy of the Duke of Argyll*)
Princess Mary, *c.* 1815. Hoppner (*Copyright reserved*)
Mrs Perdita (Mary Ann) Robinson. Romney. (*Wallace Collection*)
Charles X of France. Lawrence (*Copyright reserved*)
Charles, Archduke of Austria. Lawrence (*Copyright reserved*)
Alexander Ivanovitch, Prince Chernichev, 1818. Lawrence (*Copyright reserved*)
George IV when Prince of Wales. John Singleton Copley (*Museum of Fine Arts, Boston, Massachusetts*)
Princess Sophia, sister of George IV. Lawrence (*Copyright reserved*)
Princess Victoria, aged two, with her mother, the Duchess of Kent. Beechey (*Copyright reserved*)
Queen Adelaide, wife of William IV. Sir Martin Archer-Shee (*Copyright reserved*)
The Empress Eugénie and her ladies. Winterhalter (*Giraudon*)
The difficulties of wearing the crinoline shown in delicate sketches. (Photo *Flammarion*)
Queen Victoria and Prince Albert photographed in 1861. (*London Express News and Feature Services*)
The elegance of Queen Alexandra
The bustle becomes accentuated after the decline of the crinoline (Photo *Flammarion*)
Queen Mary in black satin (*Radio Times Hulton Picture Library*)
Edna May, leading lady in *The Belle of New York* (*Radio Times Hulton Picture Library*)
Queen Mary dressed in her own individual style (*Radio Times Hulton Picture Library*)
A genteel version of the hobble skirt (*Mansell Collection*)
Miss Camille Clifford, a stage celebrity, was a setter of Edwardian fashions (*Mansell Collection*)
An Edwardian dress of indisputable impact

FOREWORD

Down the years the glass of fashion has been a mirror of contemporary society. As the social emphasis has changed, so fashion has changed with it—not always for the best, but always as a reflection of taste and social standing.

Time was when life on one level revolved around the Courts of Europe. The Sun King, Louis XIV, epitomized this enclosed world; perhaps more than any other monarch he illuminated his royal heaven while around him moved his aristocratic and dutiful satellites. But he was not by any means alone, for other Courts of Europe set their own standards of elegance. That they often set their own standards of debauchery also was merely a sign of the times.

For several centuries, kings and princes, their queens and princesses —and their mistresses—set the fashions of the day. The class structure of other centuries was vastly more rigid than it is today, so that fashion was inevitably the private parish of the royal, the aristocratic and the rich, who were often neither royal nor aristocratic. Further down the scale the lower orders had neither the time nor the inclination and certainly not the money, to indulge even in fashionable homespun. Thus, as we look back at the visible memorials of the past, fashion and the royal Courts are seen to have been the children one of another.

In this book I have taken the Tudors as a reasonable starting-point. I have ended in 1919, for with the end of the First World War and the disappearance of most of the royal Courts of Europe, the nature and origin of fashion changed abruptly. No longer did the Courts that remained set the fashion of their day, for the 1920s saw the rise of the great couturiers, the new arbiters of fashion who were to set the trends and reflect the radical changes in the social scene. That much at least has altered beyond recall, but since there is still room for nostalgia I have tried here to look back nostalgically on the old and vanished world, for whatever its failings, that lost world has left for us a legacy of exquisite taste and memorable elegance. Finally, I should like to record my indebtedness to Mary Cathcart Borer for her research and assistance in the writing of this book.

March 1971

Norman Hartnell

CHAPTER ONE

THE TUDORS

When primitive man put on his first animal headdress and furs, he probably wanted to indicate to his fellow-men the totemic clan to which he belonged, and from that time onwards the business of clothing his body has afforded him a vast amount of interest and amusement. By clothes and other adornment he found that he was able to express the ideas of status and rank; and at the same time the sexes could be distinguished and their attractions enhanced.

As Western civilization developed, with its elaborate caste system of Royal families and nobility, above rigidly defined classes of decreasing status, clothing came to have a dual purpose. It distinguished social rank and it proclaimed the occupation of the wearer. With the passing centuries, as an increasing choice of materials for clothes became available, the art of costume developed and clothes became ever more important as a means of establishing the wearers' tastes and personalities, their wealth and their physical charms.

Yet there was a paradox about the whole business. The Royal family and the Court set the fashion and the nobility and the gentry copied them, so far as the law and their means would allow. Nevertheless, while conforming to basic fashion, they tried at the same time to express their individualities and personal preferences. This conflict is probably one of the reasons for the wide variety of fashions which flourished in England during Tudor times, when the country was fast becoming rich and prosperous, with ever-widening horizons and markets for her valuable wool, her most important item of trade.

England had no need of essential commodities in exchange, for the population, four-fifths of whom were country-folk, was well under four million and self-supporting. So the sailors brought back luxuries, which included rich fabrics from Europe and the East. To the busy quays of the port of London the city merchants imported 'jewels and precious stones, silver bullion, quicksilver, wrought silks, cloth of gold

I

and silver, gold and silver thread, camblets, grosgrams, cotton, linen fine and coarse, serges, demi-ostrades, tapestry, madder, metallic and other merceries to a great value . . . as well as carpets and brocades, spices and perfumes from India, Persia and Turkey.'

There had been a London trade in furs since Roman times and during the Middle Ages the traders of the Hanseatic League established a fur market at the Steelyard in Thames Street. Close by, the Company of Skinners was established, one of the earliest of the medieval gilds, which drew up regulations for the importing and manufacture of skins into furs.

At this time only the members of the Court and the nobility could afford to wear them. Cloaks were lined with fur and both men's tunics and women's dresses were trimmed with sable and ermine. However, as the export of wool brought increasing wealth to the country, city merchants and their wives took to wearing furs, to the great indignation of their betters, who insisted that people must dress according to their station in life. 'A gentleman must go like a gentleman, a yeoman like a yeoman and a rascal like a rascal.'

Sumptuary laws had been passed as early as the fourteenth century, decreeing that only members of the Court and the nobility might wear ermine and sable and that wives of tradesmen must wear the furs of 'lambs, rabbits, cats and foxes'. This may have been an attempt to preserve the rarer fur-bearing animals from being over-trapped, but was more likely a desperate measure to try to keep the rising middle classes in their place.

When Henry VII came to the throne more sumptuary laws were made. Citizens' wives must wear white knitted caps of woollen yarn unless their husbands were gentlemen by descent. Apprentices had to wear blue gowns in winter and blue cloaks in summer, with breeches of white broadcloth and flat caps. Servants were not allowed to wear gowns which reached below the calf of the leg. No man under the degree of knight might wear gold chains and bracelets or silk shirts, 'upon peine of forfeityre thereof' and none under the degree of gentleman any gold or silver decoration on his clothing.

Court dress at this time, during the first of the Tudors, was relatively simple and very attractive. Women had abandoned the monstrous horned and conical headdresses of late medieval times and taken to flat kerchiefs bound low round the forehead and floating back over the neck. The Queen, the beautiful Elizabeth of York, invariably wore a veil or scarf richly bordered with gems, 'put on like a hood, hanging down on each side of the face as low as the breast'. Dresses were very long, sometimes sweeping the ground, but they were simple and elegant, fitting tightly at the waist, with full skirts and sleeves drawn in at the wrist. The square neck was filled in with a fold of white linen—the partlet—and little jewellery was worn, apart from a rather wide jewelled girdle, with long ends hanging down in front. In winter long cloaks were worn and shoes were simple leather slippers.

The men's costume was a loose, full gown with hanging sleeves over tunic and hose, and they wore flat, velvet caps.

The change came early in the sixteenth century, when Henry VIII established friendly relations with the French Court and there was also a closer contact with Italy and all its magnificence of dress and social life. At first women's costume was less affected than men's and for a few more years maintained a restrained grace. Gradually, however, it became more formal and elaborate. Bodices were stiffened and cut lower in the neck. Skirts became a little shorter, to show the shoes, and were divided in front to display a beautifully embroidered kirtle. The bodice had full hanging sleeves, falling loose to show a lining of fur or brocade, and also undersleeves. These were attached separately and were very elaborate, being slashed and puffed with lawn and drawn in tightly at the wrist, with lawn ruffles.

The simple head-kerchief was replaced by a three-cornered cap built over a wire frame, under which no hair was allowed to show. For a while fashion decreed a high, bare forehead and women sometimes shaved their front hair to produce the right effect. A few years later, however, they adopted the more becoming headdress which Anne of Cleves introduced, though it was designed in Paris and known as the French hood. This was a cap, usually of some dark material, curved in front and fitting the head, but built out on either side of the face with stiffening and with broad streamers hanging down at the back. It was often trimmed with borders of silk, satin or velvet encrusted with gold and jewels, called 'biliments', and remained in fashion all through the sixteenth century. Hair was allowed to be seen again and was most often parted in the middle and fastened with jewelled pins close to the head in coiled plaits.

The Mary Stuart cap was similar but lighter. It was often made of lawn and edged with lace and the front border dipped in a curve or point over the middle of the forehead.

3

Caps like this, but made of black silk with black streamers, were worn by widows.

Clothes were already becoming costly and among the items of expenditure listed in the King's Privy Purse were many of Anne Boleyn's dresses, including a 'nightdress', or what would now be called a housecoat, of black satin, lined with taffeta and edged with velvet, costing more than £10, which was about the annual stipend of a parish priest.

When she was beheaded, she wore ' a beautiful night-robe of heavy grey damask trimmed with fur, showing a crimson kirtle beneath', and a pearl-covered headdress, which she removed before placing her head on the block.

For her lying-in-state at Hampton Court the much-loved Jane Seymour was dressed in a robe of gold tissue, with all her jewels and crown.

Yet Tudor England was essentially a man's world and it was men's costume which became so ostentatious and flamboyant. In essentials it still consisted of a doublet over a shirt, trunks and an outer coat, but these were now all of velvet or heavy silk. The coat was lined and collared with fur and the sleeves grotesquely bolstered and puffed, so that the shoulders were far too wide in proportion to the rest of the body.

Henry VIII dressed himself in the most dazzling splendour. At his coronation he wore a crimson velvet robe, trimmed with ermine, over a doublet embroidered with diamonds, rubies, emeralds and pearls, and at the Field of the Cloth of Gold, when he paid his state visit to the King of France, he wore 'a garment of Clothe of Silver, of Damaske, ribbed with Clothe of Golde, so thick as might bee'.

After this visit he decreed that men's hair should be worn close cut, as it was at the French Court, but beards came into fashion again.

During the brief reigns of Edward VI and Mary Tudor women's dress did not alter a great deal and Mary maintained the standard of regal splendour when she made her triumphal entry into London, after the arrest of Lady Jane Grey, wearing 'a gown of purple velvet, furred with powdered ermin'. Men's dress was a little more subdued, though the rich still wore velvet, satin and silk, while the middle and lower classes wore the same style in cloth, with a flat cap of cloth or velvet, for the sumptuary laws still decreed that people under the rank of a knight's eldest son must not wear satin, damask, taffeta or similar rich stuffs.

It was during Queen Elizabeth's reign that all restraint in dress vanished. In that exuberant and prosperous age there was an increasing rage for fine clothes. The Queen set the pace for she had a passion for beautiful and elaborate clothes. Not only did they please her personal vanity: she regarded them as a symbol of her royalty and of England's increasing wealth and rising power in Europe. The Court followed her and no sumptuary laws could restrain the lower ranks from copying them, so that for a time, they were relaxed. Never before or since have the people of England dressed so gorgeously.

This applied only to the towns, of course, and there were only some 800,000 town-dwellers in England at this time, 200,000 of them being Londoners. The next largest towns to London were York, Norwich and Bristol, but their populations were still very small, rising throughout the century to between fifteen and twenty thousand.

The country people in their lonely hamlets and villages were little affected by the new fashions and most of them still wore their practical worsted and russet. This was a coarse woollen material, varying in colour between natural and a reddish-brown, either spun and woven at home or by local village craftsmen. Yeomen mostly wore fustian—a mixture of wool and linen and, in later times, of wool and cotton—but their wives would sometimes manage a touch of velvet on their best dresses. However, the artisans and craftsmen, living nearer the centres of fashion, very soon became more elaborately dressed than their country cousins.

Among the wealthy and fashionable, both men and women wore a linen shirt or smock next to the skin. Over this women wore several petticoats and a boned under-bodice, which in time developed into a corset. Tight-lacing and the wearing of corsets had been practised intermittently for years and corsets were nothing less than instruments of torture, solid wooden moulds into which the long-suffering wearers managed to squeeze themselves, despite the splinters which pierced their flesh and rubbed their skin raw. They were so disastrous to health that laws were passed forbidding their use, but now French fashion, which was setting the standard throughout other parts of Europe as well as in England, decreed that waists should be compressed again. Catherine de Medici is said to have ordered her ladies-in-waiting to wear corsets which would reduce their waists to thirteen inches.

Over the Tudor boned bodice came the outer dress, consisting of a

B

kirtle or petticoat and a bodice, usually boned, stiffened and padded, which came to a point below the waistline. The neck was sometimes filled in with a partlet, but the neckline grew lower as the century progressed and the partlet was discarded. The bodice had a separate triangular piece in front, called the stomacher, which was fastened to the bodice with ribbons or hooks. The sleeves were also separate and fastened similarly at the shoulders.

Skirts grew fuller and stiffer and eventually were draped over a farthingale. The Spanish farthingale was an underskirt shaped into a cone by rings of wood, wire or whalebone of increasing size, and it was worn almost universally until the end of the century. The French farthingale was a padded roll fastened round the waist so that the skirt stood out in a wide circle and then fell abruptly to the ground, in the form of a cylinder, the hard top edge being softened by a flounce. This is the type of farthingale which Queen Elizabeth wore in her later portraits.

Skirt and bodice were made of the finest satin, silk or velvet and loaded with embroidery and jewels. The skirt was usually divided in front to reveal an underskirt which was exquisitely embroidered in the most delicate flower patterns.

Over all this women sometimes wore a loose-sleeved gown, either for extra warmth or to add dignity for some special occasion, and out-of-doors, particularly in winter, an additional cloak, with sometimes an overskirt as a protection from mud and rain.

Stockings were usually of worsted and held up by garters below the knee, but Queen Elizabeth wore silk stockings, the first woman in England to possess a pair.

Women usually went hatless out of doors, apart from their hoods, but when they did wear hats these were smaller copies of those of their menfolk, of felt or beaver trimmed with feathers, but worn more squarely on the head than the rakish angle affected by some of the Court gallants.

Towards the end of the century a court bonnet was designed. This was a velvet pill-box trimmed with ostrich feathers and jewels. An alternative was the pipkin, which was just as lavishly trimmed and had a small crown and flat brim. With both of these, women wore hairnets of gold mesh lined with silk or of silk thread or even human hair.

Queen Elizabeth adopted the French fashion for scented gloves, which was soon copied by her Court. Scent was used a great deal.

Pomanders of gold, silver or ivory, all beautifully jewelled and enamelled, were worn on the girdle and scent was also hidden in finger rings and necklaces. The favourite was that of the damask rose, which was both distilled and used in a potpourri. A cowslip cream for the skin became popular after the Queen began to use it, for it was said to preserve, beautify and whiten the skin, to remove existing wrinkles and prevent new ones. A milk of almonds, lemon and honey preserved and whitened the hands. A lotion of essential oils of rosemary, camomile, sage, thyme, southernwood and cloves made the hair grow thick and shining. An infusion of the eyebright plant made the eyes bright and sparkling.

Hairdressing became extremely elaborate. That irascible old Puritan, Philip Stubbes, author of *Anatomie of Abuses*, complained that women's hair was 'frizzled and crisped, laid out on wreaths and borders from ear to ear, propped with forks and wire' and 'on this bolstered hair, which standeth crested round about their frontiers, they apply gold wreaths, bugles and gew gaws'.

Hair was often dyed and false pieces added and when the Queen lost all her beautiful red hair and had to take to an auburn wig, false hair became the rage. Women tried to make themselves look like the Queen by wearing auburn wigs and, to acquire her fair complexion and be 'of a pale, bleake colour', powdered their skins, some even going to the lengths of indulging in sympathetic magic by swallowing 'gravel, ashes and tallow'.

When Mary Stuart was put to death, in 1587, she was found to be wearing a wig. She entered the hall at Fotheringhay Castle for her last appearance dressed in 'borrowed hair, having on her head a dressing of lawn edged with bone lace and above that a veil of the same, bowed out with wire, and her cuffs suitable; and about her neck a pomander chain and an Agnus Dei hanging at a black riband, a crucifix in her hand, a pair of beads at her girdle with a golden cross at the end. Her uppermost gown was of black satin, printed, training on the ground, with long, hanging sleeves trimmed with akorn buttons of jet and pearl, the sleeves over her arms being cut, to give sight to a pair of purple velvet underneath; her kirtle, as her gown, was of black, printed satin; her bodice of crimson satin unlaced in the back, the skirt being of crimson velvet; her stockings of worsted, watched, clocked, and edged at the top with silver, and under them a pair of white; her shoes of Spanish leather with the rough side outward'.

Despite all this finery worn by women, the men often managed to outshine them. Basically their costume consisted of a tight-fitting, waisted doublet or jacket worn over a shirt, and breeches. The breeches were an innovation by the fashionable, but countrymen continued for many years to wear their medieval hose.

Throughout the sixteenth century the doublet became increasingly stiff and padded and was pointed in front to well below the waist-line; and eventually men took to the Dutch fashion of the peascod belly, in which the front points were so heavily padded with horsehair or 'bombast' that they bulged and drooped. They were 'stuffed with four to six pounds of bombast' snarled Stubbes.

The breeches were called trunk-hose or galligaskins. They were ballooned with padding to balance the broad shoulders of the doublet and were so slashed and puffed that they were by no means easy to put on and even more difficult to wear.

Cloaks of various lengths were worn over the doublet and sometimes they were of soft, scented Spanish leather. The doublet and hose were usually of satin, taffeta or velvet and cloaks were trimmed with fur or gold braid, with coloured linings often contrasting with the doublet and hose, which sometimes matched but were often themselves of contrasting colours.

Hats were of varying remarkable shapes and trimmings and they were always worn indoors, though they were removed in the presence of royalty or a personage of higher rank.

Men wore earrings, gloves and scent, being particularly fond of civit and musk; and the dandies carried small fans, although many also wore rapiers or daggers and some even gorgets, with all their finery.

There was little difference between the shoes of men and women. They were made of various materials, silk, brocade, velvet or Spanish leather. Early in Tudor times they were flat-heeled, but later the Venetian high-heel was introduced. About 1570 'pantofles', which were a form of patten, were worn to protect the more delicate shoes. These had thick cork soles, which enabled a contemporary critic to observe that we now tread on 'corked stilts, a prisoner's pace'. Men had boots also, but they were extraordinarily loose and ungainly.

From Spain came the fashion, for both men and women, of high neck-ruffs. At first they were wired, but by about 1560 a Dutchwoman introduced starch for stiffening them. This meant that they could become larger than ever. Queen Elizabeth was particularly fond of them but objected to the fashion becoming too widespread.

In 1580 a sumptuary law forbade people to wear them larger than the prescribed size and members of the Ironmongers' and Grocers' companies were stationed at the gates of London to prevent the citizens entering the city with 'monstrous ruffs' or swords and cloaks of undue length. If they refused to reform they were liable to arrest.

The ruffs were of fine white linen or lawn and their laundering was a problem. At first they were shaped into tubular pleats with wooden or bone 'setting sticks', but in the 1570s goffering irons were made. Even so, larger ruffs needed wired props to hold them in place and ultimately they were pinned to wired frames.

As an alternative to the ruff, the Queen and her court sometimes wore large, fan-shaped collars of wired and stiffened lawn, cambric or lace, which grew in size until eventually they reached as high as the top of the head.

The colours of the rich fabrics worn by the wealthy were gorgeous, with romantic names like lady blush, marigold, popinjay blue and devil-in-the-hedge. Various shades of red and orange were popular—Bristol red, flame, lusty gallant, sanguine, carnation, gingerline, maiden's blush, scarlet, tawny, orange-tawny and bronze.

Black with silver or gold became popular at Court towards the end of the century, despite the association of black with mourning, and white was also favoured.

A true medium blue, the symbol of constancy, was the colour worn by servants and apprentices and was therefore avoided by the fashionable, although variations of blue, including lighter shades and greenish blues, were sometimes worn.

Clothes were increasingly expensive. Dresses, which were regarded as heirlooms, were sometimes given as presents. After the Earl of Essex had fallen from the Queen's favour and was in prison, his mother sent her many gifts to try and soften her heart. In the Sidney Papers we read that 'Yesterday the Couwntess of Lester sent the Queen a most curious fine gown, which was presented by my Lady Skudmore. Her Majestie liked yt well, but did not accept yt, nor refuse yt, only answered that, things standing as they did, yt was not fitt for her to desire what she did. . . .'

The Church tried to restrain the growing passion for clothes. In 1563, with the blessing of the government, it published the *Second Tome of Homilies*, which included a sermon *Against Excess of Apparel*. This could be preached by all parsons who had not a licence to preach sermons they had composed themselves and included the

9

protest that 'fashions are at these days so outrageous that neither Almighty God by his word can stay our proud curiosity in the same, neither yet godly and necessary laws, made by our princes and oft repeated with the penalties, can bridle this detestable abuse'.

The sumptuary laws had been relaxed during the early days of the new prosperity but were now revived. They included not only the restriction on the size of ruffs but decrees that only the nobility might wear imported woollen goods. Only those with an income of over £200 a year might wear 'velvet or embroidery, or pricking with gold, silver or silk'. Only those with over £100 a year might wear satin, damask, camlet or taffeta.

Many were the protests from Churchmen and writers about the extravagance of the fantastic fashions and also the fact that they were mainly copied from other European countries and were un-English. In the first act of *The Merchant of Venice*, Portia, discussing with Nerissa her English suitor Falconbridge, the young baron of England, exclaimed: 'How oddly he is suited! I think he bought his doublet in Italy, his round hose in France, his bonnet in Germany, and his behaviour every where.' And some years later, Thomas Dekker in *The Seven Deadly Sins of London* said: 'An Englishman's suit is like a traitor's body that hath been hanged, drawn and quartered, and is set up in several places: his codpiece is in Denmark; the colour of his doublet and the belly in France; the wing and narrow sleeve in Italy; the short waist hangs over a Dutch botcher's stall in Utrecht; his huge slops speak Spanish; Polonia gives him the boots; the block for his head alters faster than the feltmaker can fit him, and thereupon we are called to scorn blockheads. And thus we that mock every nation for keeping our fashion, yet steal patches from every one of them to piece out our pride, are now laughing stocks to them because their cut so scurvily becomes us.'

But the most interesting of all the comments on Elizabethan extravagance of dress comes from Philip Stubbes. The current abuses in England at this time he considered to be 'an inordinate pride in dress, whoredome, gluttonie, drunkenness, covetousness, usury, swearing, the lack of observance of the Sabbath, stage plays and interludes, the appointing of Lords of Misrule, May day festivals, Church Ales, Wakes and Feasts, the horrible vice of pestiferous dancing, music, because it allures to vanity, all games and sports, particularly on the Sabbath, and the reading of wicked books at all times'; and of all these he gives most time to his criticism of contemporary dress.

For Stubbes, clothes were given to us by a rather unimaginative Almighty for two purposes and two purposes only—to hide our shame and keep us warm. Any attempt at decoration and design he rejected as mere sinful pride. The love of clothes was 'a poison in the country'. Native wool was good enough in the old days and should be good enough now. Foreign countries bought it from us eagerly, since they had not been endowed with a commodity of such fine quality, but for English men and women a material 'if it comes not from beyond the seas it is not worth a straw' and now 'there is suche a confuse mingle mangle of apparell . . . and suche preposterous excesse thereof . . . that it is very hard to know who is noble, who is worshipfull, who is a gentleman, who is not. . . .'

Men's hats, he said, were sharp on the crown, like a church steeple, standing a quarter of a yard above the crown of the head, or flat and broad on the crown like the battlements of a house. They were made of silk, velvet, taffeta, sarcenet, wool or even beaver.

'Every article of wear is extravagantly fashioned,' he declared. 'Hats are of all fantastic shapes and some people will have no kind of hat without a great bunch of feathers of divers and sundry colours, peaking on top of their heads, not unlike coxcombs. . . . Many get a good living by dyeing and selling of them, and not a few prove themselves more than fools in the wearing of them. . . .'

Doublets were 'quilted, stuffed, bombasted and sewed, as they can neither work nor yet well play in them. . . . Some are of satin, taffeta, gold, silver . . . slashed, jagged, cut, carved, pincked and laced'.

Ruffs were 'great and monstrous', of the finest cloth that can be got for money . . . 'but if Aeolus with his blasts or Neptune with his stormes, chaunce to hit upon the crasie barke of their brused ruffes, then they goe flip, flap in the winde like ragges that flew abroad, lying upon their shoulders like the dishcloute of a slut'.

He was outraged that shirts were sometimes 'wrought throughout with needle work of silke' and could cost anything up to ten pounds, but some of this embroidery was the attractive Elizabethan 'black work', fine embroidery in black thread on white linen. Its charm was lost on Stubbes, who complained of shirts costing at least a crowne or a noble, 'and yet this is scarcely fine enough for the simplest person that is'.

He had plenty to say about the stuffed and quilted doublets which men were obliged to wear 'loose about them for the most part, otherwise they could very hardly either stoupe or decline to the grounde, so stiffe and sturdy they stand about them'.

He distinguished between Gallyhosen or galligaskins, which reached only to the knee, and Venetian hosen which reached to below the knee and were tied in with silk points.

Pantofles he spurned for their discomfort and impracticability, 'for how should they be easie when a man cannot goe steadfastly in them, without slipping and sliding at every pace, ready to fall downe?'

Coats and jerkins were of all manner of colours and fashions and Stubbes asks: 'Doe they thinke that it is lawfull for them to have millions of sundry sorts of apparell lying rottying by them, when as the poore members of Jesus Christ dye at theyr doores for want of clothing?' And this is the main cause of his discontent.

Cloaks white, red, tawny, black, green, yellow, russet, purple, violet and infinite other colours, some of 'clothe, silke, velvet, taffetie, and such like, whereof some be of the Spanish French and Dutch fashions—some shorte, scarsly reaching to the girdlestead or waste, some to the knee, and othersome trailing uppon the grounde . . .' all of them trimmed with costly lace of gold or silver, he found just as irritating.

He had much the same to say about women's clothes and prefaced his comments with a diatribe on the use of cosmetics, whereby they adulterated the Lord's handiwork. Another of the devil's inventions to entangle poor souls in the nets of perdition, was the wearing of false hair. The making of holes in the ears to hang 'rings and jewelles by' appalled him and the starch that was used for their ruffs he called the devil's liquor.

In his description of the diversity of women's gowns, so many styles are described that it is clear that the dresses were kept for a very long time and handed down from mother to daughter. They were altered and reshaped occasionally and valuable trimming and ornaments transferred from one gown to another.

Who made all these wonderfully intricate clothes? Mostly they were made at home, probably by sewing-maids. Queen Elizabeth must have had a large staff of them for, when she died in 1603, she left an enormous wardrobe of gowns and hundreds of complete costumes, including French gowns, loose gowns, kirtles, petticoats, cloaks and bodices, as well as her special Court gowns for State occasions, all of which were inherited by the wife of James I, Anne of Denmark.

Gentlewomen did much of the embroidery themselves and little girls were taught their embroidery stitches—the cross-stitch, tent-stitch, long-and-short stitch, crewel-stitch and feather-stitch—on samplers of long strips of fine linen, using linen thread and coloured silks, from the time they were very young, for embroidery was one of women's main diversions, particularly for those who could not read.

It was probably with the introduction of carpets and rugs from the East that Tudor embroideresses became so interested in patterns and so skilful in the blending of colour. Flowers were the most usual motif, in particular the Tudor rose. There were few if any pattern books as yet. Women copied flowers and plants from Nature and adapted them, and they may well have borrowed each other's samplers. They probably drew the patterns first and then copied them on to the material they were embroidering, two or three people working perhaps on a single piece, like Helena and Hermia in *A Midsummer Night's Dream*:

> We, Hermia, like two artificial gods
> Have with our needles created both one flower,
> Both on one sampler, sitting on one cushion.

In her last years Queen Elizabeth was described as having 'a face oblong, fair, but wrinkled; her bosom uncovered as all the English ladies have it till they marry'. By this time she was dictating a style of dress so excessively formal that Stubbes complained, with justification, that 'women seem not natural women, but artificial women: not women of flesh and blood, but rather puppets or mommets of rags and cloths compact together'. However, gradually, as the exuberance of the middle years of the century gave place to the sophistication and experience of the later years and the dawn of the seventeenth century, a more tasteful elegance in English costume began to emerge.

CHAPTER TWO

THE STUART COURTS
James I and Charles I

James VI of Scotland had never met his mother's illustrious cousin nor, when he suceeded to the throne of England, had he ever crossed the border, but this unattractive, uncouth Scot, brought up in the spartan, poverty-stricken Scottish Court, now prepared, with his wife, Anne of Denmark, to enter an inheritance which they believed to be of fabulous wealth. They were very soon to be disillusioned, for they found that the coffers of the English treasury were disconcertingly low.

The great wealth of land and properties which Henry VIII had acquired by the dissolution of the monasteries had been largely dissipated by munificent gifts to noblemen, who had thereby founded the fortunes of their own families. Queen Elizabeth had also made many gifts to her favoured courtiers and towards the end of her reign, as the supply was running low, their devotion became markedly cooler.

The Crown derived its income mainly from Crown lands and customs dues, and this money had to cover the expenses of government, of foreign embassies, of troops for Continental wars, of ships and their crews, as well as the Royal family's personal expenses, including the maintenance of the palaces and their gorgeous apparel.

Throughout the sixteenth century, England was bedevilled by inflation, caused by the influx of Spanish gold and silver. During the reign of Henry VIII the coinage had been debased, and although one of the first reforms of Elizabeth's reign had been the issue of a new and stable currency, it did not check the increasing cost of living. By the end of the century prices had risen threefold.

Despite these difficulties, and an income which was steadily decreasing in value, Queen Elizabeth had maintained her large Court as a centre of fashion and culture. She believed implicitly in the divine right of her sovereignty and there was a quality of awe-inspiring grandeur in her behaviour and appearance and in the strict etiquette of the Court, which was adopted by her courtiers and proudly respected by the people.

'The English are great lovers of themselves, and of everything belonging to them,' remarked an Italian visitor. 'They think there are no other men like themselves.'

Hentzner, the German tutor, described the Queen in her last years, when he was admitted to the audience chamber at Hampton Court, to watch her procession to the chapel.

'Next came the Queen, in the sixty-fifth year of her age, as we were told, very majestic. She had in her ears two pearls, with very rich drops; she wore false hair, and that red; upon her head she had a small crown. . . . She had a necklace of exceeding fine jewels . . . her air was stately, her manner of speaking mild and obliging. That day she was dressed in white silk bordered with pearls of the size of beans and over it a mantle of black silk, shot with silver thread. Her train was very long, the end of it borne by marchionesses. Instead of a chain, she had an oblong collar, of gold and jewels.'

Up until the last weeks, when she was desperately ill, the Queen maintained this aura of majesty, though at the last, her godson, Sir John Harington, found her, to his distress, 'quite disfavoured and unattired', refusing to be carried to her bed and lying on the floor, on a pile of cushions.

She died on 24 March 1603. At once a messenger set out to carry the news to King James of Scotland, at Holyrood House. He was thirty-seven years old, married to the penniless Anne, daughter of King Frederick of Denmark and Norway. Like his predecessor, James believed that he was endowed with the divine right, but he had neither the talent nor the inclination to conduct himself with regal dignity. He accepted the homage of the people but gave nothing of himself in return. He was uncouth and ill-favoured, with a shambling gait. He had a passion for hunting but rode badly. His legs were weak through bad nursing in infancy and he had to be strapped to his saddle, where he lolled slackly, making little attempt to manage his horse. 'A horse never stumbled but when he was reined,' he said. He hated the sight of naked steel and as he lived in terror of assassination his doublet and breeches were heavily padded, making him look even fatter than he was.

Among his intimates, James was not so unprepossessing as he appeared in public, for he had a great deal of learning and not a little wit, but he was slovenly in both dress and manners, he ate and drank gluttonously and untidily, and the effect on Court life and fashion was disastrous.

As soon as the coronation had taken place, King James began to examine his financial resources. He had little idea of the value of money, being mean in some matters and wildly extravagant in others. He was prepared to give large amounts he could ill afford to the handsome young men on whom he doted, yet with little aesthetic perception, he was unwilling to spend anything on improving or even maintaining the Court. He cared very little for clothes and towards the end of his life his appearance deteriorated. To the Queen he allotted £5,000 a year, for her separate household, and expected her to dress from the vast wardrobe of clothes Queen Elizabeth had left.

It is small wonder, therefore, that during the early years of the century there was no great change in the fashions seen at Court. A portrait of Anne of Denmark, painted by Paul van Somer, shows her wearing a farthingale, low-cut, pointed bodice, with elaborate sleeves and undersleeves and a stiffened, high-standing lace collar, which could well have been part of Queen Elizabeth's wardrobe, and with it she is wearing a high-crowned hat, turned up at one side and trimmed with an ostrich feather.

The Spanish and French farthingale remained in fashion, for the Queen, perhaps because she had such an excellent supply of them, declared that they were her favourite dress. They grew ever larger and more unwieldy and at a Grand Masque at Whitehall they were so large that some of the women became inextricably wedged in one of the narrow passages leading to the hall where it was taking place, so that many of the guests were never able to pass through.

King James, who thought the fashion ridiculous, issued an edict forbidding the wearing of farthingales at Court. 'The impertinent garment takes up all the room,' he grumbled: but the Queen ignored the order and the fashion continued, the favourite form being tilted a little forward. 'High at the back and low in the front, the sides wide, that I may rest my arms upon it,' as one young woman put it.

Enormous sums were being spent on imported silk and an attempt was made to start a silk industry in England, to save foreign currency. Early in his reign, James ordered the planting of a mulberry garden in Chelsea, for example, and a large mulberry garden certainly existed there during the seventeenth century, but the early experiments in English silk weaving must have been unsuccessful, for it was not until the early years of the eighteenth century that we find any evidence of a silk-weaving industry in Chelsea.

Queen Elizabeth's 'silk-woman' had knitted her mistress her first silk stockings, which had delighted her so much that the woman had promised to knit her some more. 'Do so,' said the Queen, 'for indeed I like silk stockings well, because they are pleasant, fine and delicate, and henceforth I shall wear no more cloth stockings.'

In 1599 William Lee invented a loom for knitting silk stockings and from that time most men and women of the Court took to them, even though they cost anything from £2 to £5 a pair.

The amount of money paid for clothes was still enormous in relation to incomes. A plush cloak could cost £50 and a beaver hat £4 without the trimmings, yet only the top 160 families in the country had an income of over £3,000 a year. It has been estimated that another 8,266 families had an income of about £1,000 a year, while well over 90 per cent of the population had less than £100 a year.

Among men and women of fashion the neck-ruff was still worn and clothes were lavished with trimming, lace, ribbons, braid, embroidery and jewels of all kinds. When Endymion Porter went on his trip to Spain, to try to win the hand of the Infanta for Prince Charles, he borrowed his wife's diamond necklace to wear as a hat-band.

Men wore their swords in embroidered and jewelled scabbards, their gloves were embroidered, fringed and tasselled, their shoes embroidered and trimmed with rosettes. The knee-length breeches were rather narrow at first but within a few years had become baggy and were sometimes hung with tassels and ribbons. Doublets were waisted and pointed, not unlike the women's bodices. The long silk stockings were often worn two or three pairs at a time and were gartered at the knee with silk ribbons and rosettes. London dandies wore boots of fine leather which were loose and ungainly, very different from the sensible riding boots of countrymen. Sometimes the toes were turned up, making them still more difficult to walk in, provoking the pamphleteers to sneer at 'the flapping boot tops of the rich' which 'wasted leather that would serve the bare-foot poor'.

Women's dress maintained the formality of the late Elizabethan costume, the wide skirt over the farthingale, and a rather tight-waisted bodice, like a jacket, with a flared basque and tightly fitting sleeves. The cut was relatively simple, the splendour lying in the fabric and decoration. Fabrics were often patterned and every form of slashing and lace and braid trimming was used, but the favourite form of decoration was embroidery. Black on white was still fashionable, but also embroidery with coloured silks and gold and silver thread. The naturalistic floral patterns of the Elizabethan embroiderers now became more stylized, with repeating patterns of flowers and leaves, and sometimes entire skirts of rich silk or velvet were covered with embroidery.

Up until around 1620 this formality and stiffness of dress was maintained, but the waistline gradually rose and bodices became less pointed. At the same time the men's doublets also became higher-waisted and less pointed, which meant that the peascod belly was modified and the bombast discarded. Yet clothes remained heavy, impractical and graceless, representing a strangely sterile few years in the history of fashion.

Shortly after her arrival in London, the Queen set up her separate establishment at Somerset House which, for a short time, was renamed Denmark House. Here her principal diversion was to perform, with her ladies, in the masques written for her by Ben Jonson and other talented writers and designed and produced by Inigo Jones. Her Court was described as 'a continued maskarade where the Queen and her ladies, like so many nymphs or Nereides, appeared often in various dresses, to the ravishment of the beholders and made the night more glorious than the day'.

The King's main interests remained his library and his hunting, but he enjoyed the masques. One of the most famous and technically ambitious was the Masque of Blackness produced at Whitehall Palace on Twelfth Night, 1605, when the Queen and her ladies, dressed in azure and silver and wearing jewels and ropes of pearls, appeared in a great shell, floating on waves in which tritons, sea-horses and mermaids disported themselves.

The following year, when the Queen's brother, King Christian IV of Denmark, paid a state visit to London, a masque depicting the Queen of Sheba's visit to Solomon was performed, but it had a disastrous ending, for it came after a great banquet and both King Christian and King James, as well as most of the cast, were exceedingly drunk.

'The Lady who did play the Queens part,' wrote Sir John Harington, 'did carry most precious gifts to both their Majesties; but forgetting the steppes arising to the canopy, overset her caskets into his Danish Majesties lap, and fell at his feet, tho I rather think it was in his face. Much was the hurry and confusion; cloths and napkin were at hand, to make all clean. His Majesty then got up and would dance with the Queen of Sheba; but he fell down and humbled himself before her, and was carried to an inner chamber and laid on a bed of state; which was not a little defiled with the presents of the Queen which had been bestowed on his garments; such as wine, cream, jelly, beverage, cakes, spices and other good matters. The entertainment and show went forward, and most of the presenters went backward, or fell down; wine did so occupy their upper chambers. Now did appear, in rich dress, Hope, Faith and Charity: Hope did essay to speak, but wine rendered her endeavours so feeble that she withdrew, and hoped the King would excuse her brevity: Faith was then all alone, for I am certain she was not joyned with good works, and left the court in a staggering condition; Charity came to the King's feet, and seemed to cover the multitude of sins her sisters had committed; and in some sorte she made obeysance and brought giftes, but said she would return home again, as there was no gift which heaven had not already given his Majesty. She then returned to Hope and Faith, who were both sick and spewing in the lower hall.'

When, in the following year, the beautiful little Frances Howard was married, at the age of thirteen, to the fourteen-year-old Earl of Essex, the wedding festivities included a masque at Whitehall dressed with sumptuous extravagance. The men were dressed in crimson and the women all in white, with headdresses of herons' feathers ordered especially by the King from his own hawkers. Jewels and ropes of pearls were borrowed or hired from all over the country and the Spanish ambassador, accustomed as he was to Court splendour, is reported to have been abashed in the presence of so much glittering luxury.

At the end of it all the bride was returned to her parents for a few years and the young Earl was sent abroad to finish his education.

In 1610 a new masque was written for the celebrations following the investiture of Prince Henry as Prince of Wales. Danish Anna, as the people called the Queen, was cast for Tethys, the mother of all the river gods and goddesses, and the young Countess of Essex was nymph of the river Lea.

The Queen's dress, designed by Inigo Jones and his assistants, was of silver gossamer with a sky-blue train, festooned with seaweed of gold brocade, but the Queen spoilt it all by insisting on wearing it over a farthingale, with an enormous ruff, without either of which she did not feel right.

Prince Henry was attracted to the beautiful Frances Essex, but by this time she had fallen madly in love with young Robert Carr, the handsome young man who had supplanted Philip Herbert in the King's affections. Naturally enough, he was hated by both the Queen and the Prince, and to complicate the situation it was at this point that the Earl of Essex returned to England to claim his bride. He had none of the graces of young Carr and Frances took a violent dislike to him, refusing to consummate the marriage.

Living in Paternoster Row was Anne Turner, the attractive young widow of a Cambridge doctor. She was the mistress of Sir Arthur Maynwaring, who was the father of her children. He had very little money but good connexions, and Anne was a clever dressmaker as well as a shrewd businesswoman; so that, with his help and introductions to the Court, she was able to make a good living for them all. She very soon became indispensable to Inigo Jones for his masque costumes and to the ladies of the Court, for whom she not only made dresses but proved a willing confidante. She knew all that was going on behind the scenes, gave advice freely, passed on gossip discreetly and brewed nostrums at fashionable prices. Amongst her secret brews was a yellow starch for ruffs and her yellow ruffs became immensely popular for a time.

Frances, in her distress at the return of her husband and her passion for Robert Carr, had turned to her great-uncle Henry Howard, the great Earl of Northampton, for help. He in turn sent for Anne Turner to comfort and advise his favourite niece.

The question of the annulment of the marriage was discussed. One of Carr's oldest and closest friends was Thomas Overbury, who, with Carr's help, was fast rising to an importance at Court of which Carr and many others were increasingly suspicious. The political motives in the Overbury mystery are largely conjectural, but Overbury, supporting the Prince of Wales' and the Queen's party, tried to prevent the dissolution of the Essex marriage.

In November 1612 young Prince Henry died, at only eighteen years old, leaving the highly-strung and sensitive Charles as heir to the throne. Prince Henry's death was said to be from typhoid fever though there were some at the time who hinted at poisoning. However, the period of mourning was short, for very soon afterwards his sister, Elizabeth, was married to the Elector Palatine, Frederick of Hanover, and the display of wealth and finery at the wedding is said to have cost James £100,000. Ladies of the Court spent as much as £750 on their dresses and on one gown the embroidery alone cost £50 a yard.

The legal commission considering the problem of nullifying Frances's marriage began its long sittings, and while Overbury intrigued to make them refuse the decree, the Essex family, seeing the marriage with Carr an important step nearer the throne, were in favour of it.

By 1613 Overbury had been removed from the scene by the simple expedient of his arrest and imprisonment in the Tower. Yet Frances was still mortally afraid of the harm he might do her cause, until Anne Turner, pocketing a handsome fee, comforted her with re-assurances that all would be well in the end.

Overbury became very ill. Doctors attended him in the Tower and vaguely suggested consumption, but on 15 September he died in agony.

A few weeks later the Essex marriage was annulled and on 26 December 1613 Frances and Robert, created Earl of Somerset by his doting King, were married amidst more lavish splendour. The King, though many of his servants were owed weeks of wages, gave the bride £10,000-worth of jewels and it seemed the happy ending of a fairy tale.

Yet Carr's rapid rise to fortune had made him many enemies and the mystery of Overbury's death was not forgotten. People talked. George Villiers supplanted him in the King's favour and led the whispering campaign about poor Overbury until it became a loud-voiced protest. Before many months had passed an official enquiry was demanded.

In October 1614, by which time Frances was within a few weeks of her first confinement, Anne Turner and her servant were arrested and brought to trial. In the end, Anne confessed that she had sent poisoned food to Overbury and was condemned to be hanged. The story goes that King James ordered her to wear one of her yellow ruffs for her journey to Tyburn, but it was the hangman who, with a sudden turn of vicious humour, dressed himself in a yellow band and cuffs. The crowds were not amused. Anne was young and beautiful and her penitence sobered them to a mood of transient sympathy, and from that time onwards yellow ruffs were never seen again.

Both Frances and her husband were arrested. Frances made the journey from the Tower to Westminster Hall for her trial dressed in black linsey-woolsey, the garb of penitents. Her collar and cuffs were of fine white lawn and on her head was a French hood of black crape. She confessed her guilt and was returned to the Tower. Robert Carr denied all knowledge of the plot but was kept in the Tower with Frances for the next six years, when King James set them at liberty. Robert never forgave Frances and they ended by hating each other. Frances died of cancer but Carr lived on until 1643. Their only daughter had married the Earl of Bedford and Carr lived alone, disgraced and shunned, in a house on the north side of Russell Street, part of the estate which the Earl had asked Inigo Jones to build at Covent Garden.

Early in 1619 Queen Anne died of dropsy, but the Treasury funds were so low that no money was forthcoming for a state funeral until the following May. James did not attend. Though only fifty-four, he was fast falling into senility and more than occupied with George Villiers, who was to become the first Duke of Buckingham.

James lasted for another six years and during that time the Court was debased with drink and debauchery. There were very few women to be seen there and, with no Queen to lead them, fashion showed no marked change, though dressing generally became less formal and ostentatious. Skirts were narrower, the hair was not dressed so high, bodices were not so bejewelled. Cosmetics were still crude, the powder being usually white chalk or starch. 'I wonder not so much that women paint themselves as that when they are painted, men love them,' remarked James in one of his lighter moments. Women had begun to wear masks out of doors during Queen Elizabeth's time but now they became more usual. They also took to patches. 'Some fill their visages full of them,' wrote one observer, 'varied in all manner of shapes and figures.'

Both men and women made a great display of mourning and close relations wore black clothes for a very long time, sometimes two or three years. After the loss of his wife, Sir Kenelm Digby, another resident of Covent Garden, who had been a great dresser in his day, never wore anything but a black cloth suit, black cloak and black slouch hat.

Widows wore a long black veil for the rest of their lives, unless they remarried. Their carriages were draped in black for the funeral and for several years afterwards and sometimes they took to black nightclothes too, sleeping on black beds hung with black curtains.

Charles was twenty-three when King James died in 1625. His first act as king did not endear him to Parliament, for it was to order a state funeral for his father which cost £50,000. He was still unmarried but arrangements had already been made for his marriage to Henrietta Maria, a daughter of the late Henry IV and sister of Louis XIII.

During the previous half-century Court fashions in France, similar in basic design to those in England, had been even more fantastically extravagant, particularly during the reign of Henrietta Maria's grandfather, Henry III, called by the pamphleteers 'the King of the Island of the Hermaphrodites'. He and his favourite courtiers had adopted all the feminine tricks of pearl necklaces and earrings, large ruffs and Venetian lace collars, rouge and powder, scented fans and gloves, with corsets under their busked doublets.

The women were as extravagant, Henry's sister Margaret of Valois leading the fashion for her Court ladies. At the beginning of her journey across France for her marriage to the King of Navarre she arrived in Cognac, where she had a fancy to dazzle the citizens, wearing 'her handsomest and most superb apparel, that she wore at Court on occasions of the greatest magnificence', and admitted that 'extravagance is with me a family failing'.

Henry IV had no taste for all this ostentation. He issued sumptuary laws in an attempt to reduce the import of expensive fabrics and although they affected the ordinary people of France more than the Court, the general tendency was for a quieter style of dressing.

At the age of fifteen, Henrietta was married by proxy to King Charles at Notre-Dame. Then, with a retinue of sixty French courtiers and attended by a concourse of English noblemen, led by the Duke of Buckingham, who had arrived in Paris to accompany her, she set out for her journey to England. She and King Charles met for the first time at Dover and were delighted with each other. They journeyed to Gravesend by way of Canterbury and then embarked on the Royal barge for their State entry to London.

Their happiness in each other was short-lived. The Queen was disconcerted and angry to find the great influence which the Duke of Buckingham, experienced in statecraft, had over the young King and was furiously jealous.

The marriage nearly foundered and her French courtiers did not help matters. With their support she refused to take part in the coronation unless it were performed according to the rites of the

Roman Church and in the end Charles was crowned alone. The number of her French Court grew from sixty to over four hundred and at last Charles, to the surprise and fury of Henrietta, took a firm hand and ordered them all to leave the country. It cost him many thousands of pounds to be rid of them but within a few weeks they had all departed, a good part of the Queen's large wardrobe disappearing with them.

It did nothing to improve his marriage, but then events took a strange turn. In August 1628, the Duke of Buckingham was murdered by a madman. With the main bone of contention so unexpectedly removed, Charles and his wife looked at each other again. They were both older and wiser and they fell contentedly in love with each other.

Their happy family life was reflected in the conduct of the Court. 'The face of the Court was much changed in the change of the King; for King Charles was temperate, chaste and serious, so that the fools, minions and catamites of the former Court grew out of fashion,' wrote the widow of the Cromwellian Colonel Hutchinson. The English Court became once more a centre of culture. It was a place of taste and magnificence where poetry and music, painting and architecture all had their place.

The fashions Queen Henrietta Maria had brought from France were soon to be seen in the English Court. She introduced a more attractive style of hairdressing than the Jacobean pile on top of the head. Hair was drawn back loosely from the face. The back hair was coiled into a knot, and at the sides it was dressed in short curls about the ears, with one or two left long and free, hanging down to the shoulders. Mary, Lady Verney, Lettice, Lady Falkland and Mrs Endymion Porter all took to this style of hairdressing.

Farthingales and ruffs disappeared though the stiffened lace Medici collar was to remain for some years. The long full skirt hung naturally and was more often of plain material than patterned, sometimes slashed in front to show an embroidered underskirt or petticoat. Bodices were cut low on the shoulders and trimmed with lace collars and cuffs. Sleeves were very full and waists rather high, but by the 1640s sleeves had become small again and bodices had strongly boned linings to produce a long narrow waist-line.

Out of doors women wore hooded cloaks, furs, masks, gloves and veils and for riding they adopted masculine jackets over their long skirts, and plumed felt hats which could well have been borrowed from their menfolk, but women did not venture abroad a great deal at this time.

In their portraits by Van Dyck, Abraham Bosse and Wenceslaus Hollar, as well as many other painters, including Honthorst and Daniel Mytens, these ladies of fashion are shown to be wearing the most beautiful jewellery, mainly brooches, earrings and necklaces of diamonds and pearls, but the Queen was not extravagant. In one of her letters she writes to France for a new petticoat-bodice as she has nothing but a velvet one which is worn and too tight and in another she asks for 'one dozen pairs of sweet chamois gloves and one of doeskin'.

Throughout King Charles's reign men wore fitted, hip-length coats of fine cloth, velvet or satin, ornamented with braid and jewelled buckles, either in black, which was becoming increasingly popular, or rich and glowing jewel colours. In place of the ruff, coats were trimmed with collars and cuffs of point lace and sleeves were slashed to show the fine white shirt beneath. Loose breeches reached to the knee, where they were tied with garter ribbons, and the long silk stockings were gartered with silk ribbons and rosettes. Leather boots were still loose and ungainly. Cloaks were knee-length and lined with brightly contrasting silk. Felt or beaver hats were wide-brimmed and high-crowned, with a gold and jewelled hat-band and wide, sweeping plume. Their wide leather gloves were still embroidered and scented, their hair curled and pomaded and they usually wore tight-laced, whalebone corsets to ensure a good fit for their jackets.

Moustaches and neat, pointed beards continued in favour and hair was worn long, either in the French style of a bunch of curls about the face and straggling down the back, with a bow of ribbon tied to the end of the longest curl, or the English style of a better-ordered bob of ringlets reaching no lower than the back of the collar.

The Puritans wore much simpler clothing but it was not until the days of the Commonwealth and the Restoration that the contrast in their appearance became so marked. The extremists cropped their hair and wore a severe felt hat with an untrimmed, broad, flat brim and high crown, a plain jacket and breeches of serviceable cloth in sombre colours, while the women wore long, plain dresses, mostly of grey, with white collars and cuffs, aprons and caps. However, many of the Puritans did not go to these lengths and their clothes remained as colourful as those of the Cavaliers, even during the Commonwealth, as witness the gentleman who, though his coat was of 'sad' colour, which was only another name for brown, recorded buying three yards of gold lace for a waistcoat, together with a scarlet cloak and green stockings. Neither did they all crop their hair and it has been suggested that the term Roundhead came about because so many men in the Parliamentary armies were recruited from the lower ranks of society, who had been obliged by law to wear their hair short.

The tradition of fine needlework and beautiful embroidery continued amongst Englishwomen throughout the century. Practically all women's and children's clothes were made at home and although there were professional tailors in London some of the men's clothing also was home-made. The stitching on the few garments which have survived is exquisitely fine and delicate, the most famous example being the shirt which Charles I wore for his execution, with its beautiful hemstitching.

After the household duties were finished and the midday meal eaten, women must have spent hours at their embroidery. The Puritans sometimes went to the length of embellishing their clothes with texts and holy thoughts, according to that amusing clergyman-playwright Jasper Mayne. In his play about city life during the reign of Charles I, *The City Match*, which was written in 1639, he pokes fun at a Puritan waiting-maid and makes her mistress complain:

> She works religious petticoats; for flowers
> She'll make Church histories. Her needle doth
> So sanctify my cushionets! Besides,
> My smock-sleeves have such holy embroideries,
> And are so learned that I fear, in time,
> All my apparel will be quoted by
> Some pure instructor.

In early Stuart times the Tudor rose was still used a great deal in designs, but within a few years the Oriental influence became very apparent. Patterns beautifully filling the space they were intended to cover were composed of stylized birds and animals, trees, flowers, leaves and trailing vines and were often bordered with a band of pattern based on carnations, pansies and other English garden flowers.

They are easily recognizable and very characteristic of the period. They appeared on cushions and stools, bed covers and curtains, window curtains and other hangings, worked in crewel wool and silk, the two most popular stitches being satin or crewel stitch and long-and-short stitch. Night-caps, garters and underclothes were all embroidered as well as bed linen, and handkerchiefs were either hem-stitched and embroidered with an elaborate pattern of drawn-thread work or bordered with needle-point lace.

In time the animals and flowers became more naturalistic and human figures were introduced. Patterns became subordinate to the pictorial interest and realism was introduced in the smallest details. Human figures were given wigs of human hair or the hair was embroidered in a knotted stitch to represent curls. Tiny beads were sewn into the work to represent pearl necklaces. The faces were some-times painted on smooth silk and appliquéed on to the fabric, though usually they were embroidered in the finest silk, using a small satin stitch. Figures and animals were stuffed with fragments of frayed silk to raise them and make them realistic.

These picture embroideries were sometimes worked on cushions and screens and miniature needlework pictures were used to decorate caskets and book covers. Favourite subjects were Royal pageants in which the figure of Charles I often appeared, and scenes from the Old Testament, particularly those illustrating the stories of Hagar and Ishmael, the finding of the infant Moses and Susannah and the Elders.

'Stump' work was popular for a time. It was a form of collage in which the figures were raised and often embellished with gold and silver thread.

As in Elizabethan times, little girls were taught their stitches on samplers of fine linen. Broderie anglaise or 'eyelet' embroidery was fashionable and the buttonholes were wonderfully fine.

Needlework tapestry, worked in fine wool on canvas, was very popular, the pictures being similar to those of the pictorial embroid-eries. Both James I and Charles I were interested in tapestry-making and it was at this time that the workshop for the manufacture of large tapestries on a loom was established at Mortlake. Many Flemish weavers were employed at Mortlake and they produced some won-derful wall hangings. The Archbishop of York is said to have paid £2,500 for four, representing the four seasons, and the hangings at Corfe Castle probably came from Mortlake, but some very large wall hangings in the Mortlake style were also made entirely by hand.

The Stuart embroideresses had thimbles and scissors, stilettos for their eyelet embroidery and spools for their coloured silks and wools. Special tambour needles have been found and also small wooden moulds, like short thimbles, on which they made their raised, knotted work.

As the troubles between King Charles and Parliament increased and the days of the Commonwealth approached, there was a tendency for women's dress to become more subdued, but the Cavaliers stalwartly maintained their flamboyant finery and for many years they were to outshine their womenfolk.

During the Commonwealth there were no marked changes in style but with the Restoration fashion came into its own again.

CHAPTER THREE

THE STUART COURTS
Charles II and James II

Most English people had little taste for the eleven years of Oliver Cromwell's military dictatorship, but during this time the country's home industries and overseas trade continued to develop. It was no age for the encouragement of the arts, despite the great figures of literature then at work, and although Cromwell loved music it was not allowed in the churches. Most of the theatres had been demolished and the rest were closed. There were a few surreptitious performances at the old Cockpit in Drury Lane, but on at least one occasion the army broke in, cleared the auditorium, broke up the stage, confiscated the props and clapped the players into gaol for a few days.

Yet there were advances in science and education. The society was founded in Oxford which a few years later was to be established in London as the Royal Society, under the patronage of Charles II. The first experiments in improved agriculture were made and the Russell family resumed the drainage of the Fens, which had been halted during the Civil War. Grammar schools became increasingly important and by 1660 there were fourteen hundred throughout the country, as well as private schools, though after the Restoration many of the grammar schools, apart from such long-established foundations as Winchester and Eton, which were already aristocratic, fell into disrepute, being regarded as breeding-grounds of dissent and rebellion against the Crown.

In late Tudor times some of the grammar schools had offered education to girls as well as boys, to replace the opportunities they had lost with the dissolution of the monasteries and convents, but as the Puritan spirit spread and the social position of women declined, the practice was stopped. At Uffington school, for example, there is a note in the records for 1637 that girls be refused admission, for though 'it was a common and usual course' it was 'by many conceived very uncomely and not decent'. The girls of the aristocratic families were taught at home, and for the rest there was little or no education, apart from that offered by a very few boarding-schools, teaching dancing, needlework, music and perhaps a little French.

This decline in women's status was reflected in the fashions of the day. It was a man's world. Men's clothes were more elaborate and costly and for many years the styles changed more quickly.

Yet much of the country's economy was concerned with producing the material for clothes. England's main source of wealth was still wool and out of a population of between five and five and a half million, a million men, women and children were fully occupied throughout the seventeenth century in the spinning and weaving of wool. Both were as yet cottage industries. Weaving had become exclusively men's work and the women and children, who out-numbered the men workers by eight to one, were engaged in the spinning.

Holland began to compete in the manufacture of cloth and Spain was producing some excellent merino wool, but England's main export was still woven cloth, and at the end of the century it re-presented a third of the value of the entire export trade. The industry was protected, the export of raw wool and the import of foreign-made woollen cloth being forbidden.

The trade was run by wealthy merchants who supplied the raw materials and yarn to the chapmen, who in turn distributed it to the spinners and weavers, tramping for miles or riding with their pack-horse trains through the narrow lanes and over the causeways, to reach the isolated villages and lonely farmhouses.

The wool industry was widespread, the three main centres being East Anglia, the West Country and Yorkshire. East Anglia had a tradition of weaving and spinning, passed down by the Flemish weavers who had settled there in medieval and Tudor times. Col-chester and Sudbury made baizes and serges, mainly from imported Portuguese and Italian wool, and by 1662 Colchester had ten thousand woollen workers. In Norfolk weavers produced a wide variety of woollen cloths and also made worsted stockings.

In the West, Somerset, Wiltshire, Dorset and Gloucestershire specialized in fine quality broadcloths made from the wool of the sheep flocks of the Cotswolds and Salisbury Plain and West of England cloth was exported from Bristol and other ports of the west coast to France and Italy and as far afield as the Levant.

In the West Riding of Yorkshire, the developing wool trade in Leeds, Halifax, Huddersfield, Bradford and Wakefield was not yet so important, concentrating on the manufacture of coarse, poor quality cloth for ordinary working folk.

Flax was imported from Ireland for the linen looms of Manchester, although the finest linen was imported from France.

The silk-weaving industry, founded by Flemish weavers, had become well established in East Anglia and there were other small centres throughout the country. It was not until Louis XIV exiled so many French Protestants by his revocation of the Edict of Nantes, in 1685, that a colony of refugee Huguenots settled in London and established the important Spitalfields industry.

Lace-making had been introduced from France many years earlier and was a source of additional income to many cottage women, particularly throughout Buckinghamshire, Bedfordshire and Oxfordshire; and Honiton was already famous for its beautifully fine lace.

Amongst the produce brought back by the great sailing ships of the East India Company was a variety of cotton fabrics from India. Raw cotton, or 'cotton wool' as it was called, had been imported in small quantities from the Near East for many years to make wicks for candles, and at the beginning of the century this trade was taken over by the Levant company.

Weavers used up yarn more quickly than the spinners could produce it, and early in the century chapmen reported a serious shortage of linen thread, which was used with wool to make fustian. Someone had the idea of experimenting with a cotton weft and a wool warp, and it was so successful that the Lancashire spinners were soon demanding cotton from London. Before long regular pack-horse trains were making the two-hundred-mile journey from London to Manchester, laden with 'cotton wool'.

Yet despite all this expanding trade and industry, the Commonwealth had little aptitude for finance and when the penniless King Charles arrived in England he found that, for a long time, outgoings had been exceeding national income by £1,000,000 a year, so that by 1660 the resources of the Exchequer were just over £11.

Ten days before Charles's arrival at Dover, on 26 May 1660, from the Hague, Pepys recorded: 'Mr Edward Pickering told me in what a sad, poor condition for clothes and money the king was, and all his attendants . . . their clothes not being worth forty shillings the best of them. And how overjoyed the king was when Sir J. Greenville brought him some money; so joyful that he called the Princess Royal and Duke of York to look upon it as it lay in the portmanteau before it was taken out.'

For his triumphant journey back to London the young King quickly equipped himself and his courtiers in the best of French fashions. France was by now the most important and wealthiest country in Europe, taking the place which Spain had occupied a century earlier. Louis XIV had come to the throne in 1643, at the age of five, and by 1660 he was married to the Spanish Infanta, Maria Theresa, and had already begun to plan the sumptuous palace of Versailles, where his court was to be maintained with such profligate luxury and set the fashion for the next fifty years for much of Europe.

English fashions by no means followed the French in every detail but the influence was marked. Broadly speaking, from 1660 until the end of the century, Englishman's fashion changed from the immensely baggy petticoat breeches with short jacket, to slimmer breeches with a knee-length coat and under-coat. This was the earliest form of coat and waistcoat. The Vandyke beard disappeared and the long curling locks were shorn to make way for the periwig.

Women's fashions did not change so fundamentally. With the Restoration they wore brighter colours. In many ways their dress was similar to the pre-Commonwealth days, but the skirt was no longer divided and was often set into the waist in full, deep pleats. Later it was bunched up at the sides to reveal an underskirt falling at the back into a train. Then the bunching moved to the back, like an early form of bustle. The long full sleeves were sometimes opened and caught in two or three places with ribbons and jewelled clasps and gradually bodices were cut lower on the shoulders and deeper in front.

Silks and satins, velvets, brocades and gold and silver tissue were the favoured materials and women were beginning to practise the art of blending colours subtly and skilfully.

Shoes were beautifully embroidered and decorated with rosettes of ribbon. Heels, often scarlet, became higher. In the street women wore pattens to protect them from the mud, with wooden soles and straps over the shoes. When they were first introduced these pattens were very difficult to manage but before long each pair of shoes was provided with its own pair of specially fitted pattens.

In cold weather women often used muffs and wore shawls or a fur wrap in the house and for the first few years of the Restoration, out of doors they still wore a hooded cloak.

Nightdresses had become usual by now and women wore a quantity of underclothes, though knickers had not yet been devised. The first under-garment was a long shift of linen or silk, over which went the corset, a torturing contraption of leather, laced tightly in front and stiffened with steel or whalebone. It was a fashion which endured for centuries, despite all the warnings from doctors and protests from women who preferred their comfort. In *The Gentlewoman's Companion*, published in 1675, Hannah Woolley bitterly condemned mothers and nurses who 'by cloistering you up in a steel or whalebone prison, open a door to Consumption with many other dangerous inconveniences, as Crookedness; for Mothers striving to have their daughters small in the middle, do pluck and draw their bones awry'.

She had every justification for this protest. There was the terrible example of a little girl who died at the age of two. 'I had the advice of a very able physician,' wrote her father. 'His judgment was that her iron bodice was her pain and had hindered her lungs to grow, and truly the surgeon found her breastbone pressed very deeply inwards and he said two of her ribs were broken. Both the doctor and the surgeon did conclude that going into the bodice so young . . . hastened her death.'

Yet even Hannah Woolley would not have Englishwomen 'by inconsiderate looseness run into a deformed corpulence, like the Venetian ladies who seldom lace themselves at all'.

Over the corset ladies of fashion wore a tight-fitting bodice and then a multiplicity of waist petticoats, the outer ones beautifully embroidered and trimmed with lace.

The people were delighted with their new King Charles II, so tall and slim, dark, elegant and handsome, but men's Court fashions for the first year or two of the Restoration were very odd indeed. Randall Holmes, writing in 1684, said that men's clothes at the beginning of the reign consisted of 'short-waisted doublets and petticoat breeches, the lining lower than the breeches, tied above the knee, ribbons up to pocket-holes half the length of the breeches, then ribbons all about the waistband, the shirt hanging out'.

The petticoat breeches were an awkward fashion. Pepys met a friend one day who told him 'of his mistake . . . to put both his legs through one of the knees of his breeches, and went so all day': and a character in Wycherley's play *The Gentleman Dancing-Master* remarked: 'While you wear pantaloons they make thee look and waddle, with all those gewgaw ribbons, like a great, old fat slovenly water dog.'

Bunches of ribbons were worn everywhere. On one pair of petticoat breeches 250 yards were used. Doublets had wide lace collars and with their broad-brimmed and gaily feathered hats men wore short cloaks swinging romantically from their shoulders.

The ungainly high boots gave place to long, narrow, square-toed shoes with elaborate buckles, which were worn with silk stockings gartered high with rosettes of ribbon and sometimes padded with bran to give a good calf.

Charles was crowned at Westminster Abbey on 23 April and the previous day Pepys watched the procession from the Tower to Whitehall Palace. 'It is impossible to relate the glory of this day, expressed in the clothes of them that rid . . .', he wrote. 'Embroidery and diamonds were ordinary among them. The King, in a most rich embroidered suit and cloak, looked most noble. So glorious was the show with gold and silver, that we were not able to look at it, our eyes at last being so much overcome with it.'

The following year arrangements were completed for the King's marriage to Catherine of Braganza, daughter of the Queen Regent of Portugal. Portugal had only recently freed herself from the rule of Spain and was a close ally of France. Spain protested at the match with the English throne, which was throwing the balance of power in Europe against her, and many in England were dubious of this obvious strengthening of French influence in Europe, apart from the fact that Catherine was a Roman Catholic. However, Portugal was delighted with the match, the Queen offering a rich dowry which included half a million pounds' worth of gold, the island of Bombay and a share in the Portuguese trade with Brazil and the East Indies. She also offered the port of Tangier, of which the English duly took possession, but it proved to be no great asset. Corsairs made the whole of the North African coast extremely dangerous at this time and twenty years later England abandoned Tangier 'because it had become a nest of papacy where Irish troops and Romish bastards could disport themselves unheeded'.

Escorted by Lord Sandwich, Catherine set sail for England. The gold she was to have brought with her, perhaps to the impoverished Charles her most valuable asset, never materialized. Her mother sent the excuse that the recent war with Spain had exhausted the national coffers for a time. She sent half the value in merchandise, promising the rest in gold at a future date, but it was never to come.

Charles and Catherine met for the first time at Portsmouth and there they were married. 'There is not anything in her face that can in the least shock one,' said Charles. Catherine was not beautiful but she was by no means entirely unattractive, which was more than could be said for her ladies-in-waiting, who were all quite exceptionally ugly.

According to Count Grammont, Catherine was a woman of sense, with an amiable disposition, but was lacking in personal charm and 'gave but little additional brilliance to the Court either in her person or in her retinue . . . six frights who called themselves maids of honour, and a duenna, another monster, who took the title of governess to those extraordinary beauties'.

Unfortunately for Catherine, she fell in love with Charles. All went well for the first few weeks, for only a few days after the marriage Charles's mistress, Lady Castlemaine, gave birth to his son, but when she was in the public eye again and Charles suggested that she should join Catherine's court, the trouble, not surprisingly, began. Charles was adamant. Catherine had no alternative but to suffer her presence and when later she adopted a policy of treating her with cordiality people professed to be shocked, so poor Catherine pleased no one.

Charles could not afford to maintain all the Royal palaces. Many had fallen into disrepair and their treasures had been dispersed during the Civil War and the Commonwealth. He concentrated on the renovation and refurnishing of Windsor, Hampton Court and Whitehall. Windsor was always his favourite retreat but Whitehall was the most important of the Royal palaces and much of the looted treasure was restored to it, including many Raphaels and Titians. St James's became the official residence of the Duke of York and here Catherine and her Portuguese ladies had their Catholic chapel. Charles also ordered the restoration of Greenwich Palace. Nonsuch, which was fast falling into decay, was ultimately given to Lady Castlemaine, who had it demolished for the value of the materials.

Whitehall was the centre of London's fashion and culture as the Royal Exchange was the centre of the City's commerce, and it was in the privy garden of the palace that, one day in 1662, Pepys saw 'the finest smocks and linnen petticoats of my Lady Castlemaine's, laced with rich lace at the bottom, that ever I saw; and did me good to look upon them'.

Pepys, being the son of a tailor, took a great interest in clothes. When Elizabeth wanted 'a new petticoat of the new silk striped stuff, very pretty', he went to Paternoster Row 'and bought her one, with Mr Creed's help, a very fine riche one, the best I did see there and sent it by Creed to the tailor's to be made up'.

Paternoster Row was the fashionable place for shopping. 'This street before the Fire of London,' wrote John Strype, 'was taken up by eminent Mercers, Silkmen and Lacemen; and their shops were so resorted to by the nobility and gentry in their coaches, that oft times the street was so stopp'd up that there was no passage for foot passengers.'

Pepys wrote about his new suit of purple velvet trimmed with gold and his black suit trimmed with scarlet ribbons. Like most men connected with the Court, he spent more than he could afford on clothes. 'This morning came home my fine camlet cloak with gold buttons, and a silk suit, which cost me much money, and I pray God to make me able to pay for it.'

It was in February 1664 that the Duke of York first appeared at Court in a periwig. The fashion was French and is said to have been designed by a French hairdresser to hide the Dauphin's round shoulders. Be that as it may, the fashion spread to the Courts of Europe.

'And I to White Hall to the Duke: where he first put on a periwigg today,' recorded Pepys, 'but methought his hair cut short in order thereto did look very pretty of itself, before he put on his periwigg.'

It was not until the following April that King Charles began to wear one and then they became high fashion and, in various forms, were to be worn for the next century.

The wigs were made mostly of women's hair, which became a valuable commodity. Money for live hair was advertised by the barbers and they would travel through the country-side buying it from the village girls. Men carried ivory and tortoiseshell combs to tend their precious wigs, for they were costly affairs. The very long and full French wigs had curls sometimes eighteen inches long and came in black, brown or grey, but there was a smaller form which men usually wore indoors when they were relaxing and had changed from their tight and expensive clothes into a loose robe.

36

An exquisite example of the famous Elizabethan 'blackwork'—which is of black silk
embroidery upon fine white linen—worn
here by Mary Cornwallis, with a dress of
black velvet

Although the flamboyant Henry VIII always appeared in apparel as gorgeous as this, he was still outshone by the Court ladies

Diana Cecil, Countess of Oxford, in a splendid dress with foliage-like decoration appliquéed to the two front panels to hang freely

Elizabeth Tudor loved sumptuous clothes and above are two dresses thick with encrusted precious jewels, magnificent in their ostentation and incredible in their workmanship

Below: On the right an unknown girl of 1569 dressed in high fashion for the young nobility. She wears a chic little feather-sprouting hat as does Henry, Prince of Wales, in the next century

Mary Throckmorton, Lady Scudamore, is still wearing in 1614 the Tudoresque fashion of her younger years. A dress of two differing materials, an overdress of cut velvet and an underdress and sleeves of velvet embossed metal tissue

Poor little Lady Jane Grey—who was beheaded at the age of sixteen—seems heavily clothed in dark brocades and vast fur sleeves which may well have been lynx—a somewhat impoverished pelt

The Duke of Buckingham and his family.
The Duchess and her daughter both wear
the sloping shoulder-line broadened by the
framework of the collar and the under-
padding of the banded sleeves. The Duke,
with his rich but sombre appearance, makes
a perfect foil for his womenfolk

A fringe of kiss-curls frames the pretty
French face of Queen Henrietta Maria,
wearing a becoming dress of taffeta. Her
balloon sleeves are deliciously cuffed with
garlands of leaves, probably made of net,
the edges oversewn with metal thread

A sleeveless overmantle heavily embroidered with gold along its full hem is held by Dorothy St. John, Lady Cary, across her equally magnificent dress. Minute embroidery is on the bodice and sleeves, with a different design around the skirt. An ankle-length border of heavily gold *passementerie* reveals her sharp-heeled and sharp-toed slippers

A perfect dandy is Prince Rupert in his flared tunic of cross-way cut, his voluminous sleeves embroidered and split to show yet another sleeve; the same embroidery edging his waistcoat and decorating his velvet breeches. A light touch is the Vandyke lace he wears below his knees and around his wrists and throat

Charles I retains something of the Elizabethan look about his slashed sleeves. Some time elapsed before boots became more close-fitting

Charles II, as handsome as famed, in Garter Robes. Gone are the Vandyke beard and the natural long hair—replaced by a splendid periwig falling luxuriantly to his shoulders

Plain little Catherine of Braganza was accompanied to England by six especially ugly maids of honour for her marriage to Charles II. Her hair was crimped into corrugations. This deep *berthe* collar of lace must have been very flattering. The stiffened cuffs show off her carefully posed hands

Mary of Modena, dressed in richly embroidered male riding habit, holding a feathered and beribboned hat in her right hand and a hunting crop in her left

Charles always wore black wigs although towards the end of the century they were often powdered, the powder being made from starch, burnt alabaster, plaster-of-Paris or flour, a fashion of which Louis XIV did not approve. They were scented with ambergris, musk, civet, violets, orris root, rose, bergamot, orange flower and jasmine. Apothecaries offered 'The Secret White Water' to curl them after they had been in the rain, while London's enterprising underworld trained small boys to sit astride their fathers' shoulders and snatch them from the heads of passers-by.

King Charles had much to contend with during the middle years of the 1660s—the plague, the great fire of London and the Dutch war. In the autumn of 1666 he announced a dress reform. Pepys first mentioned it on 8 October. 'The King hath yesterday in Council declared his resolution of setting a fashion for clothes which he will never alter. It will be a vest, I know not well how; but it is to teach the nobility thrift and will do good.'

Less than a fortnight later, Pepys was to see this new fashion for himself and approve of it. 'This day the King put on his new vest, and I did see several persons of the House of Lords and Commons too, great courtiers, who are in it; being a long cassocke close to the body, of black cloth, and pinked with white silk under it, and a coat over it, and the legs ruffled with black riband like a pigeon's leg; and, upon the whole, I wish the King may keep it, for it is a very fine and handsome garment.'

The fashion was a deliberate effort to shake off the influence of French fashion and rid Englishmen of the sneer that they were 'the apes of Europe'. Evelyn wrote at the time: 'To Court, it being the first time his Majesty put himself solemnly into the Eastern fashion of vest, changing doublet, stiff collar, bands and cloak, into a comely dress after the Persian mode, with girdle or straps, and shoe-strings and garters into buckles, of which some were set with precious stones, resolving never to alter it, and to leave the French mode, which has hitherto obtained to our great expense and reproach. Upon which divers courtiers and gentlemen gave his Majesty gold by way of wager that he would not persist in this resolution.'

However, the fashion remained, though with certain moderations, for shortly afterwards the King complained that the 'pinking upon white' made the members of the Court look 'too much like magpyes' and ordered a new suit in plain black velvet.

Pepys had very soon ordered the new style for himself and by

3 November was writing in his diary about his new vest 'and coat to wear with it, and belt, and silver-hilted sword', in which he liked himself mightily and so did his wife. But it was a very cold day and going up the river to Whitehall, he was 'mighty fearfull of an ague', his vest being new and thin and the coat cut 'not to meet before upon my breast'.

The ladies of the Court adopted an air of elegant negligence in their silk and satin dresses. Trains were often worn at Court. The low necks of the tight, low-waisted bodices grew lower and drooped more alluringly from the shoulders. Sir Peter Lely's portraits show the ladies with their hair arranged in soft ringlets on either side of the face. Pepys saw the Queen 'in a white waistcoat and a crimson short petticoat and her hair dressed *à la négligence* mighty pretty'.

There were some bizarre dressers amongst the Court ladies, the most notorious being the Duchess of Newcastle, author of *Poems and Fancies*. 'And first let me ask if you have seen a book newly come out made by my Lady Newcastle; For God's sake if you meet with it, send it to me; they say 'tis ten times more extravagant than her dress,' wrote Dorothy Osborne. After Dorothy had read the book she said that she was 'persuaded there are many soberer people in Bedlam'.

About 1670 muslins were imported from India and became extremely popular, the Duchess of Newcastle being particularly partial to them. At a Court party at which the King was present, Miss Hamilton announced that a lady was waiting to be admitted who 'must have at least sixty ells of gauze and silver tissue about her, not to mention a sort of pyramid upon her head, adorned with a hundred thousand baubles', and the King was 'ready to wager that it was the Duchess of Newcastle'.

It was in 1670 that Charles went to Dover to meet his greatly loved youngest sister, Henrietta, Duchess of Orleans. Amidst the festivities arranged for the meeting, the secret Treaty of Dover was drawn up, by which, for an annual subsidy of 2,000,000 livres from Louis XIV, Charles was to make a perpetual alliance between England and France.

There were nearly two hundred and fifty people in Henrietta's entourage, amongst them a maid-of-honour, Louise de Keroualle, who quickly took Charles's fancy. She returned to France with Henrietta but a few weeks later was back in England as the King's mistress, being given the title of the Duchess of Portsmouth.

The French stay at Dover was only for a few weeks but the latest

Paris fashions of Henrietta's retinue caused a vast amount of amusement and ridicule amongst the Kentish folk, many of whom were notoriously rude to all foreigners. The French ladies were wearing large circular hats which the English called cartwheels, and the gentlemen wore extremely short coats with broad waist-belts.

This same year saw the founding of the Hudson's Bay Company under a Royal Charter granted by Charles, with Prince Rupert appointed the first Governor. The first company meetings were held in Prince Rupert's private quarters in the Tower of London and here the first consignments of furs were stored. The quality and quantity of furs reaching London was so high that European dealers were soon coming to London to buy and the city became the world centre of the fur market. Apart from all the other varieties of fur the company had to offer, they held the monopoly of beaver, and men continued to wear beaver hats for the next hundred and fifty years, until they were outmoded, about the time of Waterloo, by the tall silk hat.

The Duchess of Portsmouth was an extremely elegant woman and her style of hairdressing, with tight bunches of curls on either side of a flat, central parting and two or three long curls hanging over the shoulder, was copied by many of the ladies of the Court, while bunches of false curls were sometimes worn on the forehead.

Lace caps with ribbon bows were fashionable as well as lace veils and hoods. While bodices remained much the same, with elbow-length sleeves, skirts were now bunched up both at the sides and the back.

In 1675 the beautiful Hortense Mancini, niece of Cardinal Mazarin, arrived in England, fleeing from her dour and eccentric husband, the Duc de la Meilleraye. She was now twenty-eight but as a girl there had been talk of her marriage with Charles. However, Mazarin thought his prospects as an exiled prince not good enough and when he became King of England, the Council considered her unsuitable. Now he received her with great sympathy and kindness. Her husband had appropriated her large fortune and she was almost penniless, but Charles gave her an allowance of £4,000 a year.

Somehow the King managed to keep all his high-born mistresses on good terms with each other. Only six days before his death on 6 February 1685, at the age of fifty-four, Evelyn saw him entertaining Barbara Castlemaine—now the Duchess of Cleveland—the Duchess of Portsmouth and Hortense Mancini, who used the style of the Duchesse de Mazarin, all at the same time. His more homely mistresses, such as Nell Gwynn and Moll Davis, did not mix in these high-born circles but were established conveniently near at hand, Nell Gwynn in Pall Mall, looking on to St James's Park, and Moll Davis in a smart new house in St James's Square.

James II's troubled reign was too short to have any noticeable effect on fashion. His first wife, Anne Hyde, was dead, their two daughters married, Mary to Dutch Prince William of Orange and Anne to Prince George of Denmark. His second wife was Mary of Modena, his mistress the uncomely but amusing Catherine Sedley, Countess of Dorchester, whom the Queen, though twenty-five years younger than her husband, had the strength of character to turn out of Whitehall to a house in fashionable St James's Square.

Court fashions remained much as in Charles II's time, with all the painting, powdering and patching, for throughout the seventeenth century cosmetics were used a great deal.

Evelyn observed that 'women began to paint themselves, formerly a most ignominious thing' yet it was no newer than the practice of dyeing the hair, about which Pepys was so complaining. 'This day my wife began to wear light coloured hair, quite white almost, which, though it makes her look very pretty, yet not being natural, vexes me. . . .'

Up to this time a good deal of mercury had been used in the making of cosmetics and its effect on the skin was disastrous, which explains why many of the new advertisements now made a point of stating that their preparations were 'entirely without mercury or any such harmful thing in it'.

Talc, which is still used in the preparation of face powder, had just been introduced and a concoction called 'water of Talc and Pearl' became very popular for a while.

In London the beauty doctors were setting up practice. One advertised night masks, forehead pieces, red pomatum for the lips, a paste to smooth and whiten the hands, a tooth powder to cleanse and whiten the teeth and a plaster to take off hair from any part of the body. She also 'shaped the eyebrows, making them perfectly beautiful, without any pain, and raised low foreheads as high as you please'.

The forehead pieces were strips of soft leather or linen, soaked in a mixture of spermacetti, wax and oil, and they were bound to the forehead at night-time to keep the skin in good condition and smooth out wrinkles.

Oil of vitriol was recommended to turn black hair a chestnut colour. An abrasive powder made of snuff, ashes of tobacco, gum and myrrh was used as a dentifrice. This was either rubbed on to the teeth with the fingers or applied with a toothbrush made from the fibres of a dried root of marshmallow: and dentists, both male and female, made false teeth with which, they confidently announced, one could eat.

Herbalists as well as beauty doctors now opened shop, selling herbal cosmetics and the aromatic waters of lavender, elder flower and rosemary. Scent was used a great deal, not only on the person but for linen and clothes, in presses and chests and sprinkled about the room.

Although the use of cosmetics was widespread amongst women of fashion by the end of the century, the habit came in for a great deal of criticism. When the wife of Pepys's cousin took to rouge he re-marked: 'Still very pretty, but paints red on her face, which makes me hate her.'

Queen Mary of Modena used rouge but confessed it each day to her Italian confessor.

Patching was still fashionable and the literary Duchess of New-castle had 'many black patches, because of pimples about her mouth'.

Women had used small hand mirrors by Elizabethan times and now they had toothbrushes. Without piped water washing and bath-ing were obviously not easy and except where there was a good supply of servants to fetch and carry it, there was no marked enthusiasm for the process. Mary of Modena had a bathing closet at St James's Palace, the curtains of rich Indian silk enclosing two wooden tubs. In the days of the Commonwealth the physician who had attended Charles I had tried to introduce steam baths of the kind used in Scandinavia, but both Parliament and the College of Physicians opposed the idea on the grounds that it might lower moral standards. In London there were one or two by the time of the Restoration. 'My wife busy in going with her woman to the hot-house to bathe herself after her long being in doors in the dirt,' wrote Pepys, 'so that she now pretends to a resolution of being hereafter very clean. How long it will hold I can guess.'

Yet there was a plentiful supply of soaps, including Joppa, Smyrna,

Jerusalem, Genoa, Castille, French, Curd, Irish, Bristol and Windsor, either in block or liquid forms. There were also coloured and scented 'wash balls' made from rice flour, fine flour, starch powder, orris root and the deadly white lead which was so injurious to the skin.

CHAPTER FOUR

FRENCH COURTS OF THE RENAISSANCE

The Court fashions of sixteenth-century France were, in the main, wildly extravagant and ostentatious, but there were brief periods when sumptuary laws, though never observed for long, subdued the splendour and glitter.

When Henry II came to the throne in 1547, his laws forbade the wearing of such expensive luxuries as cloth of gold and silver, gold lace and satin. His edicts regulated the fashion in strict detail, ordaining not only the types of material which the different classes were permitted to wear, but also the colours. Princes and princesses were allowed to wear costumes entirely of crimson, but nobles and their wives could wear only one crimson article of dress. Ladies of lesser rank might wear any colour but crimson and those socially beneath them had to be content with dull red or black. It must have been agonizing for the social climbers and it is small wonder that the laws were so often flouted.

When the King died, in 1559, the year after Queen Elizabeth I came to the throne of England, the brilliance of the French Court revived, its star being the superbly beautiful Diane de Poitiers, the late King's mistress. His widow, Catherine de Medici, put herself into black from head to foot for the rest of her life, which lasted through the next three troubled reigns, wearing a wide black skirt, a black pointed bodice, with large black wing-sleeves floating from her shoulders, a black collar standing high round her ruff and a black cap which came down on to her forehead in a point; and over all this flowed a long black mantle. She was a sombre figure, 'black like the night, black as her soul', yet she dominated her Court, and although black, white and grey were the popular colours and Diane de Poitiers' distinctive dress was black and white, the Court ladies glittered unrestrainedly in lace and jewels.

43

The Tuileries was sumptuously furnished, its painted and gilded walls hung with embossed and gilded Cordova leather, its parquet floors strewn with Oriental carpets. From Italy Catherine had brought her astrologer and alchemist, Cosmo Ruggiero, who, in a room in the Tuileries, connected by a secret staircase to her private apartments, concocted perfumes, creams, lotion and powders for her, and who knows what other sinister brews besides, to further her dark plots.

Despite the religious wars which ravaged the country, Catherine entertained lavishly and, surrounded by her maids of honour, the 'Queen's Flying Squadron', presided over sumptuous banquets and balls and lavishly staged tournaments. The Flying Squadron were chosen for their brains, beauty and impeccable pedigrees, and they served as alluring enchantresses to ensnare men, with promises they seldom fulfilled, into unwise confidences and confessions which were speedily reported to the Queen. They were the most glamorous spies the world had ever known and only with Catherine's permission would they permit themselves to become the mistresses of the men they were betraying.

The Court paraded in the richest clothes of silk, brocade, velvet and lace, adorned with jewels, gold and silver, and more than one foreign ambassador was moved to exclaim that 'the world had never seen anything like it before'.

The dress was elegant and greatly enhanced by the beautiful lace ruffs which Catherine had introduced from Italy. They were moderate in size as yet and the skill of the Renaissance lace-makers was superb, the three main centres of their craft being Brussels, Genoa and Venice.

Henry II's successor, his son Francis II, who had married Mary Stuart, died within a few months of his accession and in 1560 his brother, Charles IX, came to the throne.

Fashions changed little during the fourteen years of his reign, remaining as lavish and luxurious as ever, but his Court was a cruel and sinister place, the 'Court of silk and blood', during which the terrible massacre of the Huguenots on St Bartholomew's Day was allowed to take place. It was the home of intrigue and passion. Love affairs were inextricably involved with political plotting and the beauty and luxury were a mask for squalor of thought and the most ruthless cruelty.

In 1574 Henry III succeeded to the throne. As a youth during the French conquest of Poland he had proved himself a brilliant soldier.

On his way back to France he stayed for a while in Venice and there his personality underwent a strange metamorphosis, for when he arrived in Paris it was all too clear that he had contracted the 'Italian disease'. When he came to the throne he was rouged and powdered and covered with jewels, and at a court fête which took place shortly afterwards he appeared dressed as a woman, in a gown of pink damask, embroidered with pearls. The vast sleeves were tied with gold and silver threads and fastened with pearl and emerald clasps. He wore long emerald, pearl and diamond earrings. His hair and beard were dyed and scented with violet powder.

A banquet was spread under the trees of the park at Chenonceaux and here he and his beautiful young men were served by his mother's Flying Squadron, wearing dresses cut so low that they revealed their breasts and under which they were completely naked.

Henry was passionately interested in all matters of women's dress and was said to starch his wife's ruffs and dress her hair himself.

Though like his predecessors he issued sumptuary laws which were at first resented and then ignored, he led the Court into the most extraordinary fashions, reaching a point where his young men, with their scent and fans, earrings and necklaces, were hardly distinguishable from the women. Even more bizarre were his moods of contrition, when he would appear with his followers in the coarse woollen robes of the penitent flagellants.

In the end he was murdered and in 1589 Henry IV came to the throne of France.

Morally he was the exact opposite of Henry III for he was a great womanizer and for the first nine years of his reign he shocked the Court (which one would have thought was inured to the vagaries of its rulers by this time), by living openly with his mistress, Gabrielle d'Estrées and their children; and when, in 1600, he married Marie de Medici, he expected her and their children to live together, in felicitous harmony, with Gabrielle d'Estrées, his other mistresses and the numerous bastards.

'In truth, I have never seen anything more like a brothel than this Court,' declared the envoy of the Grand Duke of Tuscany.

The lives of the royal family, their dressing, their undressing and their meals, were conducted entirely in public and the corridors of the palace were crowded from morning till night with courtiers seeking preferment or favour and vying with each other in the splendour of their dress.

Fashion did not change fundamentally but grew increasingly lavish and vulgar. At the christening of the Royal children in 1606 the Queen's dress was 'covered with thirty-two thousand pearls and three thousand diamonds'. It was 'beyond rivalry and priceless', but the ladies of the Court did their valiant best to maintain the standard, spending far more than they could afford on dresses of brocade, satin and damask, flowered and edged with gold.

They wore elaborate headdresses, false hair and sometimes wigs, as well as patches and masks. Ladies were expected to wear three skirts, each of a different colour, under the gown, and farthingales made of rings of iron, wood or whalebone, 'resembling the hoops of casks', were sewn to the petticoat beneath them, making skirts hang 'like church bells'. To enhance the bell effect, hips were padded and defined by a stiff frill.

Bodices were either buttoned in front and cut square at the waist or open at the neck and cut to a deep point in front, with enormous winged sleeves hanging loose from the shoulders over tight sleeves, with padded shoulders and close-fitting cuffs.

The farthingale, which was originally a Spanish fashion, necessitated a long, slim waist, and to achieve this women poured themselves, heedless of the agonizing discomfort, into long splints of unyielding wood. Busks, stiffened bodices and corsets were later refinements of this particular form of torture.

The lace ruff or stiffened Medici collar remained very fashionable and for a time bodices were cut so low beneath them that Pope Innocent XI issued an edict enjoining 'all women, married or single, to cover their bosoms, shoulders and arms down to the wrist with non-transparent materials, on pain of excommunication'.

The indignation of His Holiness had little effect on the fashions of the French Court, however, and the names they gave to the colours of their choice show a remarkable cheerfulness in face of the agony they must have endured from their dreadful stays, as, for example, rat-colour, widow's joy, gladsome widow, doe's belly, scratched face, fading flower, dying monkey, lost time, dead olive, sick Spaniard, mortal sin, common ham and chimney-sweep.

As well as having a passion for women and for hunting, the King was an inveterate gambler. Stakes at Court were high and losses often catastrophic: yet members of the nobility who could ill afford Court life, and indeed had little taste for its dissolute licence, had to present themselves, if they wished for public office or preferment, for

46

the King held the reins of government firmly and only through him could appointments be made.

The beautiful and cultivated Marquise de Rambouillet was the first to break away from the Court and establish an independent salon, where members of the nobility who longed for a saner and more intelligent way of living were welcomed and entertained. At the age of twelve, the Marquise had married the Marquis de Rambouillet, who became the Master of the Horse at Henry IV's Court. In 1606 she moved to a mansion in the Rue Saint Thomas du Louvre. The house was entirely rebuilt and for the first time Paris was to see long windows, which afterwards were called French windows, though the Marquise had brought the idea from her native Italy. The Marquis resigned his Court post to join her and their children and from that time they were seldom seen at the Louvre.

At the Hôtel de Rambouillet the art of conversation was cultivated. At first only people of quality were admitted but eventually, as her daughter Julie grew up, men of letters were welcomed. Brains were valued as highly as noble birth and to be received there was a sign of social acceptance.

The establishment of the Hôtel Rambouillet and that of the rival salon of Madame de Loges were important in the setting of trends of thought, but did not affect the dissolute, frivolous Court life. The aristocracy of France which formed the Royal circle was still feudal, owning vast estates from which they could recruit their own armies. They had little culture, but physical bravery and a ruthless arrogance; and they were quarrelsome and jealous of each other's wealth and prestige. Their glory lay in their personal display and a man's dress could represent the value of many acres of land. They and their wives appeared at the Court functions, the fêtes, ballets, masquerades and banquets, so magnificently attired and 'so laden with precious stones that they could not move about'.

Henry IV died in 1610 leaving his heir, Louis XIII, a young child and his widow, Marie de Medici, as Queen Regent. During her Regency, Richelieu, in an attempt to stem the reckless extravagance of the Court and stop the flow of French gold to the foreign countries from which much of the finery was imported, introduced sumptuary laws which for a time were more effective than many earlier ones. There was to be no more Milanese silk braid, lace and embroidery. Gold lace, lace enriched with gold and silver and gold and silver fringes were all forbidden.

These edicts produced a revolution in women's fashion. For a short time materials were plain and, along with the farthingale, elaborate ornaments disappeared. The skirt fell in straight deep folds and over it went a basqued bodice, fastened high at the neck with a ribbon. Wide sleeves opened on to a plain tight undersleeve. The ruff or high-standing collar was replaced by a simple band of lawn.

The ladies of the Court did not maintain this austerity for long, although the costumes which Richelieu had forced their dressmakers and tailors to design for them became the costume of the bourgeoisie for many years to come and was permanently adopted by the sisters of Saint Vincent de Paul.

Women of fashion very soon adapted it so that it became a costume of grace and charm. The dress was open from neck to hem, showing a bodice of light satin ending in a rounded point, over a silk skirt. The outer skirt was very long, its fullness draped to the sides in deep folds. The puffed sleeves were tied with ribbons over lace undersleeves. Large flat collars of lawn edged with lace, falling low on the shoulders, replaced the ruffs, and cuffs to match reached from the wrist to the elbow. Ribbons were immensely popular and the favourite jewels were strings of pearls and diamond clasps.

This was the dress of the 1630s which Charles I's Henrietta Maria brought to England at the time of their marriage.

Men's fashions also altered about this time, but for the worse, ultimately developing into the short jacket and ugly beribboned petticoat breeches which were to reach England at the time of the Restoration.

Richelieu aimed to humble the French nobility. In addition to his sumptuary laws prohibiting luxury in dress, he made duelling illegal and planned to destroy the ancient feudal castles, which were potentially dangerous as strongholds of resistance.

The nobles ignored him to the best of their ability. They dressed more magnificently than ever and duelled in public, but many of their castles were seized and destroyed.

The rather simple, aloof Louis XIII had no interest in fine dress and was no match for the vast crowd of some thirteen hundred nobles who crowded the halls of the Louvre and St Germain. In summertime he was content to lead them to war but during the autumn and winter months, when campaigning came to a halt, they returned to Paris, where their principal pastimes were outshining each other in splendour of costume and gambling. As they often lost heavily, and as the necessity for sumptuous finery became ever more demanding, many became hard-pressed for money.

Yet infinitely worse was the poverty of the peasants. In 1640 Louis' brother, Gaston d'Orléans, wrote to him: 'Less than a third of your subjects in the provinces eat ordinary bread, another third lives solely on oat bread, and the remaining third is not only reduced to begging, but languishes in such lamentable want that some actually die of hunger, the others just sustain themselves on acorns, grass and such like as if they were animals. And among these the least to be pitied eat only bran and blood which they pick out of the streams in the slaughter-houses.'

After Richelieu's death, Mazarin continued his policy of trying to control the nobility. Louis XIII died in 1643, leaving his heir, Louis XIV, a child of five. The country was virtually ruled by Mazarin. The Queen Regent, Anne of Austria, was devoted to him. She almost certainly became his mistress and it is probable that she ultimately married him.

The quarrel deepened between the nobility and the King's party, led by Mazarin, who infuriated the nobility by his endless restrictions, amongst them sumptuary rules controlling the smallest details of dress. One week gimp was forbidden but guipure permitted, the next gimp was in and guipure out.

In 1648 civil war—the Fronde—broke out in France, the peasants at first joining with the nobles. The 'Fronde' was the sling that the citizens of Paris used to hurl stones at the windows of Mazarin's house and those of his adherents.

The Fronde was very different from the civil war in England. It has been described as 'the most costly and least necessary civil war in history'. The nobility conducted it in a frivolous, half-hearted way and the peasants and citizens of Paris withdrew in disgust, as it developed into desultory fighting between quarrelling groups of nobles, in which many of the grand ladies of France took part, light-heartedly adopting military fashions for their new roles as partisans.

These were years of anarchy amongst the French aristocracy. The salons closed. Anne of Austria still held her Court, but dress was free from the dictates of fashion. Apart from an ephemeral rage for details 'à la Fronde' amongst sympathizers with the rebels, there were no changes.

By October 1651, the civil war was over. The country, tired of its quarrelsome nobles, was prepared to accept the King's party and Mazarin as the party of settled government.

Louis XIV was growing up and the troubles of the Fronde had cleared the way for the policy of absolutism which he adopted throughout his long reign and the establishment of fashions which were to dazzle the whole of Europe.

CHAPTER FIVE

THE COURT OF LOUIS XIV

In 1661 Mazarin died and Louis XIV, a young man of twenty-three, took over the reins of government. He was to hold them firmly for the next fifty-four years. In 1660 he had married the Spanish Infanta Maria Theresa, a niece of Anne of Austria and also of Louis XIII, and when the Spanish nobility came to Paris for the wedding celebrations Parisians were as surprised at the sight of the Spanish farthingales of their ladies, so long out of fashion in France, as the English were to be a year or two later, when Charles II married poor Catherine of Braganza. Yet the Spaniards in their austere black velvet were considerably more elegant than the Frenchmen in their extraordinarily ugly fashions of the early 1660s—the beribboned petticoat breeches which Charles II brought to England and which were to remain in fashion for the next year or two.

For her wedding Maria Theresa was dressed in a 'gown enriched with gold, pearls, and precious stones, and was adorned with the most splendid of the crown jewels'.

She had a pretty face and she adored Louis, but she was no match in wits either for him or his succession of mistresses; and although Louis always treated her with his characteristic impeccable courtesy and a tolerant, rather paternal affection, she was to suffer agonies of jealousy throughout her married life.

Louis XIV surrounded himself with an aura of splendour and luxury. *L'État c'est moi.* The sun was his symbol, his word was law, his every wish was obeyed. Though accessible to his courtiers, he invested himself with a god-like majesty.

On Mazarin's death he allowed the sumptuary laws to lapse, so that the Court glittered again with gorgeous fabrics and rare lace, although cloth of gold and cloth of silver were permitted only for himself and his immediate circle. For the next few years women had never been more sumptuously dressed than at the French Court, where they passed their time in a round of fêtes, balls, banquets and masquerades.

> 'We often masqueraded in most delightful fashion,' wrote Mme de Montpensier. 'On one occasion, Monsieur, Mlle de Villeroy, Mlle de Gourdon, and I, wore cloth of silver with rose-coloured braid, black velvet aprons, and stomachers trimmed with gold and silver lace. Our dresses were cut like those of the Bresse peasants, with collars and cuffs of yellow cloth in the same style, but of somewhat finer quality than is used by them, and edged with Venetian lace. We had black velvet hats entirely covered with flame-coloured, pink and white feathers. My bodice was laced up with pearls and fastened with diamonds, and had diamonds all about it. Monsieur and Mlle de Villeroy also wore diamonds, and Mlle de Gourdon emeralds. Our black hair was dressed in Bresse peasant style, and we carried flame-coloured crooks ornamented with silver.'

The general form of women's dress was still the stiffened bodice cut very low on the shoulders and deep in front, shaped into a tight, pointed waist and opening to show a jewelled stomacher. The outer sleeve was short, the undersleeve, of lawn or lace, very full, caught above the elbow with ribbons and falling to just above the wrist. The skirt, cut away in the front to reveal a richly embroidered and jewelled underskirt, hung in deep pleats and was looped back at the sides with braid, ribbons and jewelled clasps, falling in a long train at the back.

This basic design was to last for another twenty years. It was in costly details that fashion changed.

Hair was usually dressed with bunches of curls at each side of the face, falling forward on to the cheeks, and a bunch of small curls over the forehead.

During the previous reign men had worn their hair long and some had taken to wigs, which were intended to simulate real hair, but by 1660 enormous periwigs, obviously artificial, came into fashion. They soon became universal at Court and, for a few more years, men still wore with them the short doublet and petticoat breeches or rhinegraves, which had been introduced by the Comte de Salm, known as 'the Rinegrave'.

However, in November 1666, only a few weeks after Charles II had introduced his new fashion for men, in order to break the domination of French fashion, Pepys was having supper and playing cards with Mr Batelier, who told him 'the newes how the King of France hath, in defiance to the King of England, caused all his footmen to be put into vests, and that the noblemen of France will do the like; which, if true, is the greatest indignity ever done by one Prince to another. . . . This makes me mighty merry, it being an ingenious kind of affront; but yet it makes me angry, to see that the King of England is become so little as to have the affront offered him.'

Research has found that both in England and France the 'Persian' mode of dress had already been worn by a few people a year or two earlier, so perhaps Pepys's indignation was unnecessary. Within the next few years the style was adopted universally at the French Court. It consisted at first of a vest, which ultimately became the waistcoat, reaching to the knees and almost hiding the breeches, which were much slimmer and cut to a better fit after someone invented fly-buttons. The vest was buttoned right down and elaborately embroidered. Over it went a somewhat plainer coat of the same length. The ruff had been replaced by a flat collar and as this was obviously impractical under a coat it was changed to an early form of lace fichu, worn unknotted, with long narrow ends hanging loose.

The hat had a shallow crown, a very wide brim and was smothered in feathers.

Louis became a dictator of fashion. His courtiers had to dress as he wished and in 1664 he distributed presents of dress materials to them. That year the *Mercure Galant* published the following fashion notes:

Dresses painted with figures and flowers are still worn, but there is more green in the bouquets of flowers. They are beginning to paint the finest linen, and this is quite a novelty, for all those we have seen hitherto were only printed.

Jet and enamel buttons are mentioned, watered ribbons, and square watches with looking-glass at the back; but this last fashion does not meet with approval, as it is thought the corners of the watch might be dangerous.

Net-work coifs were at first dotted, and afterwards open worked; this last is quite a novelty, as are also the skirts of 'point d'Angleterre,' printed on linen and mounted on silk with raised ornaments; every woman has bought some.

One of Louis's early love affairs was a mild flirtation with his sister-in-law, the English princess Henrietta, wife of Monsieur and sister of

E

Charles II. While his mother was alive, Louis kept these affairs as discreet as possible and when people began to talk about him and Henrietta, she suggested that he pretend to pay court to one of her ladies-in-waiting, Louise de la Vallière. Soon the fancy became reality and the beautiful, gentle Louise became his mistress.

She first enchanted him at a fête at Vaux in 1661, when she was seventeen, wearing a white gown 'with gold stars and leaves in Persian stitch and a pale blue sash tied in a large knot below the bosom. In her fair waving hair, falling in profusion about her neck and shoulders, she wore flowers and pearls mingled together. Large emeralds shone in her ears. Her arms were bare, and encircled above the elbow by a gold open-work bracelet, set with opals. She wore gloves of cream-coloured Brussels lace'.

Louise had several children by the King, all of whom died in infancy until in 1666 her beautiful little daughter Marie Anne was born and survived. This was the year that the Queen Mother died of cancer. Louis made Louise his official mistress and Marie Anne was legitimized, being given the title of Marie Anne de Bourbon.

Louise's greatest friend was Madame de Montespan, three years older than Louise. She had come to Court as a lady-in-waiting to Henrietta and had by this time been married to the Marquis of Montespan for four years and had two children. Her ambition was to usurp Louise and become the royal mistress. She was both beautiful and witty, and in most ways more brilliant than the gentle, clinging Louise, yet for many months she seemed to be making no impression on the King. In desperation she consulted Madame Voisin, a prosperous bourgeoise widow who, beneath the thinnest of veneers of respectability, dispensed aphrodisiacs and spells, performed abortions, got rid of unwanted live babies, supplied suitable philtres to impatient heirs, practised black magic and numbered amongst her lovers the public executioner.

Athénais de Montespan was well pleased with her visit for in 1667, when the King departed for his summer campaign in the war against the Netherlands, he appointed her lady-in-waiting to the Queen and the three went off together, leaving Louise behind. Unwisely she followed them but the King sent her home again and that summer Athénais became his mistress.

On their return to Paris he still saw Louise and, in fact, gave her another baby, but Athénais became the favourite and led the Court fashion. On one occasion she appeared wearing 'point de France and her hair in numberless curls, one on each side of the temple, falling low on her cheeks. Black ribbons in her hair, pearls which had belonged to the Maréchale de L'Hôpital, and buckles and ear-drops of magnificent diamonds'.

'Langlee, director of the royal sports,' wrote Mme de Sévigné, 'gave to Mme de Montespan a gown of gold upon gold, embroidered in gold, bordered with gold, above which was a band of gold, worked in gold mixed with a particular kind of gold; and forming the most divine material that can be conceived. . . .'

Fashion became a question of etiquette and the courtiers obeyed every dictate of the King, sometimes incurring enormous debts for their dress. One tailor made a claim on Condé, the great Duke of Bourbon, for 300,000 francs.

King Louis had already begun work on the transformation of his father's modest house at Versailles into the vast and magnificent palace it ultimately became, but it was not until about 1674 that the first apartments were ready for habitation. Colbert, who had succeeded Mazarin, was at first aghast at the huge sums of money which were being expended on the tapestries and furnishings of the château as well as the clothes of the Court, but soon took practical action by setting up factories in France to manufacture the enormous quantities of lace, silk, jewellery, carpets, furniture and tapestry which were being used.

At the Gobelin factory the tapestry and much of the furniture for Versailles was made. A soap factory was converted for the production of Savonnerie carpets. Lace factories were established at Arras, Quesnoy, Sedan, Château-Thierry Loudun, Aurillac, and the finest lace of all came from Alençon. The coarser kinds of lace which were already being made in Paris, Lyons, Normandy and Auvergne were no longer of fine enough quality for the growing extravagance of taste. All kinds of silks were made at Lyons, including a particularly lustrous type called 'donner eau'.

Fine ladies had their gowns made by men—Renaud, Sieur Villeneuve, Lallemand, Le Brun, Le Maire, Bonjuste and Chalandat were all fashionable Court dressmakers of Paris. They also used men hairdressers for a time, Sieur Champagne being the most fashionable until success went to his head and he became insufferable. He created the high headdresses which were the rage early in the reign, but women who clamoured for his services soon had reason to complain.

'Their foolish behaviour made him quite insupportable, and he made the most impertinent remarks to them; some ladies he would leave with their hair half-dressed.'

Martin followed him as a popular hairdresser and introduced the style of clusters of thick curls on each side of the face falling only to the ears and decorated with ribbons and strings of pearls. However, there were many fashionable women hairdressers as well, all of them wives of wigmakers.

Women took to long kid gloves for the first time or long silk mittens. They wore satin slippers, usually of pink or blue, with rosettes on the instep and heels which grew gradually higher, until they were well over three inches. Tallemant recorded that 'some of the Queen's ladies who, that they might wear pretty shoes, tightly bound their feet with bands of their hair, and fainted from pain in the Queen's room'.

Fans were used a great deal, beautifully painted with handles of mother-of-pearl, gold and ivory. 'There are so many ways of playing with that precious appendage,' Mme de Staël was to write in the next century, 'that by a mere movement of the fan one can tell a princess from a countess, a marchioness from a plebeian', but the principal use of the fan at Louis XIV's Court was to conceal the discomfort the user was suffering from her tight stays.

The capeline was a wide-brimmed straw hat, the brim lined with silk or satin and covered with feathers. This is probably the 'cartwheel' which so amused the people of Dover when Henrietta visited Charles II there in 1670.

About this time it was correct for a woman of rank to wear an underskirt of watered or glacé silk, with a long overskirt trailing on the ground or carried on the left arm. The underskirt had a double border of gold silk embroidery and the upper one a single border.

Henrietta died suddenly, very shortly after her visit to Dover, and it was whispered that she had been poisoned by two of Monsieur's lovers, though nothing was ever proved.

The following year he married Charlotte Elizabeth of Bavaria, daughter of the Count Palatine. Charlotte had little interest in clothes nor in her husband, whose main concerns in life were clothes, jewels and boys. Her passion was hunting and the only contribution she made to the history of fashion was the introduction of the little shoulder cape known as the palatine or pelerine. This she wore to 'avoid the immodesty of exposing her shoulders and bosom' and it became high fashion, though probably not for the same reason. In winter the palatine was of fur, in summer of lace or muslin.

Louise was still at Court but Athénais was increasingly in favour. Her husband was outraged, went into mourning and referred to his 'late' wife. The Church sympathized with the Marquis, for Louis was committing double adultery, but Louis obliged Parliament to sanction a deed of separation between the Montespans and Athénais was settled in the palace at St Germain, sharing an eight-roomed apartment with Louise.

By 1671 Louise could bear the situation no longer and fled to the convent of Chaillot, saying that she was dedicating the rest of her life to God, but Louis called her back for a reconciliation, and for a while there was harmony between the two.

Athénais was expecting her first baby by Louis, but as there was a real danger that Montespan might legally claim it, the fact was kept as secret as possible. 'She was in despair at her first accouchement,' wrote Madame de Caylus, 'consoled herself at her second, and carried impudence as far as it could be borne in all the subsequent ones.'

Athénais had a friend, well-born but impoverished, the widow Scarron, whom she asked to take the child. Madame Scarron was thirty-four, several years older than Athénais, intelligent and attractive, but with a hard, uncompromising strain in her make-up. She was very religious and most careful of her reputation. Louis did not like her and was suspicious of her friends, some of whom had been associated with the Fronde. Nor was Mme Scarron over-pleased by the invitation at first, but she needed the money and her confessor assured her that in the unusual circumstances it would be in order to accept. A house was bought for her in the Boulevard des Invalides, then a remote suburb of Paris, beautifully furnished and equipped with servants, and Mme Scarron moved in from the convent where she had been staying for economy. When Athénais' daughter was born at St Germain, Mme Scarron was waiting at the gates in a carriage to receive the baby and take it away to a secret nursery at the Boulevard des Invalides. She was a devoted nurse and genuinely fond of children but the little girl died. However, she was soon receiving Athénais' second child, the future Duc du Maine.

By 1673 the unhappy Queen had borne Louis six children, though all but the Dauphin had died at birth or during infancy. This was the year that the King went off to his summer campaign of the Dutch war with the Queen and his two mistresses—the three Queens, as the wondering populace called them—all in the same carriage, with Mme Scarron following the procession with the little boy, Athénais' first son. Athénais was pregnant again and at Tournai she gave birth to another boy, but within two days she had to join the cavalcade again, for the King had little patience with any indisposition. It was after this campaign that he gave the two children the titles of the Duc du Maine and Comte de Vexin and Mme Scarron became a permanent member of the household.

Athénais was reaching the summit of her glory. Near Versailles the King built the château of Clagny for her and raised her brothers and father to high office. Parts of the building at Versailles were near completion and by 1674 the apartments of the King, the Queen and Monsieur were ready for occupation. Athénais was given a suite next to the King's. Louise could bear no more and that year she retired from the Court and took orders in a Carmelite convent to expiate her mortal sins. She was only thirty and she remained at the convent for the next thirty-six years, dying there in 1710.

Mme Scarron approved of Louise's penance and now began what she described as 'her long struggle for the King's soul'. Her aim was to break his association with Athénais and bring him to a more chaste way of life. She found it uphill work but Louis began to show more interest in her and her views on life than he ever had before and was devoted to the Duc du Maine, whom she had reared with such loving devotion, preferring him to the Dauphin.

The long and bitter rivalry between Athénais and Mme Scarron began—fierce quarrels alternating with long periods of reconciliation and apparent friendship.

In 1679 Louis began to build Marley, a small house near Versailles, just big enough for the royal household, with twelve pavilions adjoining it, eleven for visitors and one for the bathrooms, all set in the most lovely gardens. Life was less formal at Marley but no less sumptuous, with its parties, concerts, balls, plays and gambling, and invitations were anxiously sought and highly prized.

Louis was still dictating fashion and at Marley every Court lady found a complete costume and a quantity of exquisitely fine lace in her wardrobe. 'At the royal residences,' wrote Voltaire, '. . . a princess had but to appear in some striking costume, and every lady of rank immediately endeavoured to imitate, even to outshine her.

The most extravagant sums were paid for dresses that were continually renewed.'

Yet it was still in details rather than basic design that fashion changed. There were gallants, which were little knots of ribbon. When they were arranged in tiers on each side of the stomacher they were known as 'ladders'. Furbelows, hurly-burlies and whatnots all had their day, and during the 1670s 'transparents' were very popular.

'Have you heard of transparents?' wrote Mme de Sévigné to her daughter, in 1676. 'They are complete dresses of the very finest gold or azure brocade, and over them is worn a transparent black gown, or a gown of beautiful English lace, or of chenille velvet, like that winter lace that you saw. These form a 'transparent', which is a black dress and a gold, silver or coloured dress, just as one likes, and this is the fashion.'

That same year Madame de Sévigné spent a day at Versailles and reported that Athénais de Montespan's dress 'was a French needle point lace, her hair, in a thousand curls, done up with black ribbon; she wore huge diamonds and enormous pearls'.

But Athénais was beginning to be seriously worried about Mme de Scarron's deepening friendship with Louis. She suggested they find a husband for her or a convent of which she could become head. It was too late. By this time the King did not want to lose her. Instead, he gave her a château near Chartres and made her the Marquise de Maintenon.

That summer he went off to the wars without either of them. Athénais retired to Clagny and sent for Madame Voisin again. She provided Athénais with some special love philtres she had obtained from Monsieur Galet, who was a specialist in such commodities.

The King returned from the war. Some time later he recalled suffering from severe headaches soon after his arrival at Versailles, but they did not prevent him inviting Athénais to return to her apartment there. Once more she reigned supreme, although when Mme de Maintenon returned there a few weeks later, for the winter, with the Duc du Maine, the King treated her with his usual courtesy and friendliness.

By the end of the year Louis was more concerned with Mme de Soubise, wife of François de Rohan, and the future Cardinal de Rohan appears to have been the result, but when she lost a front tooth he turned to Mme de Ludres for a brief spell. Then it was time for the next summer campaign. Athénais, again pregnant, went to stay with Mme de Maintenon, where she gave birth to the future Duchesse d'Orleans.

At Versailles the following winter Louis seemed more devoted to her than ever. 'Mme de Montespan was covered with diamonds the other day, such a brilliant divinity that one's eyes dazzled,' reported Mme de Sévigné. 'The attachment seems stronger than it has ever been; they're at the stage when people can't stop looking at each other. There can never have been another example on this earth of love starting again like theirs.'

In 1678 the Queen and Athénais accompanied the King on his summer campaign, but after a few weeks Athénais had to retire to Clagny for the birth of her sixth child by Louis, the Comte de Toulouse.

By this time she had lost her figure. She had grown fat and ill-tempered and the King was driven to finding a more amiable companion. His new love was the beautiful Mademoiselle Fontanges. He established her in a small room near his own at Versailles, hoping at first that neither Athénais nor Mme de Maintenon, not to mention the Queen, would know what was happening, but when the affair became obvious to the entire Court he created her a Duchess and she was declared a Royal Mistress.

She was an excellent rider and one day, during a royal hunting party, her elaborately dressed hair was blown into disorder. She tied it up with a ribbon, letting the ends fall over her forehead. The effect was so enchanting that the besotted King expressed his approval and started a rage for the Fontanges headdress which was soon adopted not only by the French Court but also by women of fashion in England. Gradually the original headdress was elaborated until it was made up of tiers of frills of stiff linen and lace, built up on a foundation of wire called a 'Commode'. It was attached to a linen cap worn at the back of the head, and tilted forward a little. The hair was dressed on a wire frame in front of the headdress and two streamers made of either linen or lace hung down at the back or were pinned up to the crown.

The hour of glory for poor little Fontanges was very brief. She quickly became pregnant and gave birth to a still-born child, which broke her health. The King sent her to a convent of which he appointed her sister the Abbess and there, in March 1681, she died, at the age of twenty.

The vast palace at Versailles was nearing completion and the following year the King announced that it was to be the official seat of government. Athénais still had her apartment there, but her star was waning and the King was coming more and more under the influence of Mme de Maintenon.

'Madame de Montespan was a devil incarnate,' wrote the Princess Palatine indiscreetly, in a private letter, 'but La Fontange was good and simple. It is said that the latter is dead because the former put some poison into some milk. I do not know if it is true.'

A serious scandal was shaking Paris society. In March 1679 Mme Voisin had been arrested. It was the outcome of a conference between the Chief of Police, La Reynie, and a priest who felt compelled to inform him of the alarming and increasing number of confessions of poisoning he was hearing. During the previous few years there had been several notorious cases of poisoning. The Marquise de Brinvilliers had been tortured and beheaded after confessing to murdering her father and two brothers and attempting to murder her husband and sundry other people by poisoning. Madame Bosse, who had supplied the poison, was arrested with several other grim characters and Madame Voisin's name was mentioned.

They blamed each other without compunction and gave away the names of many members of the nobility. When two of Mazarin's nieces were mentioned, Marie-Anne, Duchesse de Bouillon, and Olympe, Comtesse de Soissons, and then Athénais' maid, Mlle des Oillets, by whom it was common knowledge that the King had had a child, La Reynie went to the War Minister, Louvois, and together they went to the King.

They decided that the investigation must continue, but in strictest privacy. The most terrible secrets were unveiled. Mme Voisin seems to have been responsible for some two thousand abortions as well as the murder of scores of unwanted live babies. She practised black magic with human sacrifice, using children kidnapped from the Paris slums. Before she and Madame Bosse were put to death by torture and burning dozens more famous names were mentioned and there were many arrests. Olympe de Soissons had been a love of the King's in his youth and he warned her that a warrant had been issued against her, giving her the chance to escape to Brussels, where she remained an exile for the rest of her life.

Suddenly the trials stopped. The name of Athénais herself had been mentioned. She was accused of buying poison in order to murder the King and Fontanges. The eighty-one people still held remained in prison for the rest of their lives, chained and in solitary confinement. Thirty-six had already been burned to death after torture, four had been sent to the galleys, thirty-six fined and banished and thirty acquitted.

Neither the King nor Mme de Maintenon believed that Athénais had attempted murder but it seems very probable that she had resorted to love philtres in order to gain and keep the King's attention. He forgave her and she lived on at Versailles for another ten years, in sad eclipse, easily enough overshadowed in the sumptuous, overwhelming magnificence of that vast palace, where at times five thousand courtiers and their families were in attendance, living in quarters which, despite all the grandeur, were usually cramped and uncomfortable.

After the death of Fontanges, the King announced his disapproval of the headdress she had unwittingly made fashionable and it disappeared for a few months, only to reappear again. For the next thirty years, despite the grumblings of the King, who protested in vain against 'towering headdresses', it was worn by the fashionable ladies of France.

Louis turned to a more sober way of life, coming increasingly under the influence of the chaste and intellectual if somewhat hypocritical Mme de Maintenon. He paid more attention to his wife and made her happy for the last few years of her life, for which she was grateful both to him and Mme de Maintenon, but in 1683 she suddenly died, in the arms of Mme de Maintenon. Very shortly afterwards, probably only a few months later, Louis was secretly married to Mme de Maintenon. He was forty-eight and his new wife three years older. She had a strong vein of melancholy in her make-up and spent hours of each day alone in her small apartment or listening in silence while the King and his Ministers conducted their affairs of state there, absorbed in her needlework and seldom speaking until she was addressed.

The dullness of her life inevitably reflected on the atmosphere of the Court for a time. Her clothes were as dark and sombre as her mind and she wore a nun-like, demure coif. In this sober period, women abandoned their gaily flowered silks and satins for plain materials in dark colours.

In 1685 Louis, with the approval of most of France, revoked the Edict of Nantes and sent hundreds of French Protestants into exile to England, Holland and Germany. Most of them were members of the upper bourgeoisie, solid, worthy and intelligent people whom France could ill afford to lose. The expulsion was more political than an act of religious conviction, Louis seeing it as the removal of a potential opposition; and English trade was to benefit with the establishment of the Huguenot silk industry at Spitalfields.

Mme de Maitenon's melancholy did not prevent her from making life as difficult as possible for Athénais and, in 1691, after the last flicker of hope had died that, on the death of the Queen, Louis might have married her since she was now widowed, she left Versailles for ever, spending the remaining sixteen years of her life in penitence, devotion and good works.

The only notable change in fashion during this period came after the battle of Steinkirk in 1692, when the French defeated William of Orange. The battle achieved little and the losses on both sides were appalling and about equal. 'The country,' wrote Fénelon to the King, 'is a vast hospital!' However, Steinkirk was hailed in France as a mighty victory and when the story spread that the French officers had at first been taken by surprise and hardly had time to throw their cravats loosely about their necks before rushing into battle, a French opera singer appeared on the stage with a cravat thrown loosely over her stage dress as a tribute to their gallantry. It started the craze for 'steinkirks' which soon became lace cravats or silk neckerchiefs trimmed with lace, gold fringe or gold and silver thread.

With the Treaty of Ryswick in 1697 the long French war against the Protestants came to an end. Louis, wearying of the sombreness of life around him and still obsessed with Versailles, to which he was constantly making improvements he could now ill afford, decreed a brighter Court.

At the end of the year his eldest grandson, the Duc de Bourgogne, was married, at fifteen, to the twelve-year-old Marie Adelaide of Savoy. For her wedding she wore a dress of cloth of silver with embroidery of precious stones, so heavy that she could hardly stand in it, and her diamonds were from the royal diadem. Louis had ordered the Court to appear in their most sumptuous clothes and jewels for this event, but afterwards said that he did not understand how husbands could be fools enough to ruin themselves over clothes for their wives.

The royal grandchildren, the little dukes and duchesses, princes and princesses, were growing up and the Court became young again, gay and sumptuous. With the closing years of the century dresses were made of flowered satin and brocade, interwoven with gold and gorgeously trimmed. Bodices opened on to frilled lace underbodices and skirts were still raised and draped.

During the betrothal celebrations of Monsieur's daughter Elizabeth to the Duc de Lorraine, the Duchesse de Bourgogne, on whom the King doted, wore 'on the first day a gown of silver tissue, with gold flowers, touched with a little flame-colour and green, and in her hair the finest of the crown diamonds. The next day her gown was of grey damask with silver flowers, and she wore diamonds and emeralds. Mademoiselle wore a coat of Gros de Tours richly embroidered in gold; her skirt, of silver tissue, was embroidered in gold touched with flame-colour. She wore a splendid set of diamonds, and a mantle of gold point d'Espagne, six yards and a half long, and her train was carried by the Grand Duchess. Another time her coat and skirt were both of cloth of silver, all laced with silver. Her jewels were diamonds and rubies.'

'Towards 1700,' wrote Michelet, 'the women no longer show . . . the rich development that they so freely displayed. But the devil was no loser. If backs and shoulders are concealed from our gaze, the small portion that we are permitted to admire, and that is, as it were, offered to our inspection, is but the more attractive. There is a sort of audacity about the uncovered brow, the hair drawn back, so as to show its every root, the high comb, or diadem-cap, that seems little in harmony with the soft and childish features of the day. This childishness, so devoid of innocence, combined with the masculine Steinkirk, gives them the appearance of pets of the seraglio, or of impudent pages who have stolen women's garments.'

In 1700 Charles II of Spain died, leaving the Spanish crown to Louis's grandson Philip, the Duc de Bourgogne's younger brother. He became Philip V of Spain and in 1702 the weary and costly War of the Spanish Succession broke out, with Austria, most of Germany, Denmark, Holland and England ranged against France and Spain. It lasted until 1713, during which time France suffered one disastrous defeat after another—Blenheim, Ramillies, the retreat from Italy and the fall of Madrid. The treasury grew empty. Trade came to a standstill. The army was neither paid nor fed.

Yet at Versailles the Court remained as gay and glittering as ever and Louis, though increasingly hard-pressed for money, was still improving or extending the palace.

Fashion moved. Bodices were tighter. *Pretintailles* were appliquéed motifs stitched on to the skirt, making it unbearably heavy. There was a craze for very large brocaded patterns in gold and a variety of colours, 'Dress improvers', which were petticoats of stiffened linen, gave a becoming slimness to the waist. By 1711 farthingales were back in the form of panniers. They were made by the coopers and basket-makers and consisted of an open framework of hoops made from straw, cord, cane or whalebone, fastened together with tapes. They remained in fashion for many years, despite the protests when they first appeared and their remarkable inconvenience in crowded rooms and narrow streets. Men who had scoffed at the fashion now stiffened the wide basques of their coats with whalebone, so that they, too, began to take up more room.

Mme de Maintenon sourly commented: 'I find the females of today insupportable with their ridiculous and immodest clothes, their tobacco, their drink, their greed, their vile manners and their idle hands,' but no one listened to her, although the country and the Court were fast heading for bankruptcy.

A few people began to sell their jewellery. The King sold some of his silver furniture and gold plate. A certain amount of fake jewellery was made, perhaps to replace gems which had been sold. Someone called Jaquin invented artificial pearls by filling hollow glass beads with the sediment left in the water in which whitebait had been washed, but as it took about 20,000 whitebait to produce one pound of essence of pearls, the process was no great economy.

'Every fashion they invent is to conceal some defect,' exclaimed the valet in a comedy presented in Paris at the end of the century. 'Falbala[1] high up for those who have no hips; lower down for those who have too much. Long necks and flat chests brought in the Steinkirk; and so it is with everything.'

It was not until 1714 that the *fontange* headdress was discarded, owing, so the story goes, to the visit of two English ladies to the Court wearing their hair dressed low. The King so admired the fashion that Frenchwomen were induced to copy it.

By this time the War of the Spanish Succession was over. The Treaty of Utrecht of 1713 had left France desperately impoverished but Philip V was still on the throne of Spain. Versailles had become sad again for it had seen terrible tragedy in the Royal family during the last years of Louis's reign. In 1711 the Dauphin had died and the

---

[1] Falbala were similar to *pretintailles*.

following year his hier, the Duc de Bourgogne, and the beautiful little Duchess, as well as their four-year-old son, leaving the two-year-old Duc d'Anjou to succeed.

Louis XIV died in 1715, leaving a national debt of three thousand million livres. Mme de Maintenon retired to St Cyr, where she died five years later.

CHAPTER SIX

THE LAST OF THE STUARTS
William and Mary and Anne

In 1689, when William and Mary came to the throne of England, the magnificence of the Court of Versailles had so impressed the rest of western Europe that French fashions were worn at nearly all the Courts. French clothes had never quite regained the freedom and grace of the 1660s, but they had recovered from the brief period of austerity when Mme de Maintenon's influence was first felt. Now they were gay and colourful again, though more formal and stiff. The *fontange* headdresses gave women height and dignity, the periwigs, growing longer and more cumbersome each year, gave men a ponderous and top-heavy appearance.

Only in Spain did fashion remain behind the times. As late as 1700, when the seventeen-year-old grandson of Louis XIV left Versailles to succeed Charles II as Philip V of Spain, he arrived, on his grandfather's advice, and so as not to shock the Spaniards with French fashions, in the black velvet and white ruff which had been ordained as correct wear for a Spanish gentleman by Philip II, nearly a hundred and fifty years earlier. However, from this time onwards, as the economy of Spain revived, largely through the work of Louis XIV and Philip V, French taste in architecture, painting, furniture and dress gradually spread through Spain.

The Italian states had long been under the influence of France or Austria. The Medicis, for all their scheming, had not been able to produce a direct heir, and Tuscany, with the riches of Florence, had gone to Austria. The might of Venice had been declining slowly but inexorably for two centuries and by the end of the seventeenth century the city had become increasingly French in its fashions.

The German people had suffered terribly during the Thirty Years War of 1618 to 1648 and their numbers had been halved. At the end of the war Germany was divided into numerous small sovereign states, all of them poor, but very proud of the sovereignty they had established and the aristocracy they were in the process of creating. The common language of these Courts was French, and as the German princes recovered their fortunes or amassed new ones and were ready for self-aggrandizement, Versailles was the model of their new palaces. Regional and traditional costumes were discarded and the new fashions came from Paris.

Of Vienna at the end of the century, Herr Mathias von Wolzogen wrote: 'The splendour is more rich than artistic, everything causing trouble and requiring thought is abhorrent. More is spent on dogs, horses, and dresses than on books or works of art.'

In the Netherlands, the Dutch had prospered throughout the earlier years of the century. Narrow-minded, bigoted, unimaginative and dull they may have been, but they were hard-working and thrifty, perhaps to the point of parsimony. 'The Dutch are always buying in order to resell at once,' said the English ambassador, Sir William Temple. 'They sell the best products of their textile industry in France and buy the coarsest cloth in England for their own use.' The Dutch amassed great wealth, one of their important sources of revenue being the cultivation of the tulip. They exported thousands of tulip bulbs to France, where Louis XIII had first made the flower fashionable, and when English travellers brought them back to England they were soon as popular.

The Netherlands had offered a generous refuge to the French Huguenots, who exerted a marked French influence, particularly when they opened schools where they taught fencing, dancing, hairdressing and French cooking, and for the next few years the way of life in the Netherlands became increasingly French. The Dutch developed a taste for tapestries and beautiful marquetry furniture. The palaces at Kaisergracht and Heerengracht were built in the Louis XIV style and fashions for both men and women came from Paris, causing the older generation to complain of the corrupting influence of France and the decline of the old bourgeois austerity and pious conservatism, which had given the people of the Netherlands their strength.

By 1670 Louis and Charles II had signed their secret Treaty of Dover. That year William, the son of Charles II's sister Mary, who had married William, Prince of Orange, came to visit his uncle. He was just twenty and Mary, the daughter of the Duke of York and Ann Hyde, was eight, her little sister Anne three years younger.

In 1671 Ann Hyde died and two years later the Duke of York married the fifteen-year-old Catholic Mary of Modena.

Probably a wooden corset gives the straight
line to this heavy velvet gown and restrains
the scheming Catherine de Medici

The boy-king Louis XIII, in his thigh-
length full-gathered breeches, apparently
combines two materials in his dashing
costume of velvet stripes and panne velvet
sewn with galloon

The popular slashed sleeves, a collar-shaped
ruff and stomacher are features of the
brocade dress worn by Madame de Châtillon,
c. 1630. The material of the mantle is
cut away to reveal the sleeves beneath

A water fête—one of the pleasures of Court life at Fontainebleau depicted in tapestry in crowded detail. Henry III and Louise de Mercoeur, unsuitably clad in formal dress, attend the festivities

Wearing in this family group a somewhat hum-drum dress, relieved by a stiffened Medici collar, Marie de Medici for her children's christening wore a dress 'covered with 32 thousand pearls, 3,000 diamonds'. It was 'beyond rivalry and priceless'

The fine collar of Valenciennes lace is the one light touch on the apparel of Maria Theresa, Empress of Austria. Her robes, as well as the great cushion and table-cover, are all embroidered with fleurs-de-lys

The pretty twin sisters Henriette de Blois and Mademoiselle de Nantes wear perfectly balanced dresses for their picture by Vignon. The two exquisitely flowered brocades have on the bodice of Henriette de Blois a garland of flowers from right to left; Mademoselle de Nantes wears a corsage draped from left to right and held by chains of pearls. Ringlets of hair fall becomingly on to their shoulders

Louis XIV—'le Roi Soleil'—is seated; behind his chair is his heir, the Grand Dauphin, and to the right his eldest grandson, the Duc de Bourgogne, in vivid vermilion. His eldest surviving great-grandson, the Duc de Bretagne, in an elaborate dress and top-heavy plumes, is led by his governess

The Sun King ablaze in all his glory

A woman of great character, Madame de Sevigné, 'intellectual and religious', evidently had a feminine weakness for pearls

Madame de Maintenon, patroness of letters, wears a black mantilla with her voluminous and sombre dress, relieved by lace collar and double cuffs. Her young niece looks happy in her satin dress and long train

Kneller, as well as Hoppner, Lely and Ramsey, delighted in picturing the passing fashions of the day; the example here shows Mary Bentinck, Countess of Essex, manipulating her floating taffetas

Good Queen Anne, who reputedly bathed only three times in her life, was crippled with gout on her coronation day, and did not care vastly for fashion anyhow

Guipure lace and loops of jewels form a becoming bustline to the satin dress worn here by the Princess of Orange before she became Queen Mary, the spouse of William III

Simon Belle's portrait of Matthew Prior, *c.* 1705, is a glorious mingling of all the nasturtium tones of orange and gold. He sits in a flame-coloured chair, wearing a tight-fitting coat of tawny velvet, encrusted with gold lace. His flowered waistcoat and large square cuffs are embroidered with green leaves and coral flowers. His enormous periwig of silky curls flows down to his chest in orange magnificence

The graceful folds of this flowing dress, worn by the beautiful Mary Isabella, Duchess of Rutland, suggest a preference for simplicity. The only extravagance is the turban of folded gauze and uncurled ostrich feathers

The timeless silhouette of fitted bodice and bouffant skirt, softened with flounced sleeves, is worn by Anne, Princess Royal in her portrait by Amigoni, c. 1734

The following year war broke out again, with France and England allied against the Netherlands. In England the war was extremely unpopular, for there was an almost superstitious terror of papacy by this time. Though Princess Mary and Princess Anne had been brought up as Protestants, the Duke of York, heir to the throne, made no secret of his Roman Catholicism and most people suspected, quite rightly, that the King also was a Catholic at heart. In 1674, therefore, Charles deemed it prudent to make a separate peace with Holland. By this time William, who had proved himself a valiant soldier, had become head of the Dutch Republic. Two years later, when Princess Mary was fifteen and her cousin William twenty-seven, Charles II astonished Europe by announcing their betrothal.

The Duke of York had little say in the matter and Mary none at all. To the King it seemed the best solution for ensuring a Protestant Stuart succession. When Louis told the English ambassador that James had given his daughter to his greatest enemy, the ambassador assured him that James 'did not know of the King's decision until an hour before it was proclaimed, nor did the King himself above two hours previously'. Matters had to be decided quickly and secretly lest they should come to the ears of Louise de Kéroualle, by now the Duchess of Portsmouth, the King's mistress and a spy for Louis XIV.

So Princess Mary, weeping broken-heartedly, was married and went off to Holland with her unattractive, ill-tempered, asthmatic husband who, for all his lack of grace and amiability, was French-speaking and more French than Dutch in his upbringing and education.

Mary remained in Holland for the next twelve years, her sister Anne living in London, where, in 1683, at the age of eighteen, she was married to the thirty-year-old Prince George of Denmark. King Charles thought little of Prince George, but he and Anne settled down comfortably together in the Cockpit, the extension to White-hall Palace built where Downing Street now runs.

Mary's life in Holland was far from enviable, partly because of her husband's neglect and partly because of the political problems which raged over the succession. Her loyalties were divided between her husband and her father, but by 1689, when King Charles was dead and James had been forced to abdicate in favour of herself and William as joint monarchs of England, she had become completely subservient to him and apparently in love.

The English courtiers who welcomed William and Mary were as

F

elegant as those they brought with them and there was little difference in their style of dress.

Men were wearing a knee-length coat, long-sleeved with wide cuffs, shaped to a rather low waist, over a sleeved waistcoat or vest of about the same length, buttoned from neck to hem. Breeches were slim and close-fitting, fastened at the side of the knee with a buckle or buttons. They were very often of black velvet and were almost hidden by the coat.

Shirts were cut very full in the body and sleeve, with ruffles of lawn or lace at the wrist. The ends of the cravat hung loosely over a knot of ribbon and later, when the steinkirk was in fashion, it was held with a brooch or folded loosely with the ends slipped through a button-hole of the coat.

Long stockings were held by garters or fastened to the breeches with tapes or buttons. Sometimes men wore two pairs, the inner pair fastened to the breeches and the outer pair gartered.

Boots were out of fashion except for riding and at Court men wore long, square-toed leather shoes, with high red heels and long tongues reaching four or five inches up the instep, lined with silk or with leather in a contrasting colour.

Periwigs, which had become an essential article of dress, grew increasingly bulky and artificial-looking and by the 1690s they rose above the forehead in two peaks. Underneath the periwigs hair was closely cut. There were very few beards to be seen and no moustaches for a long time to come.

Gloves were plain and ribbons fast disappearing, though they still trimmed the fur muffs which fashionable men used in winter, often attached to their sword-belt. They carried malacca canes and had taken to snuff, carried in elegant snuff boxes, as well as paint and patches and lace handkerchiefs, which no gentleman would refer to except as a *mouchoir*.

Cloaks were no longer the swaggering, dramatic articles of dress they had been in Cavalier days, but were long and utilitarian, to be worn in winter purely for warmth, particularly when travelling.

As periwigs grew larger hats became a problem. The low-crowned, broad-brimmed felt hat was still in fashion, turned up in front or at the side, but the practice of wearing hats in the house and at meal times came to an end.

Women's dress was still the long, pointed, tight-fitting bodice, cut low on the shoulders, sometimes draped with a lace or gauze scarf or a deep, falling collar of lace. Bodices were either fastened in front with bows of ribbon or jewelled clasps, or laced at the back; and sometimes basques were cut into splayed tabs. Sleeves had been short and puffed, with an undersleeve of deep falls of lace reaching to the elbow, or else elbow-length, closely gathered at the shoulder and elbow, but now there was a fancy for plain, straight, elbow-length sleeves, ending in a fall of ruffled lace.

By the 1680s the skirt had become a bustle, very similar to those of Victorian times, but by the 1690s panniers were being worn, as in France, with the skirt and beribboned petticoat beneath it trailing backwards on the ground.

In the Netherlands women had adopted the practical fashion of a neat little velvet jacket, edged with fur or swansdown, to wear over their thin silk or damask dresses.

The loose kerchiefs and hoods had given way to the elaborate *fontange* or 'commode', each part of which was given a French nickname, as in Paris. Hair was dressed high on the brow in a peak either side of a central parting, matching the new style of the men's periwigs, and it was pinned close to the head at the sides.

Shoes were high-heeled with pointed toes; and for state occasions they were of embroidered satin or brocade, fastened with a jewelled buckle or ribbons. For less formal wear they were of fine Morocco leather. Stockings of thread or silk were brightly coloured.

Small aprons of lace or embroidered silk edged with gold lace were fashionable, as well as elbow-length gloves of fine leather or silk, in white or pale colours, or lace mittens.

Some women still wore masks, particularly when out riding in the country, where fashion changed very slowly. Masks were also still seen occasionally at the theatre, but the fashion was dying and they were coming to be regarded as rather disreputable.

Women wore muffs and furs and pattens in the winter. They painted and patched and wore long, very broad scarves, which they sometimes draped over their 'commodes' when they were out of doors: and in summer-time they took to fringed silk parasols.

The English people were not impressed with their new king when he arrived at St James's, for he was unprepossessing, rather short, thin, sickly-looking and pock-marked. He did nothing to ingratiate himself with them for he was anything but gregarious.

When Queen Mary arrived in England shortly afterwards she

made a far better impression. Landing at Gravesend, she was escorted to Greenwich Palace, where Princess Anne and Prince George of Denmark were waiting to greet her. The royal sisters met with 'transports of affection' which, wrote Lady Sarah Churchill, 'soon fell off'.

From Greenwich Mary arrived by river at Whitehall Palace and appeared so excited and pleased at the prospect of becoming Queen, with so little regret for her father and step-mother and their infant son, living in exile in Paris, at the expense of Louis XIV, that people were shocked.

'She came into Whitehall laughing and jolly, as to a wedding, so as to seem quite transported. She rose early the next morning, and in her undress, as it was reported . . . went from room to room to see the convenience of Whitehall,' wrote Evelyn.

To Bishop Burnet she confessed that she had been warned by letters from England that she must adopt this attitude of appearing delighted at the prospect of being Queen. 'Alas! They did little know me who thought me guilty of that,' she declared. 'My heart is not made for a kingdom, and my inclination leads me to a retired, quiet life.'

King James and the Queen had left so hurriedly that most of their personal possessions and clothes were still at the palace, but when, shortly afterwards, James sent a message begging his daughter to send them over to Paris, the request, according to Clarendon, 'was utterly neglected'.

It was soon apparent that there was to be very little Court life. William made his asthma the excuse for leaving Whitehall Palace as soon as possible and settling at Hampton Court. Here he consulted Christopher Wren, with a view to rebuilding Wolsey's crumbling old Tudor Palace and making it a place to compare in grandeur with Versailles. The government was none too pleased with this idea, not only because of the vast expense involved but because it was going to be extremely inconvenient for the King to be so far from London. William compromised. Wren began some necessary work at Hampton Court in order to make the royal quarters habitable and comfortable, before embarking on his main alterations and additions, and William bought Nottingham House, near the little village of Kensington, from Lord Nottingham, instructing Wren to convert it into a small, domestic palace. Here he would be within reasonably easy access of London and the new Kensington Palace would obviously be too small for a large Court. He could lead the solitary life he preferred.

During the next six years he was campaigning in Ireland or the Continent during the summer months and while he was abroad he left Mary to manage affairs of State. This she did extremely well, but she attempted only a little entertainment. The English Court was small and dull and, cut off from France by the wars, it created no new fashions except that Queen Mary did launch the fashion for collecting china. She had a very fine collection of delftware as well as Oriental porcelain, which was being brought to Europe during these years by the ships of the East India Companies.

The craze for collecting quickly spread amongst leaders of fashion. In 1693 Evelyn saw the Queen's collection and also her rare Chinese and Indian cabinets. Very soon English china cabinets were being made for the first time, with glass doors and walnut legs, turned in the characteristic 'inverted cup' of the William and Mary period. There was also a fashion for Dutch marquetry for a few years and Mary introduced Indian printed calicoes and chintzes for curtains and bed hangings.

During her few leisure hours, her relaxation was embroidery and when Celia Fiennes visited Hampton Court she described 'the hangings, Chaires, Stooles and Screen the same, all of satten stitch done in worsteds, beasts, birds, images and ffruites all wrought very ffinely by Queen Mary and her maids of honour', as well as the green and white damask window curtains, the Presence Chamber with the low screen 'to keep company off the bed wch is scarlet velvet', and the dressing-room hung with yellow damask.

Queen Mary was nearly six feet tall, three or four inches taller than William, and had a regal and stately presence, but she did not make her mark as a leader of fashion. In fact, the Bishop of Gloucester praised her for her sobriety and lack of vanity, being particularly pleased with her because she did not indulge in 'such childish vanities as Spotted Faces'. There is, in fact, an entry in the Privy Purse account for 1694 for 'a paper of patches one shilling', but perhaps she was just experimenting. There is also a bill 'for a Pockett Glass with a gold frame the Back lined with chagreen, garnished with gold pins £6, and for a Gold pach-box with an agatt stone cover £10'.

The Bishop also praised her economy in clothes and she was certainly not above having some renovated. That same year Daniell

Browne charged one pound ten shillings for 'putting a Rich Ermine Mantle into a new Outside', but a few weeks later he was charging her £11 for a 'Rich Sable Back Muff' and £6 'For Lyneing Her Majesty's petticoate with Choyce Squirrill Bellys.' In four months she bought thirty-six pairs of slippers made of gold lace and satin.

The alterations at Kensington Palace were completed in 1694, but only a few weeks after William and Mary moved into residence Mary died suddenly, of smallpox. She was only thirty-two and childless.

Anne had agreed that King William should continue to reign and she now became the next in succession.

For the next eight years King William reigned alone. He became increasingly unsociable, except with his handful of intimate men friends. He took to pretty hard drinking of Dutch gin and though a few formal entertainments were held at the Court, there was nothing left of the early Stuart gaiety and spontaneity.

In 1698 Whitehall Palace, which had been seriously damaged by fire a few years earlier, was completely destroyed by fire, except for the banqueting hall. 'This is ye only thing left of ye vast Building which by accident or Carelessness, if not designe, has Laid it in ashes together with Exceeding Rich furniture of antiquity, as alsoe ye greate and good Queen Mary's Closet and Curious treasures,' wrote Celia Fiennes.

The design to which she referred was the rumour that the destruction of the palace had been a deliberate act of arson on the part of the Papists, while those who disliked the King whispered that he had caused it himself in order to put an end to the custom of dining in public, which he detested.

When Queen Mary died work had been halted at Hampton Court but now, with the loss of Whitehall, it was resumed, though to a far less ambitious plan, and by 1702 Wren's work was finished.

William loved Hampton Court and went there every week to watch the progress of the alterations and ride in the park, but early in 1702, with his work just finished, his horse stumbled and threw him. He suffered a broken collar-bone, and although he was able to return to Kensington Palace, he never recovered from the accident and died a fortnight later.

Princess Anne was proclaimed Queen of England. She was thirty-seven and had had eleven miscarriages and six children, all of whom had died in infancy except the Duke of Gloucester, born in 1689, who had survived until 1700. Her sister Mary had also had two miscarriages and there seems little doubt that they both suffered from inherited venereal disease. In addition, Anne was tormented with gout and was so fat by this time, not only through childbearing, but from too much food and drink, that she could never have become a leader of fashion. She was not interested in dress, wisely kept to plain clothes and did not care for jewels, except on State occasions.

At her coronation she was so afflicted by gout that she had to be carried for part of the procession. Celia Fiennes described it all in detail—the blue cloth spread from Westminster Hall to the Abbey, the procession of guards and chaplains, aldermen, lawyers, gentlemen of the Privy Council, the judges and the choirs. The baronesses wore crimson velvet robes lined with ermine, long trains lined with white sarsenet, sleeves open and tied with silver cords and tassels, with undersleeves of fine point lace, stomachers covered with diamonds, diamond necklaces, diamonds in their hair and diamonds and jewels in their coronets.

The Queen was carried in an elbow-chair covered with crimson velvet, with a low back over which her robes were spread. Her mantle was of crimson velvet lined with ermine, her dress of gold tissue embroidered with jewels, her train six yards long. Her hair 'well dress'd with Diamonds mixed in ye haire wch at ye Least motion Brill'd and flamed'.

She left her chair at the Abbey door and was helped to the altar, and after the crowning she retired to King Edward's Chapel for private prayer. Then her crimson cloak was changed for a purple one, she took to her chair again and was borne to Westminster Hall, where she summoned Prince George to take his place beside her for the banquet.

Too frequent conceptions, gout, the tortuous plots of her scheming Ministers and bitter quarrels with Sarah Marlborough shadowed Anne's life, but she had the strength of will ultimately to break with the overpowering, tempestuous Sarah and retain the services of the plain, red-nosed Mrs Masham, who had been the cause of much of the trouble, appointing the Duchess of Somerset as her new Mistress of Robes: and she dealt with her Ministers to the best of her ability.

The Queen and Prince George visited Bath on several occasions, to take the waters, an exercise which was conducted with a good deal more decorum at the end of the seventeenth century than in earlier years. At the Cross Bath, which was one of the biggest, wrote Celia Fiennes, there were seats in the middle for the men and ladies sat round the edge. 'There is a serjeant belonging to ye baths that all the bathing tyme walked in galleryes and takes notice order is observed and punishes ye rude. . . .'

The people of England loved Queen Anne, but she was too sick a woman to make long journeys throughout the country, as her predecessors had done, and she saw very few of her people, whose numbers had now risen to five and a half million. Four-fifths of them were still country-dwellers and of those working in industries by far the most were engaged in the making of materials or items of clothing.

Celia Fiennes, during her travels at the turn of the century, described the lace-makers of Buckinghamshire, Hertfordshire and Bedfordshire. In Canterbury she saw twenty silk weavers' looms in one house 'with severall fine flower'd silks, very good ones, and its a very Ingenious art to fix the warps and Chaine in their Loomes to Cast their work into such figures and flowers. There stands a boy by Every Loome and pulls up and down threads wch are fastened to the weaving, and so pulls the Chaine to the Exact form for ye shuttle to work through'.

In 1681 a Discourse on Trade had reported: 'The English formerly wore or used little silk in City or Country, only persons of quality pretended to it; but as our national Gaudery hath increased, it grew more and more into mode and is now the common wear . . . and our women, who generally govern in this case, must have foreign silks. . . . Of the same humour are their gallants.'

It is not surprising, therefore, that the new English silk industry, given a tremendous impetus by the fresh influx of Huguenots after 1685, was flourishing. By the last year of Queen Anne's reign the silk manufacture in this country was 'come to be above twenty times as great as it was in the year 1664'.

The Spitalfields weavers made velvet, which had hitherto been imported from France and Italy, and also beautiful brocades, often interwoven with gold and silver threads. They wove watered silk and shot silk, the favourite colours being claret, rose-pink, old gold, dead-leaf and brown, and they also made delicately patterned floral brocades.

In Manchester, cotton weaving began to be important, the raw cotton being imported from Asia Minor and the Levant and also from the East Indies. Printed calicoes were first made in this country in 1676, the earliest having a weft of cotton and a warp of linen thread. A little later cotton chintzes, of which Queen Anne was very fond, were being made. Less fashionable ladies wore clothes 'in calico or printed linen, moved to it as well for the cheapness as for the lightness of the cloth and the gaiety of the colours'.

Inevitably, the English manufacturers were soon demanding protective laws to safeguard their wares against the competition of the East India Company's imports and the East India Company was protesting at the threat to its trade.

As well as these patterned materials, the first striped stuffs appeared. About 1670 muslins were imported from India and were very popular, but they were not manufactured in this country till late in the eighteenth century.

In the course of her travels Celia Fiennes visited Derby where they 'make quantities of gloves', to Honiton where they make the 'fine bone lace in imitation of the Antwerp and Flanders lace and indeed I think its as fine—it only will not wash so fine, wch must be the fault in ye thread'. In Suffolk and Norfolk 'the ordinary people . . . knitt much and spin, some wth ye Rock and fusoe as the French does, others at their wheeles out in the streets and Lanes as one passes. In Norwich they spin Crapes, Callimancoes and damasks wch is ye whole business of the place. Indeed they are arrived to a great perfection in worke, so fine and thinn and glossy; their pieces are 27 yards in Length and their price is from 30 shillings to 3 pound as they are in ffineness; A man Can weave 13 yards a day, I saw some weaveing; they are all Employ'd in spinning, knitting, weaveing, dying, scouring or bleaching stuffs'. Norwich 'lookes like what it is—a Rich, thriveing Industrious place. . . . They have besides ye town hall a hall distinct wch is the scaling hall where their stuffs are all measured, and if they hold their breadths and Lengths they are sealed, but if they are defective there is a fine Layd on ye owner and a private marke on ye stuff wch shews its defficiency.'

Winchester, she said, had a 'peculiar art of dying ye best purples' and at Exeter she found 'as vast a trade in serges as in Coapes, Callamanco and damaske at Norwich'. In the Large Market House set on stone pillars 'they lay their packs of serges. Just by it is another walke wth in pillars wch is for the yarne, the whole town and Country is Employed for at Least 20 miles round in spinning, weaveing, dressing and scouring, fulling and Drying of the serges. It turns the most money in a weeke of any thing in England. One weeke with another there is 10000 pound paid in ready money, Sometymes 15000 pound. The weavers bring in their serges and must have their money wch they Employ to provide them yarne to goe to work againe. . . . There is a prodigious quantity of their serges they never bring into the market but are in hired roomes wch are noted for it, for it would be impossible to have it altogether. The Carryers I met going wth it, as thick, all Entring into town wth their Loaded horses, they bring them all just from the Loome and soe they are put into the ffulling-mills. . . .'

Some of these woollens were dyed in Exeter and she saw vats of black, yellow, blue and green dyes as well as a very fine scarlet, but most were sent to London for dyeing.

Nottingham was given over to the weaving of stockings—'a very Ingenious art.' Manchester was busy with the manufacture of 'linnen Cloth and Cottentickings' and Leeds, esteemed the 'Wealthyest town of its bigness in the Country, its manufacture is ye woollen Cloth— the Yorkshire Cloth in wch they are all Employ'd and are Esteemed very Rich and Very proud.'

Woad was still used for blue and green dyes and she saw a large plantation of it in Gloucestershire, where during the harvest season two or three families lived in huts on the site, plucking the leaves, letting them dry in the wind in a penthouse, and then grinding them into a paste which was made into balls for dyeing.

In 1708 Prince George died at Kensington Palace, of asthma, and for the next six years Anne was alone, a sick woman growing yearly more obese, more racked with pain. The Court grew even duller. 'She has laid down the splendour of a court too much, and eats privately; so that except on Sundays, and a few hours twice or thrice a week at night in the drawing-room, she appears so little, that her court is as it were abandoned,' wrote Bishop Burnet.

The centre of fashion and culture were now to be found in the great London mansions and country houses and it was the rich noblemen who were the patrons of the artists and writers.

In July 1714 the Queen presided at a Council meeting of her quarrelling Ministers, during which Robert Harley, Earl of Oxford, openly accused Henry St John, Lord Bolingbroke, of corruption. The bitter recriminations went on until two o'clock in the morning. As it broke up the Queen felt ill. She took to her bed and never recovered. On 1 August, at the age of forty-nine, she died, and the long reign of the Stuarts came to an end.

On the world of fashion she left little mark, though the superb domestic architecture and walnut furniture of her reign are now part of the nation's heritage. By the time she died, men's clothes were becoming more utilitarian and they wore mostly fine woollen coats and breeches, though velvet and silk for important occasions. Women, in addition to the wide range of silks, satins and velvets now available, took to the fine linen and fashionable cotton cloths which were being spun and woven in Lancashire.

Women tended to stay indoors a great deal when the weather was bad, for the streets were very dirty and muddy, but on fine days the mercers' shops in the City, particularly those on Ludgate Hill, were an increasing attraction. Here could be bought satins and silver tissues, damasks, brocades, poplins, crêpes and plushes, serges and other woollen materials, Indian gauzes and all manner of cottons, muslins and exquisitely fine linens. There was home-made bone lace, and Mechlin and Brussels lace appeared in London for the first time in Queen Anne's reign, while gold and silver lace became so heavy and expensive that in the end its manufacture was forbidden.

Ladies wore chatelaines when out shopping, to carry their money, but they often paid by instalments and the tally man was no unusual sight on Monday mornings.

Fashion changed very slowly for the country people in their isolated hamlets and villages, for their clothes were designed for practicability and years of hard wear. The plain countryman wore a round, plain felt hat, broadcloth coat, woollen trousers, hand-knitted, worsted stockings and sturdy leather shoes fastened with strong buckles; and his wife wore a long, full skirt of some dark material, perhaps trimmed with braid, a dark, basqued jacket of the same material, a long white apron and white cap; and when out of doors she put on a long, warm cloak, a flat felt hat, tied over her cap, and wooden clogs.

Farm labourers wore a heavy linen smock which was little different from the tunic of medieval peasants, and some of them were still wearing the medieval leggings of twisted cloth.

In the towns, women took more notice of fashion. The wife of an ordinary citizen wore a plain cloth skirt and bodice with an apron, cap and large felt hat, but she probably wore high-heeled shoes and perhaps a linen fichu and cuffs. The wife of a small merchant, slightly higher in social rank, probably possessed a skirt slashed in front to show an embroidered petticoat, a pair of long, loose leather gloves and a pair of shoes trimmed with rosettes of ribbon, but her husband had plainer tastes and usually wore 'a long open gown, with hanging sleeves, skull cap and less frippery'.

A maidservant's dress was a short gown, a large apron, a tippet and gypsy hat, tied over a white cap, and the common livery of a footman was a bright blue tunic or skirted coat, frogged, with knee breeches and white stockings.

CHAPTER SEVEN

THE HANOVERIANS
George I and George II

Throughout the reigns of George I and George II Versailles continued to set the fashion throughout the Courts of Europe, for the Courts of the Regency and of Louis XV were as gay and extravagant as in the early years of Louis XIV's reign.

When Queen Anne died there were many who expected that James II's son, recognized by Louis XIV as James III, would succeed. All through her reign the controversy had raged, but eventually the succession was declared in favour of James I's Protestant granddaughter Sophia, who had married Ernest Augustus, Elector of Hanover.

By 1702 she was seventy-three years old. Gilbert Burnet, Bishop of Salisbury, described her as 'the most knowing and entertaining woman of the age' and John Toland wrote of her: 'She steps as firm and erect as any young lady, has not one wrinkle in her face, which is still very agreeable, nor one tooth out of her head, and reads without spectacles, as I have often seen her do . . . and you cannot turn yourself in the Palace without meeting some monument of her industry, all the chairs of the Presence Chamber being wrought with her own hands. . . . The ornaments of the altar in the Electoral chapel are all of her work. . . .'

Her eldest son, George, was born in 1660 and had been sent to England in 1680 as a possible husband for Anne, but nothing came of the idea, for though he had already shown great physical courage as a soldier he was far from handsome. Neither Ann nor her father was enthusiastic and William of Orange, by devious secret diplomacy, did all he could to prevent the betrothal plans. Two years later George married the sixteen-year-old Sophia Dorothea, daughter of the Duke of Celle, thus uniting two aristocratic German families which for years had been enemies. Their first child, the future George II of England, was born in 1683, and very soon afterwards

George was recalled to service in the Imperial army. During the next few years he spent very little time with his young wife, though another child—a daughter—was born a year or so later.

In 1688 there arrived at the Court of Hanover the handsome Count Philip Königsmark and he and Sophia Dorothea were soon in love. By 1691 they were exchanging indiscreet letters which were inevitably discovered: and with George still away at the wars, his father, Ernest Augustus, had the couple watched. On 1 July 1694, Königsmark, who had been on a visit to the Elector of Saxony, returned to Hanover. That same night he left his house to visit Sophia Dorothea at the Leine Palace and was never seen again.

According to Horace Walpole's later account of what happened, Königsmark had been strangled immediately on leaving her, by the old Elector's order, and buried under the floor.

Sophia Dorothea, still only twenty-eight, was banished to exile in the lonely, desolate Ahlden Castle, where she remained until her death in 1726. She was divorced and never saw her children again.

In 1698 Ernest Augustus died and George, at the age of thirty-eight, already a distinguished soldier, became Elector of Hanover; and when his father-in-law died a few years later, he succeeded also to the Dukedom of Brunswick-Celle. Ernest Augustus had loved everything that was French. He had a Parisian *maître d'hôtel* and liked to choose dresses for his wife and mistresses which were in the latest French styles.

The Court of Celle was as French as Versailles at this time, for Sophia Dorothea's mother was a Frenchwoman who had appointed many Frenchmen to her household; and the Court of Brunswick was very similar in its tastes and fashions.

After his father's death, George maintained his Court with the same splendour. 'The Court in general is extremely polite; and even in Germany it is accounted the best,' wrote Toland, and Lady Mary Wortley Montagu said that George dined and supped in public and was 'very affable and good-natured'.

There was a theatre in the Leine Palace built after the style of the Vienna Opera House, 'visited as a rarity by all travellers, as being the best painted and the best contrived in Europe'. 'Nobody pays money that goes to a place there, the Prince, as in some other Courts of Germany, being at all the expense to entertain the town as well as the Court.'[1]

---

[1] John Toland, *Account of the Courts of Prussia and Hanover*, 1705.

'The King's company of French comedians play here every night,' wrote Lady Mary. 'They are very well-dressed and some of them not ill actors.'

It is not surprising, therefore, that the clothes of the German courtiers, the periwigs, knee-length coats and waistcoats, breeches, stockings and shoes of the men, and the tight bodices and wide silk skirts of the women were so similar to those at Versailles. Of the women, Lady Mary wrote: 'All the women have literally rosy cheeks, snowy foreheads and bosoms, jet eye-brows and scarlet lips, to which they generally add coal-black hair. These perfections never leave them till the hour of their deaths, and have a very fine effect by candle-light, but I could wish they were handsome with a little more variety.'

On 8 June 1714, the old Electress Sophia died at the age of eighty-three, and less than two months later Queen Anne died. Sophia, who loved England and wanted to be Queen, did not live long enough to realize her dream, but her son and heir now found himself George I of England. He was fifty-four and not entirely pleased at the prospect. He loved Hanover and his palaces. He was popular and his Court well ordered and prosperous. He spoke no English and had no inclination to learn it. He understood nothing of the English constitution but was well aware of the strength of the Jacobite opposition.

However, leaving his brother at the head of a Council of Regency in Hanover, he set forth for England with his son, whom he heartily disliked, and who was soon to be Prince of Wales.

Prince George's wife, Caroline of Brunswick-Anspach, also arrived with her younger children, though the eldest boy was left behind in Hanover to finish his education.

The people of London gave the King and Prince George a warm welcome during their formal drive through London to St James's Palace, but they were disappointed by the King's homely appearance, for many could remember the elegant Charles II, who had died only thirty years earlier.

The majority thought that King George was a better proposition than a Catholic king, but that was as far as they would go. They disliked him for his quiet, pedestrian ways and the dullness of the Court, over which the Countess of Darlington, the King's half-sister, and the Duchess of Kendal whom it is thought he married 'with the left hand', both plain and elderly, now presided. The English loved pageantry but George avoided showing himself in public whenever possible, particularly as the crowds usually booed him. England never forgave him for being a foreigner and speaking a foreign language, nor for his obvious preference for Hanover.

George on his part distrusted the scheming English Ministers and kept himself aloof from the details of State administration, partly, no doubt, because of the language problem and also because he felt that at any time he might be turned off the throne.

At the coronation on 20 October, there was a splendid gathering of peers and peeresses of every shade of political opinion, from fervent Jacobite to stalwart Hanoverian, but the Jacobites were 'very peevish with everybody that spoke to them', and when the Archbishop went round the throne, demanding the consent of the people, Lady Dorchester muttered under her breath to Lady Cowper, wife of the Lord Chancellor and Lady-in-Waiting to the Princess of Wales: 'Does the old Fool think that Anybody here will say no . . . when there are so many drawn swords.'

Lady Dorchester was James II's former mistress, Catherine Sedley, and this was the occasion when she came face to face with the Duchess of Portsmouth and Lady Orkney, a mistress of William III's. 'Good God!' she cried. 'Who would have thought we three whores would have met together here!'

George I awaited the outcome of the Jacobite rebellion the following year with great calm, for he would not have minded relinquishing the English crown in the least and returning to Hanover, where his Court was maintained in all its comfort and friendliness.

There was sharp jealousy between the German and English women at Court. The Countess of Buckenburgh said that 'English women did not look like women of quality,' wrote Lady Cowper in her diary in April 1716, 'but made themselves look as pitifully and sneakingly as they could; that they hold their heads down, and look always in a fright, whereas those that are foreigners hold up their heads and hold out their breasts, and make themselves look as great and stately as they can, and more nobly and more like quality than others'. To which Lady Deloraine replied, 'We show our quality by our birth and titles, Madam, not by sticking out our bosoms.'

In 1716 George returned to Hanover, leaving the Prince of Wales as Regent, and when he came back the bitter quarrel developed between them which was never properly healed. The Prince had gained a certain amount of popularity during the King's absence and his father accused him of assuming too much power. The following year he ordered him to leave St James's Palace but insisted on the grandchildren remaining there, so the Prince of Wales and Princess Caroline established themselves at Leicester House, a mansion on the north side of where Leicester Square now lies, and here they held a rival court, which was at least younger and gayer than that at St James's, though it never approached the fashion and brilliance of the earlier Stuart Courts. The process begun in William and Mary's time and continued during that of Queen Anne was not to be reversed. While seekers for preferment at Court found access through bribery of the German courtiers, particularly the women, the centres of English culture and intellectual life and also of fashion were far away from the Court, in the magnificent Palladian mansions which the nobility were building for themselves during these years, many of them re-fashioned from their earlier Tudor and Jacobean ancestral homes.

George I's pleasures were simple. He loved hunting, but for him the happiest time of the day was in the evening when he retired to the Duchess of Kendal's apartments and played cards. 'In private life he would have been called an honest blockhead,' wrote Lady Mary Wortley Montagu, 'and Fortune, that made him a king, added nothing to his happiness, only prejudiced his honesty, and shortened his days. . . . Our customs and laws were all mysteries to him, which he neither tried to understand, nor was capable of understanding if he had endeavoured to. He was passively good-natured, and wished all mankind enjoyed quiet, if they would let him do so. The mistress that followed him hither was so much of his own temper, that I do not wonder at the engagement between them. She was duller than himself, and consequently did not find out that he was so. . . .'

In a letter to Louis XV in 1724 Comte de Broghe wrote: 'The King has no predilection for the English nation, and never receives in private any English of either sex; none even of his principal officers are admitted to his chamber of a morning to dress him, nor in the evening to undress him. These offices are performed by the Turks, who are his valets de chambre, and who give him everything he wants in private.'

Not for King George I the elaborate ritual of Versailles, where members of the nobility, already effete, with few duties left to them but their obsolescent privileges, still attended the king night and morning, holding the towel while he washed his hands and helping him on and off with his clothes.

George returned to Hanover again in 1719, 1720 and 1723, and in

1726 was preparing for another visit. It was about this time that, as Horace Walpole put it, 'he paid the English the compliment of choosing from among them a mistress'. She was Anne Brett, a dark-eyed beauty who was duly installed in St James's Palace and promised a coronet, but before the issue between her and the Duchess of Kendal could be joined he left for Hanover. The night before his departure, Horace Walpole, then a child of ten, was taken, as a special privilege, to see him. 'The person of the King is as perfect in my memory as if I saw him but yesterday,' wrote Horace in later years. 'It was that of an elderly man, rather pale, and exactly like his pictures on coins; not tall; of an aspect rather good than august; with a dark tie-wig, a plain coat, waistcoat and breeches of snuff-coloured cloth, with stockings of the same colour, and a blue riband over all. So entirely was he my object that I do not believe I once looked at the Duchess, but as I could not avoid seeing her on entering the room, I remember that just beyond his Majesty stood a very tall, lean, ill-favoured old lady; but I did not retain the least idea of her features, nor know of what colour her dress was.'

The next morning the King departed for Hanover with the Duchess of Kendal. Many years earlier a French fortune-teller, perhaps at the instigation of the Duke and Duchess of Celle, who adored their daughter Sophia Dorothea, had warned George to take good care of her, for he would not long outlive her. She had died at Ahlden only a few months earlier and George, who had never forgotten the warning, had a very strong premonition of his own approaching death. When he left England he told the Prince and Princess of Wales that he would never see them again. In fact, he never reached the Leine Palace. He died of a stroke at the home of his brother, at Osnabruck.

The accession of George II made little impact on the people of England, for the Court had become remote and alien. However, the coronation was a glittering affair, for the new king, unlike his father, wanted to impress himself upon the country as a kingly figure. This was a fairly difficult task, for he was by no means attractive, but he was adorned in velvet and jewels, and diamonds were hired from London jewellers to add to the liberal supply which were stitched to the Queen's dress.

George II had few attractive qualities, but like his father, he was a brave soldier and in 1743 he commanded the British and Hanoverian forces at the battle of Dettingen, the last English king to command in the field. He had no interest in the fascinating and vital scientific and sociological developments of the eighteenth century, nor in the superb work of the writers, artists and architects. He never read a book and it irritated him to see Queen Charlotte reading. He was, however, fond of music, and appointed Handel as Court musician.

The King and Queen settled into a Court routine, staying at St James's during the winter, Kensington during the spring and summer and Hampton Court in the autumn: and they also built White Lodge as a private retreat. The Prince of Wales joined the Court from Germany but was as unpopular with his father as George II had been with George I. There were occasional drawing-rooms and receptions at the Court but mainly the evenings were passed in playing cards—basset, quadrille, cribbage and commerce. The main social event of the year was the King's birthday. This was a gala evening, when everyone was expected to wear new clothes and dress their servants in new liveries. The King would appear in scarlet and gold and the Queen in a low-cut court dress of silk and velvet, embroidered with jewels. And after that the Court sank back into its normal routine.

In 1734 their eldest daughter, the Princess Royal, was married to the Prince of Orange. The Prince was a deformed dwarf and the Princess and her mother and sisters wept at the prospect. 'The Prince of Orange's whole retinue was as magnificent as gold and silver varied in brocade, lace, and embroidery could make them, and the jewels he gave the Princess of immense value, particularly the necklace, which was so large that twenty-two diamonds made the whole round of her neck,' recorded Lord Hervey.

'The Prince of Orange was a less shocking and less ridiculous figure in this pompous procession and at supper than one could naturally have expected such an Aesop, in such trappings and such eminence, to have appeared. He had a long peruke like hair that flowed all over his back, and hid the roundness of it; and as his countenance was not bad there was nothing very strikingly disagreeable but his stature.

'But when he was undressed, and came into his nightgown and nightcap into the room to go to bed, the appearance he made was as indescribable as the astonished countenances of everybody who beheld him. From the make of his brocaded gown, and the make of his back, he looked behind as if he had no head, and before as if he had no neck and no legs.'

Two years later a marriage was arranged for the Prince of Wales. He was now twenty-nine and his parents selected for his bride the seventeen-year-old Princess Augusta of Saxe-Gotha, whom he had never seen and who spoke no word of English. However, when she arrived the Prince seemed well satisfied with her. They were married at nine o'clock at night in the Chapel of St James's and then, Lord Hervey writes: 'The King went after supper to the Princess's apartment whilst the Queen undressed the Princess, and when they were in bed everybody passed through their bed-chamber to see them, where there was nothing remarkable but the Prince's nightcap, which was some inches higher than any grenadier's cap in the whole army.'

The following year Princess Augusta was pregnant. The King and Queen were determined that the child should be born at Hampton Court, the Prince of Wales equally resolved that it should be born at St James's. At the end of July 1737, with the Royal family all in residence at Hampton Court and expecting the birth to be in September, Princess Augusta had the first signs of labour two months prematurely. In the greatest secrecy the Prince ordered a coach, and although Augusta was already in labour and begging the Prince 'for God's sake . . . to let her stay quiet where she was', she was bundled into it, with a Lady-in-Waiting, two dressers and a man midwife, and rushed off to London. They arrived at St James's at ten o'clock at night. Nothing was ready and the Princess was laid between two table-cloths where, three quarters of an hour later, she gave birth to a daughter.

Both the Princess and the baby survived, but the King and Queen were so outraged at the Prince's cruel stupidity that they banished him from the Court and he ultimately bought Norfolk House in St James's Square.

From the time of his accession, George II paid many visits to Hanover, making the journey about every three years and staying for several months at a time. On one of these trips he became infatuated with Madame Walmoden and began an affair of which he related every detail to the long-suffering Queen Caroline, in letters of forty or fifty and sometimes sixty pages.

He acquainted her of the 'growth of his passion, the progress of his applications, and their success, of every word as well as every action that passed—so minute a description of her person, that had the Queen been a painter she might have drawn her rival's picture at six hundred miles' distance,' wrote Lord Hervey.

Moreover, not content with Walmoden, the King also asked the Queen to arrange that when the Prince of Modena paid a visit to England later in the year, she would ask him to bring his wife, as he had heard she was 'pretty free of her person' and 'he had the greatest inclination imaginable to pay his addresses to her. . . . Un plaisir que je suis sür, ma chère Caroline, vous serez bein aise de me procurer, quand je vous dis combien je le souhaite.'

Back in England the King discarded Lady Suffolk and took to Lady Deloraine, the Princesses' governess, for a short time, but when Queen Caroline died, in 1737, he sent for Madame Walmoden. She was soon established in the Duchess of Kendal's apartments at St James's Palace and created the Countess of Yarmouth. Such elements of culture as Queen Caroline had been able to introduce to the Court now vanished completely. For the next twenty-three years of his reign George II passed his days in a dull routine, playing cards every evening with his small intimate circle of the Princesses, Lady Yarmouth, one or two of the late Queen's Ladies-in-Waiting and a few officers of his household.

'Every Saturday in summer, he carried that uniform party, but without his daughters, to dine at Richmond: they went in coaches and six, in the middle of the day, with the heavy horseguards kicking up the dust about them—dined, walked an hour in the garden, returned in the same dusty parade; and his Majesty fancied himself the most gallant and lively prince in Europe,' wrote Horace Walpole.

Perhaps the most festive occasions of these years were the visits to Ranelagh Gardens, which had been opened in 1742. In 1749 was the Gala masquerade and on this occasion there were said to be two thousand visitors to honour the royal party. It was so successful that another masquerade was held a few weeks later. Again the King attended and also his brother, the Duke of Cumberland, dressed in an 'Old English habit, but so enormously corpulent that he looked like Cacofaco, the drunken captain in *Rule a Wife and Have a Wife.*' All the ladies of the Court were there 'in vast beauty, Miss Pitt with a red veil which made her look gloriously handsome. . . . Miss Chudleigh was 'Iphigenia and so lightly clad that you would have taken her for Andromeda. The maids of honour were so offended that they would not speak to her,' recorded Horace Walpole.

These were very rare events for the King, however, and as he grew older the Court grew even duller. Many of the rooms in the palaces were closed and the days passed in a dim, monotonous domestic round.

In 1751 the Prince of Wales, who by now had moved from Norfolk House to Leicester House, suddenly died, and in 1760 George II, now seventy-six years old, was found dead on the floor of his bedroom.

Throughout the forty-six years of the reign of the first two Georges men's basic costume of knee-length, flared coat over a long waistcoat and neat, knee-length breeches changed hardly at all. Neither King was particularly interested in clothes and their Courts had little influence on the small turns of fashion which varied the appearance from year to year. These were introduced by members of the aristocracy, particularly those who were able to visit Paris, which was still the arbiter of taste and the source of such new ideas as were adopted in London.

The greatest change in men's clothing was that it became more practical. Except for State occasions, coats of silk, satin and velvet gave place to coats of fine cloth. Silk cravats replaced lace fichus and periwigs were smaller.

The long curls of the periwig of the seventeenth and early years of the eighteenth centuries were obviously difficult to manage and soldiers devised a campaign wig in which the back curls were tied back in a knot. The Ramillies wig was a further simplification, with the hair worn in a pigtail. The bob-wig was worn a great deal by clergymen and scholars and a familiar example is depicted in Reynolds's portrait of Dr Johnson. Here the hair was frizzed at the sides, rather than curled, and ended in a roll at the nape of the neck. In the 'tye' wig the hair was arranged in rolls of curls at the side and tied at the back in a pigtail. The bag wig looked very much the same from the front, but the back hair was pushed into a black silk bag.

Although most men wore their hair close-cropped under their wigs there were exceptions. Louis XIV is said to have kept his own hair long and threaded it through holes in his periwig, so that the real and artificial hair mingled, and in a letter written from Hanover in 1720, Joseph Wilcocks wrote to Bishop Kennet: 'The King of Prussia has paid a visit here of about ten days; he has a brisk, enterprising look, wears a short waistcoat, narrow hat, and broad sword, and has his own hair tied back, and obliges all his soldiers and officers of his army to do the like; and because his army is clothed in blue, he generally wears the same colour himself.'

The bob-wigs of the 1730s looked more like natural hair and were considerably cheaper. They were worn almost universally by professional men and ordinary citizens, shopkeepers and apprentices, and for formal occasions they were usually powdered. Sometimes the natural hair was left in front and the join between this and the wig was concealed by the powder.

At home, when men discarded both formal clothes and wigs, they wore an embroidered cap or turban to keep their shaven heads warm and a loose silk robe.

The coat was close-fitting to the waist and then flared out to the knees and was usually worn unbuttoned. It was collarless with sometimes a narrow standing band round the neck. For some years, cuffs were very large and buttoned back on to the sleeve to show a lace-edged, frilled shirt cuff. The waistcoat was of a different and usually richer material than the coat and was sometimes embroidered. It was usually worn buttoned or half-buttoned over the shirt and until the 1750s was nearly as long as the coat. Breeches were cut to just below the knee and were fairly tight and inconspicuous, worn with rolled stockings and shoes. The characteristic hat was the tricorn, which began large and tended to grow smaller, and men wore long, circular capes.

In the country men's coats were cut away in front for freedom of movement, especially when riding, and they wore stout leather boots fitted to the calves.

There was no regulation dress for special occasions yet. At Court, men wore the best they had. Army officers mainly wore red coats, but this was also a popular colour for civilians, and it was not until the end of George II's reign that the Navy was put into uniform.

People living in the country were always anxious for the latest news of London fashions. In the middle years of the eighteenth century Henry Purefoy was lord of the manor of Shalstone, a village near Brackley, about five miles from Buckingham. His letters show the pains he took to keep abreast of fashion and the considerable difficulties it involved.

In a letter of 1747 to Mr Garrett, periwig maker at Buckingham, he complained that 'The new Periwigg you made me has some Hair on the top of the Crown that don't curl and when I put on my Hat or the wind blows it stares and rises all up. I have minded other folk's periwigs and I think I should have another row of Curls higher towards ye Crown. Pray don't make my other wigs so, for you must alter this that I have.'

This same barber had a year's contract for keeping Henry's head shaved.

A few years later, the Reverend William Cole of Bletchley was making a note in his diary that he had sent his two French wigs to his London barber to be altered, 'they being made so miserably I could not wear them'.

Henry Purefoy was always writing to his tailor in London for the latest fashion news and asking for patterns of 'super fine cloth'. 'Do they button their Cloathes with Silver or Gold Buttons or continue to wear laced waistcoats of silk or cloth?' he asks. On another occasion he is complaining bitterly: 'The Gold laced waistcoat you made mee last year has done you no credit in the making, it gapes so intolerably before at the bottom, when I button it at ye waistbone of my breeches and stand upright it gapes at the bottom beyond my breeches and everybody takes notice of it. As to my size I am partly the same bignesse as I was when in Town last, but you made the last cloathes a little too straight.'

Less than a month later he had more complaints. His new breeches are too short at the knee and 'the green waistcoat is a very poor silk. . . . The sleeves of the coat come quite down to my wrist and are a great deall longer than ye coat you made me last year . . . let mee know if they wear their coat sleeves longer than they did last year. . . .'

He asked his London hatter to send him a 'fashionable sized Beaver hatt of the very best sort, it must be 26 inches and an half round the outside of the Crown. The last you sent me they tell mee was not all Beaver. . . .' And from the laceman at the Golden Ball, near Arundel Street in the Strand, he ordered, amongst other things, five yards of silver lace to bind a waistcoat 'as good and fashionable as any is worn'.

Mr Rowbotham sent Henry a hat that was too small in the head and the brim was only four inches wide. 'The gentlemen here wear 'em with a larger Brim but I desire you will enquire whether that is the fashionable size or No,' wrote back Henry.

On another occasion he bought the cloth, lining, buttons and thread in London and sent them all to a tailor in Brackley, with a pair of breeches for a pattern and exact details of how the suit was to be made, including the request for a buttonhole for his watch fob. From London he ordered a dozen printed cambric pocket handkerchiefs about 2s. od. a piece for common use, as well as cambric and Holland for nightshirts and cambric for shirt ruffles. At the same time he ordered fine white thread stockings and white thread gloves for his mother and cotton to make her some wrappers.

By 1745 Henry had grown much fatter. He was now using Mr Fell of Chipping Norton to tailor his clothes and complained that his coat was 'all too little about the belly'. And a little later his grey breeches were 'too shallow in the seat and must be let out'.

Henry had at least six handsomely embroidered waistcoats and in 1748 he was needing another beaver hat from London, which cost him £1.4s.0d. 'Your last Beavor Hat you sent me cracked sadly at the edges and I was forced to have it pared (off). I hope I shall have no reason to complain of anything of that sort in the Hat you now send,' he wrote sharply.

Women's clothing throughout these early Georgian years was very attractive, with low-cut stiff bodice, loose, elbow-length sleeves trimmed with deep ruffles of lace, and a long full skirt, often open in front and draped back in folds over side panniers to show a flowered petticoat. The *fontanges* headdress remained in fashion till about 1720 and then disappeared; and for the next fifty years women wore their hair neatly pinned to the head and covered with a small lace cap.

By the 1720s there was a great increase of imported Indian calicoes, brought home by the East India Company. As in Queen Anne's time, an Act was passed to prohibit their importation and protect the English cotton manufactures, but they were then smuggled into the country in large quantities and the law made little difference. Fashion prevailed.

A wide overdress became fashionable at this time, which hung lightly and gracefully from the shoulders and was sometimes fastened in front, over the main costume, with bows of ribbons. At first it was worn only in the house but it became so popular that the 'contouche' was soon seen everywhere, made of wool, taffeta or silk at first and then of the lighter Indian muslins or silks which were so suitable for this enchantingly delicate and informal fashion, so often depicted by Watteau.

In cold weather women wore a cloak and hood which for many years was invariably scarlet and called a cardinal.

By 1730 the farthingale was back. The side panniers were replaced by circular hoops which, with the passing years, grew ever larger. The hoop was a petticoat stiffened with whalebone, and whalebone was also used to stiffen the corset, which was as formidable as ever, laced at the back and reinforced with a stout wire round the top. With the arrival of the hoop women were able to discard some of the cumbersome petticoats they had worn to give fullness to the skirt. Some dispensed with them altogether and wore nothing under their hoops but gartered stockings and a plain linen shift, worn underneath the corset. Scotch and Irish linen were available but were rather coarse, and the finest linen at this time, though a good deal more expensive, came from Holland.

As happened in France, hoops were violently denounced from the pulpits, but with no effect, and for the next fifty years they were worn by nearly every woman, even the country housewives in the remotest villages, where fashion took a long time to penetrate.

By George II's time bodices were cut very low, to expose most of the bosom, and Queen Caroline's magnificent figure was said to be her chief attraction for her husband. She had a great fancy for flowered silks, particularly gold and silver and coloured flowers on a white ground, and this gave a lead to those who still looked to the Court for guidance in fashion, but in the main the aristocracy, and the wealthy middle classes who liked to copy them, dressed as they fancied, within the limits of the accepted style, without designing any new forms.

Regardless of the rigours of the English climate, most women now preferred the thinner silks, muslins and cottons. They were certainly a great deal lighter in weight than the richer silks, damasks and brocades, for the voluminous skirts were now taking yards of material, and cotton was sometimes quilted with wadding to give extra warmth.

Up until the 1730s stockings of all colours were worn, green being particularly popular, but after this time there was a craze for white stockings, of silk, worsted or thread, which lasted until the end of the century, despite more disapproval from the parsons, who seemed to see something immodest in them. Shoes were high-heeled and rather clumsy, with the heel far under the instep for comfortable walking, so women wore slippers in the house. Pattens and overshoes afforded some protection from muddy roads, but Mrs Purefoy, Henry's mother, writing from Shalstone in 1735, complained that 'every place is now so deep in dirt where one walks that my Galloshoes are of no service to me'.

In 1741 she was writing to a shop in Covent Garden for 'a very good whale bone hoop Petticoat of the newest fashion', which was to be sent by the Buckingham carrier, Mrs Eagles, 'who inns at the George in Smithfield and leaves London on Tuesday morning about 4 a.m.' From her milliner in the Old Bailey she ordered a long hood trimmed with black lace and on another occasion an ermine tippet. 'They say Sattins are much worn, I desire to know if they be?' she asks, and if they are she wants patterns of green satin.

False teeth were a problem and Mrs Purefoy, with a trust born perhaps of desperation, sent to Mr Coryndon, 'Operator for ye Teeth near the new Church in ye Strand', for a new set of teeth, marking on a piece of wood the places where her own teeth remained and giving the measurement of her gums on a piece of tape. But when the set arrived, she complained that the spaces he had left did not match with her own teeth and the bite was too high on the two 'hind' teeth.

Henry had a good collection of spectacles—horn, tortoiseshell and silver-rimmed—which were sent to London from time to time to be repaired, but the lenses, which were Concave Number Six, he bought separately and preferred to put in himself.

Cotton was as fashionable for furnishing as for clothes. At his parsonage at Bletchley, Mr Cole's bed was 'a beautiful Stained Cotton with Birds and Trees and Flowers'. In the next bedroom was 'a most beautiful stained Cotton of Crimson and White by a Copper Plate, having Parrots, and Baskets of Flowers. . . .' and in another room he 'laid the old, gloomy blackish Bed aside, and put up an almost new Blew and White Cotton Bed'.

At the beginning of Georgian times, the best shopping districts for all these materials was still the City—the Royal Exchange, St Paul's Churchyard and Ludgate Hill—but by the middle of the century the mercers and woollen drapers around Covent Garden were high fashion.

In 1753 His Grace the Duke of Bedford was buying cloth—blue, claret, white and blossom-colour—from Gabriel Fouace at the Pearl and Crown in Bedford Street, Covent Garden, at 17s. od. a yard, and also from James Morris at the Black Spread Eagle and King's Arms in Russell Street. One of the most famous mercers was Hinchliff and Croft of Henrietta Street, who sold brocade to the Duke at 25s. a yard, Genoa velvet at 27s. and an ordinary silk for everyday wear, known as 'tabby', for only 9s. 6d. a yard. Another excellent Mercer's shop was Mason, Lucas and Higgons at the Lamb in Chandos Street, where Mother Maberley had kept The Hole In the Wall, the tavern where Claude Duval had been arrested in the previous century.

Although far less gold lace and embroidery was used, it was still worn for special occasions and was very costly, compared with the prices of plain cloth and silk. In November 1757, for example, the Duke was charged 64 guineas 'to embroider a rich suit of crimson velvet with gold'. Waistcoats embroidered with gold and silver and silver buttons were all expensive and on one occasion the dresses of the little Bedford children were sewn with yards of gold and silver braid, which was sold by weight. Gold lace was sold by Peter Bunnell, the laceman at the Golden Cock in Bedford Street, Covent Garden, at 18s. a yard, but he gave good value for old lace, which was often used again on new clothes.

The tailors were men and also many of the embroiderers, but most of the mantua-makers were women. Elizabeth and Jane Munday charged Lady Caroline Russell eight shillings for making a crêpe gown, with six shillings extra for the body and sleeve linings and for pinking the ruffles. Making a bombazine gown and coat and a pink and silver gown and coat both cost fourteen shillings.

The sacque—another name for the *contouche*—needed very skilful cutting and for these Lady Caroline went to a professional male sacque maker. In October 1758 he charged her £1. 10s. 6d. for making a black silk sacque and petticoat, with extras, and in January 1759 £1. 11s. od. for making a bombazine sacque. Her riding habits were made by William Thompson and the one she ordered in 1758 cost her £10. 19s. 5d, which included £1. 11s. 2d. for gold and silver buttons.

It was a blue and white riding habit worn by her mother, the Duchess, which decided George II to order a special blue and white uniform for the commissioned officers of the Royal Navy. The matter had been under discussion for some time and blue with red and red with blue had both been suggested as possible colour schemes, but, said the Duke, 'the King having seen my Duchess riding in the park a few days ago in a habit of blue faced with white, the dress took the fancy of His Majesty, who has appointed it for the uniform of the Royal Navy'.

Fashionable retailing was moving west again. Although the Duke first bought his hats from William Finch at the corner of Tavistock Street and Covent Garden, by 1759 he was buying them in St James's Street, from Mr James Lock, where a fine beaver hat cost him £1. os. od. and six double cockades nine shillings.

The history of women's hats had hardly begun yet but by the middle of the century they had taken to milkmaid straw hats, tied with ribbons over their lace caps. This marked the beginning of the Luton straw hat industry and in all the surrounding villages cottage women spent their spare time plaiting straw for the hat makers, who collected the plaits each week at the nearest markets. Pay was low and Lady Caroline was able to buy a straw hat from her milliner for three shillings.

Tapestry work in wool and silk was as popular during the eighteenth century as in Stuart times and was used to cover chairs, settees, fire-screens and stools and also for carpets.

Early in the century mainly floral patterns were used, the leaves and flowers being less stylized than in the Jacobean work. To upholster the furniture of the famous cabinet-makers—Chippendale and Hepplewhite, and, later in the century, Adam and Sheraton—a great deal of beautiful needlework was done, still using naturalistic flowers but sometimes introducing classical motifs as well, particularly vases. Human figures were occasionally worked, reminiscent of those introduced by the French weavers in the Cluny and Gobelin looms.

French hand tapestry work at this time was of extreme delicacy and the designs were copied by English embroideresses. They were mainly floral, sometimes with stylized leaves curving into long scrolls which outlined the whole pattern, sometimes, as in the old French brocade patterns, arranged in bands of tiny flower sprays on alternating background colours, to produce the stripes which Hepplewhite admired so much.

Another style of needlework for upholstery was Florentine work, in which a repeating pattern of a geometric shape—the Vandyke, oyster, melon or fleur-de-lis—completely covered the canvas.

As in earlier days, little girls were expected to work at their samplers. About 1720 woollen canvas was used and also a transparent gauze stiffened with gum, which was known as tiffany. This made for finer work and samplers were often very decorative, the best of them being framed. They were embroidered with carefully designed letters and numbers. Then followed the Lord's Prayer, the Creed, the Ten Commandments or one or two Biblical texts. Towards the end of the century attractive little Georgian houses were embroidered, sometimes with trees and landscape background. Maps were also worked and the sampler was nearly always finished with a neat floral border, with the embroideress's name in the corner and the date.

CHAPTER EIGHT

THE COURTS OF LOUIS XV AND LOUIS XVI

When Louis XIV lay on his deathbed he asked to see his heir, the future Louis XV, a small boy of five years old. 'Mignon, you are going to be a great King,' he said. 'Do not copy me in my love of building or in my love of wars; on the contrary, try to live peacefully with your neighbours. Remember your duty and your obligation to God; see that your subjects honour Him. Take good advice and follow it. Try and improve the lot of your people, as I, unfortunately, have never been able to do.'

If Louis XV had taken this advice, the history of France might have been very different. Unfortunately, he did not. The Regent was Louis XIV's nephew, Philippe II d'Orléans, but in 1723, when the young King was only thirteen years old, he was declared of age and the Regency ended, Philippe dying in the same year.

The French government was desperately short of money. Louis XIV had left the country on the verge of bankruptcy and during the years of the Regency there had been financial chaos. Yet the Court was maintained in all its splendour and, with the old King dead and Madame de Maintenon living in retreat at St Cyr, it was gayer and more extravagant than ever.

The young King's bride was Marie Leszczyńska, daughter of the former King of Poland, who had been chased from his throne by the Elector of Saxony. She was twenty-two, a charming and sweet-natured woman but nearly seven years older than the King. She was driven across Europe to her new home through a rain-drenched countryside, where months of bad weather had brought famine to thousands of peasants. On more than one occasion her carriage fell into a water-hole and she had to be rescued from drowning, but when the King rode out from Fontainebleau to meet her, he was well pleased with her appearance in her dress of silver brocade. She had already been married by proxy, but the following day the marriage was solemnized again, and for this occasion she was dressed in purple velvet embroidered with golden lilies, the young King wearing a gold brocade coat and white feathered hat, ornamented with an enormous diamond.

Louis XIV had decreed the fashion of the Court for both men and women, but during the wild and giddy days of the Regency and the reign of Louis XV, women took matters into their own hands.

By about 1718 enormous panniers were fashionable, so that women were again taking up too much room. Their panniers were at least six feet from side to side, making the skirts about eighteen feet in circumference. They were monstrously inconvenient and called forth criticism both from the Church and the pamphleteers.

'The fashion is owned, even by those who are most devoted to it, to be very inconvenient,' wrote one critic. 'Panniers are most uncomfortable, both for the wearer and for everyone else.'

Criticisms of this kind made no difference at all. The fashion lasted for another fifty years and was ended only by the Revolution. At first the panniers were made from osier or cane hoops, like a bird-cage, and then whalebone was used. So widespread was the fashion that the whalebone industry became very profitable for Holland and as early as June 1722, the States-General of the Netherlands authorized a loan of 600,000 florins in support of a 'company established in East Friesland for the whale fishery, the trade in which increased daily by reason of the demand for whalebone used in the construction of hoops for women'.

The increasing size of the panniers, involving ever more material, meant that the cut of the dress had to be adjusted and the light Indian silks were found to be more comfortable than the heavy satins, brocades and velvets, while the loose hanging *contouche* or sacque, draped over the panniers, looked charming in flowered lawn or muslin, or in white or rose-coloured silk.

With these panniered dresses, hair was at first neatly curled and close to the head, dressed rather high and powdered. In summer women wore light mantles and carried sunshades, in winter they took to fur pelisses. Stockings were embroidered and shoes high-heeled. Particularly at Court, women wore lavish make-up, with far too much rouge and too many patches, the position of each patch having a particular significance. The patch in the corner of the eye was the 'impassioned' patch, in the middle of the cheek 'the gallant', on the lips 'the coquette'.

High headdresses came into fashion for a short time during the 1730s although they did not compare with the monstrous fashions of the 1770s. Nevertheless, they were complicated affairs which sometimes took an entire day to complete. The Comtesse de Mailly is said to have gone to bed each night with her hair dressed and wearing all her diamonds, and according to *Le Mercure de France* in 1730, 'ladies could not sit in their carriages but were obliged to kneel'.

'Their woolly white hair and fiery faces,' wrote Lady Mary Wortley Montagu, always very much to the point, 'makes them look more like skinned sheep than human beings.'

Marie Leszczyńska introduced the fashion of the polonaise from Poland, but generally speaking, from 1725 to 1775 there was little change in the basic fashion of the wide skirt laden with flounced frills and ribbons and the Watteau 'sac'. Bodices were long-waisted over a tight corset and cut low in front, most often with square necks. Sleeves were elbow length and, like the neck, trimmed with deep lace ruffles.

Men's dress was equally rich and elaborate. When the Duc de Richelieu, French Ambassador to Austria, presented his credentials at the Court of Vienna in 1725, he drove through the city 'preceded by running footmen in velvet uniforms, frogged with silver; then fifty grooms with silver swords at their sides; then a dozen *heyduques*, valets dressed in the Hungarian style, with short boots, tall plumed caps, and silver maces; a dozen pages; the ambassador himself, in a suit of cloth-of-gold. . . .'

Yet behind the glittering façade of Louis XV's Court there was the most appalling corruption and immorality. It was frivolous, ostentatious and in the end depraved. The King was a mean and devious character, with no political sense, no moral courage and no social conscience.

Between 1727 and 1737 the Queen had ten children. 'Toujours coucher, toujours grosse, toujour accoucher,' she protested and henceforth refused to share her husband's bed, partly because she did not want any more children and partly because she believed he had contracted syphilis.

Louise Julie de Mailly was selected as the King's mistress and given apartments at Versailles, but the King was far from generous to her. Her husband, the Marquis de Mailly, was disappointed at the poor

For Elizabeth 1, quite a simple dress. Heavily padded, but with a diaphanous collar behind the white ruff. Her long strands of pearls fall most gracefully on to the stiffened basque of the farthingale

Mary Fitzalan, Duchess of Norfolk. An embroidered yoke above the lovely neck-line of the flame velvet dress stresses the simplicity of the dress and echoes the golden glitter of the huge sleeves, composed of two brocades

Her little attendant, resplendent in bright red, admires his Queen
Henrietta Maria in her sombre yet sumptuous dress of almost black,
indigo and silvery white

*Louise de Kérouaille, the King's mistress of Breton origin, later
became the Duchess of Portsmouth. She wears a curious combination of
colours, carrot-brown with harebell blue*

This very posed group of Mademoiselle Louise de la Vallière and her
children is by Mignard

James Stuart's little sister wears a very grown-up dress and train and surprisingly enough her headdress is similar to that made famous by Mlle Fontanges, one of Louis XIV's mistresses. It is made of stiff lace and linen frills built up on a foundation of wire

Mary, Countess Howe, posed for Gainsborough in a rustle of pink taffetas and silver-blue gauze.

At this Ball to celebrate the wedding of the Duc de Joyeuse, his lady sweeps along in the glitter of gathered satin, her arms unhampered by the weighty sleeves

Marie-Antoinette, a supreme fashion-setter, epitomizes femininity

The Empress Marie Louise chose an easy-fitting dress for painting her husband Napoleon

George III's young sons wore a scaled-down version of their father's clothes. The small girls were a little less formal

This lovely picture shows the beautiful Empress Elizabeth of Austria – with diamond stars in her auburn hair – wearing one of the most romantic dresses ever painted

*At the wedding of H.R.H. Victoria, Princess Royal, to Prince
Frederick William of Prussia in 1858 the bride wears the traditional
white satin festooned with heavy garlands of orange blossom. Queen
Victoria is in lavender blue with an overskirt of Honiton lace. Next to
her is a lovely dress of pale pink satin and then a magnificent dress of
aquamarine moiré velvet banded with pink roses*

Tissot's almost photographic paintings reveal how entranced he was by coquettish silhouettes

financial return and the Spanish ambassador, after attending her toilet one day, remarked that her chemise was in holes.

In 1740 a cold and windy summer was followed by a disastrous harvest. 'More have died of want within two years than were killed in all the wars of Louis XIV,' recorded Argenson, but the Court continued its unending round of vapid gaiety. Louise Julie's sister, Felicity, became the King's mistress for a time, but she died in child-birth within a year and Louise Julie returned to favour. Then her youngest sister, Marie-Anne, supplanted her in the King's affections and Louise Julie had to leave the Court. Marie-Anne was a great success for a time. The King gave her the Duchy of Châteauroux and amongst the presents he lavished on his new Duchess was a pearl necklace worth 100,000 livres.

Though France could ill afford to take part in another war, she now became involved in the War of the Austrian Succession and Marie-Anne urged the King to join the campaign at Metz, in order to show himself to the people of France as a man of courage and action. He finally agreed and the most elaborate preparations were made at Metz for his reception. The burgesses were formed into four batta-lions, the officers being put into hastily tailored uniforms of scarlet coats edged with gold braid, white vests and gaiters, and hats a-glitter with gold braid and cockades. Two separate corps were made from four hundred young men from the better families, their ages ranging from nine to thirty, and they were distinguished by the silver buttons on their coats and the blue and white cockades. Before them went an ensign, bearing a white taffeta standard embroidered with an eagle and the sun, and a band of hautboys, bassoons and tambours, while the commanding officer of this colourful army wore wide gold braid on his blue coat and silver moiré waistcoat.

It was all lavish and impractical and silly and proved a waste of time in the end for the King was taken ill at Metz. Still being mort-ally afraid of meeting his God while living with a mistress, he sent Marie-Anne away. The people of Metz had in any case been deeply shocked at her arrival with the King's retinue, so she had to depart in an undignified and hurried secrecy for fear of being attacked.

The Queen, dressing herself and her ladies-in-waiting as enticingly as she could, in soft shades of pink and coloured ribbons, hurried to Metz to be with her sick husband and try to encourage him to a more Christian way of life.

When he was feeling ill this was not difficult and he was touchingly

H

penitent, but as soon as he was well again he found that he had no wish to be reformed after all.

'I can well believe that as long as the King is a little weak in the head, he will be very devout,' wrote the unrepentant and perceptive Marie-Anne, 'but as soon as he recovers, I wager that I shall run furiously in his head, and at length, he will not be able to resist asking what has become of me. If he recovers, he will make me public reparation for the present insult. Up to now I have conducted myself with dignity: I shall always preserve that; it is the sole means of making myself respected, of regaining general admiration, and of retaining the consideration I deserve.'

She was right. The King returned to her, but at the end of that year, 1744, she died of a sudden fever.

It was at this time that a bride was chosen for the fifteen-year-old Dauphin. She was the eighteen-year-old Infanta Maria Theresa Rafaela of Spain. The Duc de Richelieu travelled to Orleans to meet her, carrying a vast quantity of small presents for her to distribute— fans, gold watches, gold scent bottles, jewelled snuff-boxes and similar extravagant toys. The Duc also had instructions from the King that she must wear rouge, so that her fair skin did not make her look inspid among the heavily made-up Court ladies.

The Dauphin was well content with his bride, but the following year she died in childbirth, and no sooner was she buried than arrangements were made for him to marry the fifteen-year-old Marie-Josephe, daughter of Augusta of Saxony. Once more it was the task of the Duc de Richelieu to bring her to France. 'My son has set his heart on her,' wrote the King to the Duke, and I gather that he would prefer her to be sweet-smelling: he has urged Madame de Brances [the bride's dame d'Honneur] to see that she has a bath before he meets her, which confirms my suspicion that the poor late-lamented did not do this often enough.'

This was the year that the King met Madame de Pompadour. She was then twenty-three, and for the next nineteen years she reigned as Louis's mistress, cordially hated by nearly everyone and living in mortal fear of losing her ascendancy over him, of being supplanted, even of being poisoned.

Yet she lived in fabulous luxury and her clothes, though setting no basic new fashions, were delicate and beautiful. The famous portrait of her by Boucher, painted in 1759, shows the manifold labour of stitching which went into the bows and lace flounces of the dress, which was still the divided skirt over a farthingale, open in front to reveal a beautifully decorated underskirt or petticoat, a long-waisted, tight bodice, cut very low in front, with a stomacher ornamented with ribbon bows and elbow-length sleeves trimmed with ruffles of lace.

The King gave La Pompadour her châteaux at Montretout, at La Celle, at Bellevue and Crécy. She built hermitages at Versailles, Fontainebleau and Compiègne and bought mansions at Versailles and in the Champs Elysées which were decorated and furnished with staggering extravagance.

The finances of the country were steadily deteriorating and the national debt was rising. Money collected from taxes was squandered and no Minister dare complain, for she had the power to enforce his dismissal. Early in the century the French fleet had been equal to that of England and Holland together, but during the 1750s, after years of neglect, it was less than half that of Great Britain alone. Commerce and industry were stagnating. The population figures were declining through famine and plague and one-tenth of the people had been reduced to beggary. But La Pompadour lived at the rate of 2,000,000 livres a year.

Worse still, she began to meddle in politics. Anxious to be on terms of friendship and equality with Maria Theresa of Austria and Elizabeth, Empress of Russia, she engineered the alliance of Austria, Russia and France against George II of England and Frederick of Prussia, which sparked off the Seven Years War. By the end of it, in 1763, France had lost much of her colonial empire—her valuable trading establishments in India and thousands of square miles in Canada and the Mississippi basin.

To keep the King amused, while his kingdom was reeling to catastrophe, La Pompadour organized her famous theatricals in which dukes and duchesses took part but she was always the star, yet before the war ended she knew that her looks were fading and that the tuberculosis from which she had been suffering for a long time would soon kill her. She spent more money, ordered more clothes.

There was little intellectual life to be found at the Court after the time of Mme de Maintenon, but women of intelligence held sway in the salons. They were not blue-stockings, but deftly combined intelligence with grace. They cultivated the art of conversation and exercised taste in their surroundings, their cuisine and their clothes.

The women of the salons were the important promoters of the Encyclopaedia, Madame de Geoffrin being regarded as the mother of the Encyclopaedists. She was of humble origins, the daughter of the valet of the Dauphin, who had married and been widowed while still young, but it was not until middle age that she established her salon.

Her predecessor in the intellectual world of Paris was Madame de Tencin, who had continued the tradition of the Hôtel Rambouillet, after a few years of dissipation in her youth. She was an extremely intelligent woman and foretold the fate of France many years before the Revolution broke out. 'Unless God visibly stretches out his hand, it is a physical impossibility to prevent the downfall of the State,' she said and Saint-Beuve remarked of her that 'she knew the end of the game in everything'.

As she lay dying, she said 'Madame Geoffrin comes here to pick up what I shall leave.'

'Madame Geoffrin . . . is an extraordinary woman with more common sense than I have almost ever met with,' wrote Horace Walpole.

'Her toilette can be summed up as the most careful simplicity combined with the most irreproachable neatness,' said another writer. 'Invariably dressed in a dress sombre of hue and severe in cut, the collar and cuffs of the plainest and finest linen, her silver hair half covered by a cap fastened by strings under the chin, she presented the most prepossessing figure of old age it was possible to imagine. Her tastes and her years went together like two well-matched horses.'

On Mondays she gave dinners to writers and on Wednesdays to artists. She had a keen and critical mind and took an intelligent and practical interest in their work and their well-being. Voltaire, D'Alembert and Diderot all gathered regularly at her salon and one of her closest friends was Stanislas Poniatowski, father of Marie Leszczyńska, who for a few years was made King of Poland. 'Mamma, I am King; come and see me,' he wrote and at the age of sixty-seven she set forth from Paris to Poland.

So renowned was Madame de Geoffrin that at Vienna Maria Theresa came to meet her and present her daughters, one of whom was the young Marie Antoinette.

'There are three things the women of Paris throw out of the window,' she once said, 'their health, their time and their money.'

Her successor was Madame du Deffand, at one time a mistress of the Regent, who in middle-age became blind and relied therefore more especially on good conversation for the entertainment of her guests at her supper parties, which she held three times a week. In

1754 she acquired a companion, Julie de L'Espinasse, a girl of twenty-two, who later conquered the old woman's court and established her own salon. Many great men loved her, but she broke her heart in a hopeless passion for a man who became bored by her excessive devotion, and she died comparatively young.

The salon of Madame D'Epinay now became the most brilliant in Paris. She was the friend of Rousseau, Voltaire, Grimm, Galiani, D'Holbach, Duclos and Diderot. Her salon was the resort not only of the Encyclopaedists but of the Diplomatic Corps, and among her many admirers was Catherine of Russia. Catherine was deeply interested in the work of all the Encyclopaedists, of whom she was the patroness. She recognized that these philosophers were setting the scene for nineteenth-century Europe and was particularly interested in and sympathetic to their political views. With Grimm she maintained a regular correspondence, sending him a large dossier every three months by courier.

In Paris, Mme de Pompadour lived in a world far removed from the intellectual life of Mme D'Epinay. Her health was deteriorating and the King was beginning to lose interest.

In 1764 she died, at the age of forty-two. The King showed no emotion. As the body of the ravishing Pompadour, which had once been pink and white and delicate as a piece of Dresden china, was driven away from Versailles to Paris, on a wild and windy day, he stood at one of the palace windows and remarked: 'The Marquise will not have fine weather for her journey.'

Even the Queen was shocked by his heartlessness. 'There was no question here of what no longer exists, any more than if she had never existed,' she said. 'Of such is the world; it is not worth the trouble of loving it.'

Horace Walpole wrote of the Marquise de Pompadour: 'Grace, beauty, address, art, ambition, all met in that charming woman. She governed him (Louis XV) more than he had ever been governed but by Cardinal Fleury: she engaged in all politics, she gave life and agreeableness to all; she amassed vast treasures herself, she was the cause of squandering vast treasures, in varying scenes of pleasure to divert the gloom of a temper which was verging nearer to the age of devotion. The Clergy hated her, for she countenanced the Parliament; the people imputed oppressions to her; the Dauphin, who was a bigot, and who loved his mother, affected to shock her.'

In 1765 a young woman called Beauvarnier became the mistress of the Comte Jean du Barry, who also 'sublet her charms to M. le duc de Richelieu and M. le Marquis de Villeroy, during the daytime only. . . . It is difficult to resist her pretty looks, her air of sweetness and honesty; the marquis has swallowed the hook, and the pair of them shower her with presents every day. She is currently well supplied with diamonds, expensively dressed, has a carriage *à la Grecque*, Du Barry keeps a good table and lives well, and everything is fine.' Thus wrote Louis Marais, the police inspector who had recently undertaken the supervision of the Paris brothels.

The Du Barry was born at Vaucouleurs in 1743, the illigitimate daughter of a woman called Bécu. She changed her name to Beauvarnier and worked as a shop girl before joining the Comte du Barry, and some time in 1767 she was introduced to the King by his valet-de-chambre. She was of too humble birth to be received openly at Court so it was arranged that she should marry a title. Jean du Barry would have obliged but he was already married, so his brother, the Comte Guillaume, was brought up from Languedoc, married to Jeanne and sent home again, while the bride, being now the Countess du Barry, was socially acceptable at Court as the King's mistress and duly presented. Yet the people of France despised the King for associating with a mistress of such low-born stock, and the throne lost such vestiges of dignity which still surrounded it.

In 1774 the King lay dying of smallpox. Always a coward and still afraid of meeting his God while not in a state of grace, he dismissed the Du Barry, who was sitting faithfully by his bedside, and she departed in tears. A few days later he died and she was committed to a convent from which she was allowed no communication with the outside world.

Louis's nineteen-year-old grandson now became Louis XVI. His wife, the eighteen-year-old daughter of Maria Theresa of Austria, was the ill-starred Marie Antoinette.

Marie Antoinette had begun to set the fashion when she was still the Dauphine. Now she was supreme and every style that she and her dressmaker and milliner created was slavishly copied by the Court, for she had become a social cult.

The Revolution had become inevitable long before Marie Antoinette ever set foot in France, but there is little doubt that the extravagance of the Court fashions of the next fifteen years, for which she was largely responsible, helped to fan the flames.

While the Pompadour panniers were still fashionable, she created the craze for the high headdress. First the hair was brushed up so that it stood on end, being kept in place by a tie of ribbon. This was the hedgehog style. As others copied her, she and her hairdresser, Leonard, devised more styles with equally ridiculous names— jardin a l'Anglaise, parterre, forest, enamelled meadows, foaming torrents, cabriolet, mad dog, sportsman-in-a-bush and so forth. When the hair had been dressed, the woman had to hide her face in a paper bag while her hair was covered with a thick coating of powder.

Headdresses grew steadily sillier and larger. 'The pouf au senti-ment' became a Court favourite. It was composed of various orna-ments fastened in the hair, such as birds, butterflies, cardboard Cupids, branches of trees and even vegetables. The 'Cascade of Saint-Cloud' was 'a cataract of powdered ringlets' falling from the top of the head; the kitchen-garden style had bunches of vegetables hooked to the side curls. The craziest of them all was the coiffure 'à la Belle Poule' which was created in honour of the victory of the frigate *La Belle Poule* over the *Arethusa* in 1778. This headdress con-sisted of a model of a ship in full sail, reposing on waves of thick curls.

Eventually these monstrous structures became so high and so heavy that, for the second time in a century, women had either to kneel when riding in their carriages or sit with their heads hanging down. At the theatre they were a menace. Lenoir, Lieutenant of Police, wrote a letter to the actors of the Italian theatre which began: 'There are constant complaints of the size of headdresses and hats which, being loaded with plumes, ribbons and flowers, intercept the view of the spectators in the pit. . . .' though it is not clear what the actors could do about it.

Hairdressing was becoming a profession and the ladies' hair-dressers considered themselves an infinitely superior breed to the male wig-makers and barbers.

'The art of dressing a lady's hair can be attained only by a man of genius, and is consequently a liberal and free art. Moreover, the arrangement of the hair and curls is not the whole of our work. We have the treasures of Golconda in our hands, for we arrange the diamonds, the crescents, the sultanas, and aigrettes,' wrote one of them, who was obviously getting a bit above himself.

The Queen was very partial to feathers in her headdress and these were often at least eighteen inches tall. The Court ladies did their best to keep up. 'It was a fine sight to see that forest of plumes in the Versailles Gallery, waving with the least breath of air,' wrote one of the ladies, rather naïvely. 'It looked like a moving garden of bright-coloured flowers, gently caressed by the zephyrs.'

Less articulate, perhaps, but as sincere were the growing number of mothers and husbands who felt that the Queen's mania for clothes was bringing them all to ruin.

The craze was spreading through every rank in Paris and many women took to buying second-hand clothes in a more lavish style than they could have afforded to have had made, and also elaborate second-hand shoes which were invariably too small for them.

Fashion was declared to be the 'veritable demon which torments this country'.

After the birth of one of her children, the Queen decided to have her hair cut off and wore a 'coiffure à l'enfant'. It meant more business for the hairdressers as dozens copied her and had their hair cut. More hairstyles were invented—'au plaisir des dames', 'à l'urgence' and 'à la paresseuse'—and now the milliners had their turn, for hats became important and they were furiously busy bringing out such styles as 'grandes prétensions', 'bandeau d'amour', the 'Carmelite', the 'lever de la Reine', the 'novice de Cythère' and the 'prêtresse de Vénus'.

Certain colours had their day, too. When the Queen appeared one day in a dress of purplish-brown, the King remarked that the flea colour suited her admirably. The story goes that the next day every woman at Court appeared in a flea- or puce-coloured gown. It was so popular and so practical that the fashion soon spread through the country and kept the dyers in business for a long time.

For the starving people of France the most enraging of all the fashions must have been the Queen's craze for playing at shepherdesses at the Trianon, when all the women dressed themselves as operetta milkmaids or shepherdesses and wore their hair 'à la laitière' or 'à la Paysanne de la cour'.

By about 1780 straw bonnets, imported from Italy, became the rage. They were trimmed with flowers, ribbons and feathers and were of all manner of shapes. Between 1784 and 1786 the fashion in shape changed seventeen times.

During the 1780s panniers went out of fashion, being replaced by a roll on each hip and at the back, to give padding to the skirt. Then, just before the Revolution, English fashions arrived in Paris. Women in London had adopted masculine styles and Frenchwomen now wore the same tight-waisted jackets and waistcoats and driving coats with large lapels and triple collars, cut tight to the waist and very long at the back. They took to enormous fichus which, above their tight waists, made them look like pouter pigeons.

Colours were light and bright, fabrics included satin, silk, Indian silks and muslins, and by 1787 they were nearly all striped.

Women still wore a great deal of powdered hair, often with curls framing the face or hanging down behind, but they now took to the most enormous hats, with wide brims and vast, unwieldy crowns, laden with every conceivable kind of ornament. The turban hat, striped, feathered and trimmed with a gauze scarf, was equally hideous and ridiculous.

It was in these extraordinary clothes that, as their world was about to disintegrate in the Revolution, the great ladies of France would promenade or drive to Longchamps, attended by a turbanned footman to carry the parasol and preceded by a running footman in tights and a plumed cap, carrying a long, gold-tipped cane.

CHAPTER NINE

THE REVOLUTION, THE DIRECTORY AND THE EMPIRE

By the late 1780s the line of women's dresses was straighter and the bodices were short-waisted and cut very low to show a wider expanse of bosom, which was sometimes covered with a gauze kerchief. Arms were either bare or covered from shoulder to wrist with a long, tight sleeve. A few of the more dashing leaders of fashion had adopted the masculine style of the English riding-habit, with waistcoat and collared greatcoat, but, as the threat of the Revolution drew closer, most women took to simple straight dresses in subdued colours.

When the Revolution broke, women had neither the heart nor the opportunity to consider fashion for the first few months. After the arrest of the Queen, her dressmaker, Mlle Rose Bertin, and her staff fled to London, and the women of Paris aimed to be as inconspicuous as possible.

At first the bourgeoisie were in control. In the realm of fashion, the aim was for women to look as much alike as possible. Henceforth, dress must not distinguish women of rank and wealth. Powder and paint were forbidden, as well as dresses of silk or white muslin, for they savoured of the aristocracy. Brocades, silk, tissues and velvets all disappeared and women wore mainly cambrics and cottons, Indian prints and lawns.

Women took to Charlotte Corday caps or went bareheaded, except for a Greek fillet or bandeau trimmed with a large tricoloured cockade. Charlotte Corday belonged to an ancient Norman family, an intelligent and liberal-minded young woman who was a great admirer of Rousseau and intensely interested in the fashion for Classicism and its political philosophy. As she watched the hundreds of political prisoners committed to the guillotine, she declared: 'They have killed all those who would have given us freedom; they are executioners, nothing else.'

She became associated with the Girondists and was soon obsessed with the idea that there would be no salvation for France while Marat was still alive. Travelling secretly to Paris, she sought an interview with him. Marat was ill at the time but after her second request, in which she said she would 'put it in his power to do France a great service', he agreed to see her. He received her in his bath—though history does not say why—with his devoted Simonne Everard, whom he had 'married in the sight of Heaven', close at hand. Charlotte stabbed him to the heart and he died instantly.

She submitted calmly to her arrest and at her trial said she had 'killed one man to save a hundred thousand; a villain to save innocents, a savage wild beast to give my country repose. I was a Republican before the Revolution; I never wanted energy'.

As a murderess, she had to wear a red dress for her execution in the Place de la Revolution, and 'her calm smile was only disturbed by a blush when the assistants took the handkerchief from her neck before the axe fell'.

A later occupant of Charlotte Corday's cell was another Girondist, the beautiful Madame Roland, whose last words at the scaffold were: 'Oh, Liberty! O Liberty! What crimes are committed in thy name!'

Despite these tragedies, it was not long before fashion began to show itself again. The smallest event was made an excuse for inventing a new device. When a swallow pursued by a sparrowhawk fell exhausted on to the Pont Neuf a headdress 'à l'hirondelle' was at once designed, composed of two little gauze wings, stretched on steel springs, on either side of the head.

After the storming of the Bastille, fragments of the stones taken from the ruins were set in gold and silver and sold as necklaces and bracelets.

A dressmaker of the Palais Royal created a 'Federal Uniform' for ladies, a simple, enveloping garment, with a sash its only ornament. Hats trimmed with red, white and blue flowers, feathers and ribbons were on sale, to honour 'the nation and the charms of liberty'.

A Mme Rispal advertised in the *Journal de Paris*, offering dresses in African silk and Chinese satin, and undertaking to make dresses in a variety of styles, such as à la Nina, à la Sultane and à la Cavalière, but these were all very simple and low-priced Republican garments.

The years of austerity were not long. By 1794 the Reign of Terror was over and in 1795 the Directory was formed, with the upper bourgeoisie now in power. Suddenly the mood changed. All was gaiety and in the reaction the social life of Paris was a ceaseless round of balls, parties and concerts, though there were new faces now in the fashionable resorts, many of them belonging to parvenus, enjoying the delights of high life for the first time. These were the days of the Incroyables and the Merveilleuses, both of whom had appeared tentatively before the Robespierre régime, but now came into their own. The Incroyables were the young Dandies, with their high-collared coats and huge cravats, who were copying the English fashions. The Merveilleuses were the young women who worshipped antiquity and dressed themselves like the women of ancient Greece and Rome.

Dresses were straight sheaths of muslin, so high-waisted that the girdle was a ribbon tied under the bosom. They were transparent and often slit at the sides from the waist to the hem. They were cut very low, with the bosom either partially or fully exposed, and they were sleeveless. Feet were usually bare except for Roman sandals and toe rings.

Citizeness Tallien, close friend of the future Empress Josephine, became the queen of fashion in Paris. She appeared at Frascati's in a transparent muslin dress *à la Grecque*, underneath which she wore flesh-coloured tights with golden circlets for garters, antique buskins and rings on each of her toes.

For a time this was the ordinary outdoor dress of the 'Merveilleuses', under which they wore either the 'carthaginian' chemise or no chemise at all. The belt, worn high under the bosom, was about two inches wide and set with brilliants.

As a variation, the skirt, instead of being slit at the sides, was raised at one side to well above the knee, where it was held in position by a cameo, to display the left leg.

The dress was held on the shoulders with cameos and the bare arms were covered with bracelets.

Mme Tallien's costume of a gauze chemise over pink tights with gold garters came to be known as the 'Female Savage' and became increasingly popular. More women took to wearing a bare bosom, but the climax came when a young man wearing only a loin-cloth walked through the streets of Paris accompanying two young women who were stark naked. It was the ultimate bid for freedom but the citizens of Paris thought it was taking the idea too far. The 'Merveilleuses' had to flee for their lives and the dressmakers breathed again.

With the Athenian dress, women wore their hair *à la Grecque*—

curled, bejewelled and held in a net. There was a rage for blonde wigs which were slightly powdered. Mme Tallien possessed thirty of them, of every shade from ash blonde to brassy gold, each of them costing twenty-five louis, and fair wigs became the symbol of the counter-revolution against the Jacobins.

New styles of hairdressing were 'à la Victoire' and 'à la Sacrifice', brushed up at the back and forward over the top of the head, like the hair of a victim decapitated by the guillotine. At the famous 'Bal des Victimes', to which no one was admitted who had not lost a parent or near relative by the guillotine during the Terror, all the women wore their hair in this fashion, with the macabre addition of a red ribbon round the neck and a red shawl, a note of frivolity born of despair.

Two more dressmakers appeared on the scene, Mme Nancy and Mme Raimbout, both of whom employed sculptors to help them model their dresses in the style of the Greek and Roman frescoes and statues.

The Roman dress was rather more discreet than the transparent tunics of the Athenians and was worn by women in government circles anxious to maintain their dignity. Yet with neither style, while the craze lasted, did they wear anything more protective in the evenings than a light shawl, and many succumbed to pleurisy and pneumonia.

As there was no possibility of making a pocket in these flimsy dresses someone invented the reticule, a little bag decorated with spangles and embroidery, in which women could carry a purse and handkerchief.

Suddenly the fair wig was out of fashion. In its place came the 'Titus' hair cut. This, according to *Le Bon Genre*, which was the official organ of fashion during the Directory, consisted in 'having the hair cut close to the roots, so as to restore its natural stiffness to the tube, and make it grow in a perpendicular direction'. So women of fashion now cropped their hair short, leaving only a few straggling locks to fall forward on the forehead.

With this scanty dress and naked bosom, some women, perhaps to keep the milliners in business, took to wearing a bulky cravat twisted several times round the neck and a huge plumed hat, the effect being utterly incongruous.

The politics of France were as irrational as women's dress. The Revolution of 1789, the September massacres, the execution of the King and Queen and the abolition of the monarchy, the Terror of

Robespierre and the Directory, followed each other all within six years. By 1792 Revolutionary France had been caught up in fresh European wars, in which the young General Napoleon Bonaparte swiftly gained power and fame by his astonishing victories. By 1799 he had become First Consul. He was thirty and had been married for three years to the beautiful Creole, Josephine, who was six years older than her husband.

Women still wore their transparent classical dresses, with bare neck and no sleeves. They still suffered from pleurisy and pneumonia, even after they had taken to cashmere shawls. The only notable change in fashion was in detail, after Napoleon's Egyptian campaign of 1798. A few Egyptian and Turkish motifs were introduced into embroidery and jewellery, but the Egyptian influence was more noticeable in furnishings than in dress, for the costume was little different from the Greek. David's portrait of Madame Récamier, whose salon was so successful during the days of the Directory and the First Empire, gives an excellent picture of the classical dress at its best and most restrained.

From their comparatively modest home in the Rue de la Victoire, the Bonapartes moved to the Luxembourg Palace, where Napoleon, as First Consul, established a court which became increasingly impressive and regal. He expected women to dress to a high standard of luxury, with a lavish display of pearls and diamonds at State functions, and he disliked any suggestion of economy.

'Madame la Maréchale,' he said one day to an embarrassed woman, 'your cloak is superb. I have seen it a good many times before.'

Napoleon suddenly became a dictator of fashion. He decided that the flimsy gauze shifts and tunics which French women were still wearing, in the hope that they made them look like Greek and Roman goddesses, were not respectable nor becoming to the new dignity of the State. Moreover, the craze for Indian muslins was benefiting British trade and French silks and satins were being neglected.

He began a subtle campaign and saw to it that it was well advertised in the government-controlled Press.

In an issue of *Les Variétés* appeared the following paragraph: 'On the occasion of a recent reception at the Luxembourg, the First Consul ordered the fires stoked higher and higher, until one of the footmen observed that it was impossible to cram more logs into the fireplaces.

'Very well, then,' Bonaparte replied, in a voice resounding

throughout the gallery, 'I wanted to be sure to get it warm enough, because the weather is cold and these ladies are practically naked.'[1]

Shortly afterwards there appeared in *Le Moniteur*, the Consular news organ, a note that 'Bonaparte has voiced his displeasure at the sight of naked women in his salon. . . . The ladies today are dressing to please the First Consul.'[2]

Mme Despaulx, the modiste who decreed Paris fashions at this time, was put out of countenance, for she had recently declared that nudity was 'the most elegant and the most dressy of all fashion'. However, Napoleon's wish prevailed and from this time onwards Frenchwomen were more covered.

He took a great pride in Josephine's appearance, for she had a flair for dress, and he would often urge her to appear at her 'dazzling best in jewellery and costume' for certain important occasions, yet some of their bitterest quarrels were about her wild extravagance. Bourienne, his secretary, who often had to act as a buffer between the two of them over these matters, was shocked on one occasion to find an unpaid milliner's bill for thirty-eight expensive hats in one month. Josephine was always in debt and her creditors charged high prices, knowing full well that they would have to wait a long time for their money. Her mania for spending 'was almost the sole cause of her unhappiness', said Bourienne.

Napoleon loved to see women in white and Josephine seldom wore any other colour, while during the weekend parties at Malmaison the white dress was almost a uniform for all the women guests. Josephine's couturier was Leroy and his reputation was made after she appeared at a formal ball at Malmaison in her rose-petal gown. This was made from hundreds of fresh rose petals of palest pink, sewn on to a foundation of white satin.

During the first years of the Consulate, these Sunday night balls at Malmaison were the highlight of the summer season, and in the carriages which streamed from Paris to Malmaison, women glittered in their pearls and jewels and diamonds. When, in 1800, Napoleon's sister Caroline was married to General Murat, Napoleon gave the bride a magnificent diamond necklace which he had originally given to Josephine, so Josephine recompensed herself by buying Marie Antoinette's superb pearls, worth 250,000 francs, raising the money for them by clandestine trafficking in army contracts.

[1] Frances Mossikor, *Napoleon and Josephine*, Gollancz, 1963.
[2] Ibid.

In January 1801, at one of the festivities associated with the establishment of the Civil Code, Josephine was dazzling in a white satin dress covered with little twists of pearl-tipped toucan feathers. She wore a headdress of pearls and feathers and necklace, earrings and bracelets of Oriental rubies.

Napoleon and his Court were becoming more regal every year. In 1803, during a state visit to Belgium, Josephine appeared for the first time in the French Crown jewels, which till then had been kept in hiding since Marie Antoinette had surrendered them to the National Convention in 1791.

Then, in 1804, the first French Empire was declared, with Napoleon as Emperor and Josephine as Empress. He was thirty-five and she was in her forty-first year. It was a far cry from the Republican mood of only fifteen years earlier. The Empire was, in fact, an accident of war. The army was of paramount importance to France and Napoleon was proving himself an incomparable war leader.

For the inaugural ceremony of the order of the Legion of Honour he chose Bastille Day, 14 July 1804. 'In radiant sunlight, Empress Josephine made her appearance in a cloud of pale-pink tulle, sparkling with silver stars, an extremely low-cut gown, as was the fashion, and an arrangement of diamond wheat-ears in her hair,' wrote Claire de Rémusat. 'I heard many people remark that that day she outshone her entire entourage.'

As the day of the Coronation drew near, 'it is impossible to imagine the excitement, the gaiety and the revelry that prevailed in Paris at that time,' said Laure Junot.

'The Empress,' wrote Claire de Rémusat, 'called in the greatest artists and artisans of the day to confer with her on the design of the official costume for the court ladies as well as of her own: the long mantle to cover our dresses, the gold- or silver-embroidered lace or tulle ruff, called a chérusque, rising high from the shoulders to frame the neck and face. . . .'

In the spring of the following year, during a period of reconciliation after Napoleon had ended his brief affair with Madame Duchâtel, Laure Junot described Josephine's dress one night at St Cloud. 'Josephine was a vision in misty-white *mousseline de l'Inde*, with a narrow lamé border like a rivulet of gold around the hemline of the pleated skirt, a gold-and-black enamelled lion's head at each shoulder and another as a clasp for the golden belt. Her coiffure was like that of an antique cameo, curls spilling out of a golden circlet,

The music-loving sisters Princess Louisa (on the left) and Princess Caroline (on the right), hold manuscripts of music, and a 'sittern' or English guitar. Louisa's bodice is almost completely of gathered lace, and Caroline's dress is embellished with yards of ruched taffeta, similar to the extravagant fashions of Madame de Pompadour

The studio of Kneller produced a somewhat unflattering portrait of George I. The Garter Robes reveal an assortment of satin garments worn beneath them, and great attention is paid to the cylindrical shoes, elongated and cut off square

Marie Antoinette, trailing her satins on the dusty ground, enjoys playing the part of the country girl, feeding the chickens at the Petit Trianon

The embroidered and costly dress of Marie Leszczyńska, Polish wife of Louis XV, is made even more sumptuous by the wearing of an underskirt entirely of ermine

Surely the ultimate in romantic and roseate *robes de style* is this enchantingly pretty picture frock, magnificent in its impact yet simple in its design because it is merely festooned with delicate garlands of fragile roses and rosebuds. Worn by the Queen's Lady-in-Waiting

In the reign of Louis XVI a lady of the Court wears an extremely complicated outdoor costume with an equally elaborate hat

Le Comte de Vaudreuil wears a velvet coat in deep cobalt blue mixed with grey, embroidered with gold galloon and lightly edged with ermine, and breeches in the same velvet. His waistcoat is almost solid gold, with touches of silver and edged with ermine like his coat.

The collar and bows at his neck are dull silk in a mole-colour; and to complete a colourful array, his black shoes have vermilion heels and diamanté buckles

Madame Roland, looking almost modern, was the leader of the young intellectuals and all members of the Gironde during the revolution. She was imprisoned for five months during which time she wrote her unfinished memoirs. She was guillotined in 1793

Marie Pauline Borghese, Napoleon's sister, emphasizes the empire line of her fringed and embroidered satin dress and overskirt by a jewelled belt

The Archduchess Maria-Louisa before leaving Austria for her marriage in France to Napoleon, gives jewels and trinkets to her brothers and sisters. This otherwise purely Empire dress, hemmed with its garland of roses, retains a modified version of the flattering Medici collar

The *Incroyables* were the young dandies, in absurdly large cravats and high-collared coats in imitation of the English fashions; the *Merveilleuses* wore dresses which faintly suggested their wearers' admiration for ancient Greece and Rome

For the first time women's dresses gave freedom of movement to the arms and body. Madame Récamier languishes on one of her renowned sofas, a beautiful exponent of easy fashion

The dress of Marie Murat, Queen of Naples and another of Napoleon's sisters, shows the fundamental change in contour of the contemporary clothes

Isabella, Marchioness of Hertford, poses gracefully in sprigged silk. Bouffant sleeves cut in one with the bodice and narrowing towards the wrist harmonize with the double panniers of the over-dress

Queen Charlotte, c. 1779, wears a lovely dress of taffeta gauze and lace, with tightly fitted bodice, the neckline edged with fine lace and tied with a well-proportioned bow. Her coiffure is topped by a curiously beribboned cap

and she wore a golden serpent for a necklace, with matching earrings and bracelets. If there was a striking simplicity in her costume, it was simplicity of the most artful kind; if it was tremendously becoming, it was because Josephine always adapted the mode to her person—one explanation for her reputation as the most elegant of women.

'It was clear that the Emperor was as struck as I by her charming ensemble, for he went to her as he entered the room, kissed her on the shoulder and the brow, and led her to the mirror over the mantel, so that he might see her from all sides at the same time.'[1]

By May of that year, Josephine was Queen of Italy as well as Empress of France, but for her these were empty years. She had given Napoleon no heir and there was talk of divorce, so that he could marry again and have a son. At the time of their marriage he had adored her, but she had not been in love with him, nor even faithful during the first few years. With the passing of time, as his ardent passion for her had cooled, she had fallen in love with him. Now she was tortured by dread of the future. The European war had flared up again and he was away campaigning. Her son and daughter by her previous marriage, with their children, were all miles away from Paris, and she lived in a lonely grandeur, isolated by her high station and with no one close enough to her to give her true companionship.

She spent hours in her dressing-room and bathroom, attended by a pedicurist, manicurist and masseuse. She had four maids, one chief wardrobe mistress and Malvina, a mulatto from Martinique, her close personal servant and main confidante. Her make-up was elaborate, comprising face-masks, emollients and astringents, powders, rouge and skin-whiteners. In the morning her resident hairdresser, Herbault, dressed her hair. In the late afternoon Duplan visited the palace to create her flowered, feathered or jewelled evening coiffure.

In 1809 an inventory of her wardrobe listed 676 dresses and 49 Court costumes for special State occasions, 252 hats or headdresses, 60 cashmere shawls, 785 pairs of slippers, 413 pairs of stockings and 498 embroidered or lace-trimmed chemises. Clothes had become one of her main interests in life and Claire de Rémusat remarked, rather acidly: 'It was fortunate for the Empress that she could always find distraction from her problems in the selection and modelling of some dazzling new creation.'

As the moment she dreaded—the decision on the divorce—drew

---

[1] Mossiker, *Napoleon and Josephine.*

nearer, she spent more and more money on clothes and *objets d'arts*, until her debts amounted to four million francs.

Yet she never lost her grace and charm. When she travelled through southern Germany to meet her husband in Bavaria, she appeared to the peasants of the Black Forest 'like a fairy queen, glittering in pearls and diamonds, in a cloak the colour of dawn and a gown the colour of sunlight'.

The divorce came at the end of 1809 and Josephine retired to Malmaison, desperately sad and lonelier than ever, seeking solace in the beautiful gardens, for she had become a devoted and knowledge-able gardener by this time. In April 1810 Napoleon married Marie Louise of Austria, who duly presented him with a son—the King of Rome—the following year, but after his happiness in the possession of an heir, Napoleon had no further cause for rejoicing in the remain-ing years of his life. His misfortunes and those of France followed quickly.

In October 1812 began the terrible retreat from Moscow, during which Napoleon lost all but fifty thousand of his army of nearly half a million men. On 30 March 1814 came the capitulation of Paris, the restoration of the Bourbon monarchy, with the Count de Provence, Louis XVI's brother, now proclaimed Louis XVIII, and Napoleon's banishment to Elba. Marie Louise did not join him there with their son, as he had begged her to, but retired to Vienna with her lover, Count von Neipperg.

Josephine was allowed to stay at Malmaison, but on 29 May, only a few weeks after Napoleon's exile to Elba, she suddenly succumbed to an attack of diphtheria.

During the Empire, the fashion as worn by Josephine had elegance, but she was far cleverer with clothes than most of her contemporaries, as well as having an infinitely greater amount of money to spend and the advantage of the finest couturier of the day.

Generally speaking, the Empire fashions were not attractive. Everyone wore the shapeless sack dress with the waist close under the arms, and eventually the bosom seemed to be pushed up under the chin.

Extravagance and ostentation prevailed in all ranks of society and at the numerous balls and public festivities women's dress was magni-ficent in its display of diamonds and precious stones, though mostly in poor taste.

Rouge disappeared and women used white powder to give them a pale and interesting look. With the end of the Titus coiffure they took to false hair-pieces, particularly those whose hair would not grow satisfactorily after being so ruthlessly cropped.

Josephine set the fashion for white dresses, particularly for ball gowns, many of which were trimmed with costly Valenciennes lace. The arms were covered with long white gloves and slippers were of white satin.

Dance dresses were sometimes only ankle length but day dresses swept the ground and were worn with cashmere shawls. Spencers and 'hussar vests', pelisses and top-coats were other alternatives for keeping warm. Mostly they were trimmed with fur, the fashionable furs at this time being astrakhan, marten and sable.

It was during the Empire that the manufacture of artificial flowers developed in France. Before this time they had come mainly from Italy, but a Frenchman developed a new method of manufacture and they became extremely popular, and were used to trim ball dresses, bonnets and hats.

The shawls from Kashmir were extremely costly and after a number of experiments a method of manufacture from the hair of Kirghiz goats from Russia was developed, so that the French-made shawls were almost indistinguishable from the real thing.

A third important development in the fashion world was the establishment of the cotton industry at Rouen, where machinery was installed in place of the old hand looms and spinning wheels, and large quantities of cheap printed cotton were produced.

The biggest mistakes of Empire fashions were the hats. Sometimes, inspired by the victorious French armies, they were made like helmets, decorated with a wreath of flowers and surmounted by a great tuft of feathers. Sometimes they were made like shakos. Worst of all were the huge cabriolet hats with wide drooping brims, like poke bonnets, stretching far beyond the face and almost submerging it, and mighty tubular crowns, taller than a shako, topped by a curling ostrich feather.

As an alternative, milliners offered Turkish turbans. That brilliant and endearing character Madame de Staël took to a turban in her later years. When she was presented at Court, on her marriage, she tore the flounce of her dress and spoilt her third curtsey. At this social mishap, she incurred the lasting dislike of Marie Antoinette by laughing, though Germaine was a most devoted Royalist and displayed great courage during the Revolution. She was arrested and brought before Robespierre, but her friends, including Tallien, helped her to escape.

The last fling of fashion in Napoleon's lifetime was during the Hundred Days, when his supporters wore violets in their caps and bonnets or pinned to their bodices, while the Bourbon supporters wore dresses with eighteen tucks in the skirt, in honour of Louis XVIII, with bonnets of white silk, striped with plaited straw, and small, square cashmere shawls.

CHAPTER TEN

THE HANOVERIANS
George III and George IV

When George III came to the throne in 1760, Louis XV was still reigning in France and Madame Pompadour was at the height of her power. England was in the midst of the Seven Years War and most things French were anathema, yet the fashions amongst the nobility and upper classes were very much the same in London and Paris as in the other capitals of Western Europe. These were the years of hoops, low-cut, long-waisted bodices laced over stomachers, and elbow-length sleeves with deep lace ruffles. In England, women, rich and poor, wore small gypsy hats over neatly dressed curls and little shoulder-length capes in cold weather. Men were still wearing their tricorn hats, knee-length coats over somewhat shorter waistcoats, neat knee-breeches and stockings, with flat-heeled shoes or riding boots.

George II's eldest son, the Prince of Wales, had died in 1751, so it was his grandson who at the age of twenty-two became George III. England knew little about the new King, for he had always been sternly repressed by his grandfather, who cared for him no more than he had for the Prince of Wales. However, he was fairly good-looking and he had been born in England and spoke English fluently. People decided that he was probably preferable to the first two Georges and were prepared to like him.

He was a virtuous young man, a fact which pleased the middle and lower ranks of society, even if the Court circles and aristocracy found it somewhat depressing. He had fallen deeply in love with the beautiful Lady Sarah Lennox, sister of the Duke of Richmond, who was living at Holland House.

However, the Queen Mother and her mouthpiece Lord Bute had no intention of allowing George to choose his own bride and at the first hint of the romance she sent her private ambassador to Hanover to find a wife for him from among the available princesses. The choice fell on the seventeen-year-old Charlotte of Mecklenburg-Strelitz, and 'so complete was the King's deference to the will of his mother, that he blindly accepted the bride she had chosen for him'.

Queen Charlotte was very young and very nervous when she arrived in England, but she was not unintelligent. 'Very sensible, cheerful and remarkably genteel,' reported Walpole, but she was no beauty—small and thin, with a pale, homely face, a rather flat nose and a large mouth.

After a stormy nine-day crossing from Cuxhaven, the bridal party landed at Harwich and proceeded to London, and when the royal coach met them at Romford she was seen to be dressed 'in the English style, wearing a fly cap with rich lace lappets, a stomacher ornamented with diamonds and a gold brocade suit of clothes with a white ground'.

The wedding took place at nine o'clock on the evening of her arrival in London and while she was dressing for the ceremony, at St James's Palace, 'she was told the King liked some particular manner of dress,' reported Walpole, 'whereupon she replied: "Let him dress himself; I shall dress as I please".' When she was told the King liked early hours, she said that she did not, and 'qu'elle ne voloit pas se coucher avec les voiles'. But this show of spirit did not last. She very soon learnt that she must conform and became the most submissive of wives.

For her marriage she wore a diamond tiara, necklace and stomacher which were valued at £60,000. Of her dress, Walpole said: 'An endless mantle of violet-coloured velvet, lined with ermine, and attempted to be fastened on her shoulder by a bunch of large pearls, dragged itself and almost the rest of her clothes halfway down her waist,' so that 'the spectators knew as much of her upper half as the King himself'.

The coronation took place a fortnight after the wedding in 'a muddle of splendour' which depressed the King and even more the Queen, for she was suffering from toothache. The Duke of Bedford was Lord High Constable of England for the day, and according to Horace Walpole, the performance of Lord Effingham, Lord Talbot and the Duke of Bedford at the coronation was 'woeful', although the Duke was 'the least ridiculous of the three'. Lord Bolingbroke, he said, 'had put rouge upon his wife and the Duchess of Bedford', and the Duchess of Queensberry reported to him that 'the Duchess of Bedford looked like an orange peach, half red and half yellow', which was probably nothing but jealousy, for the Duchess had taken great pains with her dress. It had been made by the Queen's robe and habit maker, James Spilsbury. The hooped skirt was of cloth of silver and her silver coat was trimmed with point d'Espagne. The dress was flounced with silver net, which with the gold and silver tassels came from Kempe Brydges, the lace maker at the Three Crowns on the corner of Bedford Street, Covent Garden. Her eighteen-year-old daughter, Lady Caroline Russell, who had been a bridesmaid at the wedding a fortnight earlier, wore a hooped skirt embroidered with silver and a tight bodice of a 'very rich embroidered material'.

To Horace Walpole the whole concourse of nobility at the Abbey seemed like Bartholomew's Fair, but he was feeling disgruntled that day. He had spent the whole night in Palace Yard, had not slept a wink and had been up at six o'clock.

These descriptions of dresses were invaluable, however, for fashion plates did not appear until 1770, when they were first published by the English *Lady's Magazine*. Not long afterwards they were also being issued in France, but before this time information regarding the latest fashions had been so difficult to come by that Marie Antoinette's dressmaker, Rose Bertin, had found it worth her while to travel across Europe each year, in a large *Berline*, with her collection of dolls dressed in replicas of her latest creations.

George III and Queen Charlotte soon settled down to a life of deep domestic contentment. In later years, the Queen was to reveal a hard, unimaginative streak in her character. She was unforgiving to her sons, over-possessive, domineering and intensely selfish in her treatment of her daughters: and during the King's bouts of insanity she was frightened and unable to treat him with the kindliness and tact which her daughters showed. However, during the early years of the marriage they were a devoted couple, happy and proud of their rapidly increasing family.

Both loved the simple life and in 1762 the King bought Buckingham House for £21,000 from Charles Herbert Sheffield, the natural son of the Duke of Buckingham, and they very soon moved there from St James's Palace. All the family, except the Prince of Wales, were born there. St James's was maintained only for Court days and occasions of Court ceremony. Ultimately Buckingham House was legally settled by Act of Parliament on Queen Charlotte in exchange for Somerset House, and for several years it was known as the Queen's House or the Queen's Palace.

Within twenty-two years the King and Queen had fifteen children, nine boys and six girls, though the two youngest boys died in infancy. The surviving boys were George, Prince of Wales, Frederick, Duke of York, William, Duke of Clarence, Edward, Duke of Kent, Ernest, Duke of Cumberland, Augustus, Duke of Sussex, and Adolphus, Duke of Cambridge. The daughters were Princess Charlotte, Princess Augusta, Princess Elizabeth, Princess Sophia, Princess Amelia and Princess Mary.

As the children grew up and were allotted their various apartments, Buckingham House was not large enough to hold them all. In 1771, therefore, the King converted the old Dutch House at Kew into Kew Palace for a summer Royal residence. The princes lived with their tutors in houses on Kew Green and here also were housed the concourse of teachers, governesses, chaplains, equerries and ladies-in-waiting, so that Richmond and Kew soon became highly popular resorts for people anxious to catch a glimpse of the Royal family.

The King and Queen were happy at Kew, living simply and frugally. The Court had long since decided that the Royal pair were not going to provide them with much fun and were certainly not to be leaders of fashion and culture. The princes soon grew restive but the princesses remained submissive for many years.

In 1763 came the end of the Seven Years War; Englishwomen began to visit Paris again and French milliners and dressmakers arrived in London. One of the most useful fashions they brought with them was an adjustable farthingale which could be raised on either side when passing in and out of narrow doorways or getting into a carriage. The satirists had already suggested many devices to ease the lot of women condemned to this awkward fashion, one of which was a coach with a removable roof, through which ladies could be dropped from above by means of a frame and pulley, rather like a gibbet. They complained that necks and shoulders were too bare, and cosmetics were always a subject for ridicule.

In the late 1760s and the 1770s English women took to the French fashion of elaborate and highly complicated hair dressing. Hair was piled on to the top of the head over large wire frames stuffed with tow, wool and hemp. The whole erection was then well greased and dusted with grey or white powder and decorated with flowers and feathers, and enormous false curls were fixed on either side of the face.

This was a gift for the satirists. In 1768 the 'New Foundling Hospital for Wit' published the following lament of a disillusioned lover.

> When he views your tresses thin,
>   Tortur'd by some French friseur;
> Horse-hair, hemp and wool within,
>   Garnished with a diamond skewer
>
> When he scents the mingled steam
>   Which your plaster'd heads are rich in,
> Lard and meal and clouted cream,
>   Can he love a walking kitchen?

These elaborate structures were left intact for weeks and before long were unromantically verminous.

Women went to extraordinary lengths to create a sensation, incorporating in their headdresses objects just as unlikely as those the Frenchwomen were wearing, such as glass models of ships and buildings, and it would take a hairdresser three or four hours to complete a really fashionable arrangement.

Hats were as large as the headdresses, with wide, sweeping, tilted brims and huge ostrich feathers, immortalised in Gainsborough's portraits of the Duchess of Devonshire and Mrs Siddons. Fanny Burney, for all her lack of interest in clothes, also wore a 'Gainsborough hat' and one day, when she met George II's physician at a tea party, he exclaimed: 'My dear Miss Burney, how glad I am to see you! But why do you wear this great thing over your face? (Turning up my hat) Why, it prevented my knowing you.'

Caps now came into fashion, as monstrous as the huge piles of hair they covered, spreading out at the sides and festooned with ribbons and sundry ornaments. In 1780 the 'Bird of Paradise' cap was worn by Mary Ann Robinson, the lovely Perdita with whom the Prince of Wales was so infatuated before he met Mrs Fitzherbert. It was a vast, cylindrical creation of goffered muslin. And about the same time Mrs Cosway, the artist, wife of the miniaturist, Richard Cosway, was wearing an equally huge ovoid creation, draping either side of the face like looped-back window curtains and surmounted by a rosette on the forehead, the rest of the cap rising even higher and entirely covering the back of the head.

The longest-lasting fashion in bonnet caps was the black silk 'calash' invented by the Duchess of Bedford. It was shaped like the hood of a carriage and strengthened with whalebone hoops. By pulling a string in front, it could be drawn up and forward to shield the face, like a poke bonnet, without flattening the hair, or thrown backwards to form a frame to the headdress. Either way it was very odd-looking and extremely ugly, but it was worn until well into the 1780s, for the high headdresses lasted for a long time.

Everyone wore hats. One of the first things Sophie v. la Roche did when she visited London in 1786 was to buy one, for she noted that 'women here may not go without a hat. So the land with the greatest freedom of thought, creed and custom is yet to some measure fettered by convention. Meanwhile, I am very glad that women of my age [she was in her fifties] wear caps under their hats, and that I shall not have much trouble or expense with my coiffure.'

Sacques and hoops were out of fashion by the 1780s, except at Court, where the Queen insisted on them. Elsewhere, the hoops were at first replaced by a pad on each hip and then by a single pad at the back, making a preposterous bustle. With the enormously broad-brimmed hats of the late 1770s and the 1780s, Englishwomen copied Paris by puffing out their bodices with folds of linen and gauze to create the illusion of possessing enormous busts. These were balanced by the grotesque bustles and the lampoonists at once suggested that the space behind could be used for smuggling. In fact the shape of the dress bore little relation to the form of the human frame. A caricature of 1786, entitled *The Bum-bailiff Outwitted*, shows a bailiff seizing a woman from behind, while she sinks down through her dress, slips out of it and crawls away between his legs, leaving him holding nothing but the bustle and skirt, surmounted by a puffed-out bodice, vast headdress and even more enormous feathered hat. By 1787 bosoms, posteriors and hats were larger than ever and one bright caricaturist drew a woman sheltering her entire family from the rain under her bustle and hat.

On the Queen's birthday, in 1781, Mrs Thrale sent Fanny Burney a note to say she would be dressing for the Drawing Room at Court at the house of her cousin, Mrs Davenant, in Red Lion Square, and Fanny was invited to watch the proceedings. 'Mrs. Thrale's dress is magnificent and not heavy,' wrote Fanny in her diary. 'Part of the trimming is composed of grebe feathers made up in bells for tassels which are remarkably elegant.'

Mrs Thrale told her that the Court dress had been 'copied in a Spitalfields loom from one of Captain Burney's specimens of goods from Hawaii, and "trimmed" with grebe skins and gold to the tune of £65—the trimming only.'

In 1786 Sophie v. La Roche watched her friend the Countess Reventlow, wife of the Danish ambassador, dress for St James's, on the occasion of the anniversary celebrations of the King's coronation. Sophie regretted that the King did not follow the French fashion of allowing visitors to watch the party from the gallery, for she had seen Louis XVI's receptions at Versailles, and being full of curiosity, with a German thirst for facts, wanted to compare it with the procedure at St James's. Insatiable for details, she was able to note that 'the ladies' hoops did not differ at all, for the London ones are just as large as those in Paris; the train, however, which at Versailles trails as a mark of respect, is here held up for the same reason, and only the Queen allows hers to hang loose. The Countess's skirt of silver floss was already fixed to the hoop. It was trimmed with twining roses of silver and the sack with sleeves was also of silver floss, trimmed with rich blonde lace, flowers and pearls.'

When headdresses grew smaller again—though they remained rather high and elaborate for a long time—mob caps, which were useful to cover the hair when it was not properly dressed and curled, were very large and ugly, drooping at the back more like ungainly hoods than the neat little caps of earlier times.

During the 1780s there was a reaction in England to all the fussy ornament of dress which had accompanied the farthingale and polonaise, and simple muslin dresses became popular for everyday wear. They were plain or striped, with a full skirt and natural waist-line, sashed with a long, broad ribbon. When Sophie lunched at Richmond with the Reventlows there was a family of Burths in the party and she was so struck with Miss Burth's 'really sylphlike costume' that she described it in detail—'a white skirt with wide border on which she herself had painted trailing roses; a bodice of pink and white striped taffeta, with pearls on the seams and bindings of the short sleeves; the simple straw hat adorned with real roses and a ribbon like the skirt.'

The English Court being small, domestic and rather dull, the upper ranks of English society did not hover round it as the French nobility did at Versailles. Instead, many of them spent most of their time in their country mansions, following country pursuits, particularly fox-hunting. Inevitably they developed a fashion for simpler and more practical clothes. Men took all the embroidery off their coats, discarded their lace ruffles and white silk stockings and took to plain cloth and stout boots, before very long exchanging their tricorns for tall hats. Though the women's skirts were long and full, in the country they too were very plain, and with them they wore jackets like a man's riding coat and a man's beaver hat, with serviceable walking shoes. This was the fashion that Frenchwomen adopted in the late 1780s, just before the Revolution, when everything English was popular and high fashion.

At the time of the accession of George III, men of fashion in London were wearing a small tricorn over a neat wig, with close-rolled curls and a short queue. Coats, waistcoats and breeches were elegant and well-cut, and cloth was increasingly used, satin, silk and velvet being reserved mainly for important Court functions and similar gala occasions. During the 1770s the cut of the coat was simpler but the colours brighter. Waistcoats were shorter and the front of the coat was cut away like the riding coat, eventually developing into the tail coat.

During the early 1770s the beaux and fribbles of George II's reign appeared in a new guise as the Macaronis. These young men, having done the Grand Tour, which included a visit to Italy, had formed themselves into a club, largely given over to gambling, and on the club's menu macaroni, a dish new to England, was always to be found. Their dress was grotesque and 'the family of Macaroni' was described as a 'many-headed monster in Pall Mall, produced by the demoniac committee of depraved taste and exaggerated fancy, conceived in the courts of France and Italy and brought forth in England'.

Horace Walpole said that their appearance was due to the enormous wealth which had come from India and was being spent 'so recklessly that it was quickly being dissipated'.

In 1772 the Macaronis were wearing very small tricorns, tilted steeply forward on the forehead, with an enormous knot of artificial hair fixed behind it, to vie with the women's hairdressing. They carried very tall walking-sticks with long tassels. Their jackets and waistcoats were short and skimpy, frogged and braided and decorated with tassels and enormous silver buttons, and their breeches were cut to an extremely tight fit. Their skirts and large ruffles and their thin little pumps were ornamented with large buckles of silver, gold or pinchbeck, set with real or imitation jewels.

Contemporary with the Macaronis were the Bucks, who cultivated a slovenly disregard for dress and were seldom clean, exhibiting a marked aversion to soap and water.

The Macaronis and the Bucks disappeared from the fashion scene soon after this, but by the time of the Regency another race of dandies had appeared, who were again called 'Beaux'.

As early as 1763 the peruke-makers were complaining that gentlemen were taking to wearing their own hair, with a resulting decline in business, and apart from a few small flurries of fancy, it is true to say that wigs tended to become smaller as the century wore on. They were simpler, flat over the head, with a curl on either side above the ears and a short queue. Many deplored the decline of the wig, for it was considered to add to a man's dignity. Physicians had kept to the full-bottomed wig, to give them an appearance of wisdom, and in 1778 Boswell complained that they were discarding them. 'There is a general levity in the age,' he said. 'We have *physicians* now in bag-wigs.'

From about the 1780s the side curls were sometimes replaced by a long, horizontal curl stretching from ear to ear. Alternatively the wig was dressed in a rather untidy, shapeless crop. The final blow to the fashion came in 1795 when Pitt imposed his powder tax. Soon after that only members of the legal profession and the Church were wearing wigs and the pigtail was given up, except by the Army and Navy, who wore it for a few more years.

By 1780 men of fashion were wearing a high-waisted, double-breasted coat with pointed lapels. It had no stiffening and hung straight at the back to the knees, but was cut away in the front like the coats worn by the nobility and gentry in the country. The elaborate cuffs had disappeared and only a small shirt-frill showed below the edge of the sleeve. A jabot or frilled shirt showed above the waistcoat and when the jacket was buttoned the waistcoat, although hip-length by now, showed below the front. The back of the coat collar was standing and its height tended to increase for a time.

Long heavy overcoats with large cuffs and a flat collar, with two or three overlapping capes, were worn in cold weather.

There was little change in the cut of the tight breeches, which were fastened at the knee with buckles and buttons and worn with neatly rolled stockings, held up by concealed garters, and flat-heeled shoes or riding boots.

The advent of shoe-laces caused concern amongst the families of buckle-makers and a newspaper of the time hoped that 'the fashion for shoe laces will not become prevalent, as so many shoe buckle manufacturing families will be wiped out'. There was an attempt to ban them but Sophie v. La Roche found a splendid example of the British genius for compromise in the solving of this problem. 'There are men who dodge the ban upon the coming fashion of tying shoes with laces, which threatens to ruin buckle-makers,' she wrote, 'by wearing a buckle on one foot and a shoe lace on the other.'

By the 1770s men were growing tired of their tricorns, even though they varied the size and the angle at which they wore them. They punched them into bicorns and wore them straight across their heads like Napoleon or they perched them fore and aft and looked like British admirals. But the day of the tricorn was over and towards the end of the century it disappeared, to be replaced by a hat with a round crown and rather broad, turned-up brim, and then by the hat with a high, tapering crown, the forerunner of the nineteenth-century top hat.

The top hat was first worn in London in 1797 by its designer, a haberdasher, and it caused such a sensation that he was charged with a breach of the peace, for having, according to the *St James's Gazette*, 'appeared in the public highway wearing upon his head a tall structure having a shining lustre and calculated to frighten timid people. Several women had fainted at the sight, children screamed, dogs yelped and a small boy had his arms broken'.

However, by the time of Waterloo tall silk hats had safely arrived and the long reign of the beaver hat was over. The new silk hats were broad-brimmed at first and the crown was wider at the top than the base.

It was in 1786 that Fanny Burney was invited to become second keeper of the robes to Queen Charlotte, at a salary of £200 a year, a footman, apartments in the palace and a coach which she shared with her colleague, Mrs Schwellenberg.

This was the year that Sophie v. La Roche was in London and she was entranced with the shops. The fashionable shopping districts were still moving westwards from the City and Covent Garden to Oxford Street, New Bond Street, which had been built in 1721 as an extension of Old Bond Street, Piccadilly and the streets round St James's Square, where people of fashion were moving into the newly-built mansions.

Sophie loved to look at the shops in Oxford Street.

'We strolled up and down lovely Oxford Street this evening,' she wrote. 'Just imagine, dear children, a street taking half an hour to cover from end to end, with double rows of brightly shining lamps, in the middle of which stand an equally long row of beautifully lacquered coaches, and on either side of these there is room for two coaches to pass one another; and the pavement, inlaid with flag-stones, can stand six people deep and allows one to gaze at the splendidly lit shop fronts in comfort. First one passes a watchmaker's, then a silk or fan store, now a silversmith's, a china or glass shop. The spirit booths are particularly tempting, for the English are in any case fond of strong drink. . . .

'Up to eleven o'clock at night there are so many people along this street as at Frankfort during the fair, not to mention the eternal stream of coaches. The arrangement of the shops in good perspective, with their adjoining living-rooms, makes a very pleasant sight. For right through the excellently illuminated shop one can see many a charming family-scene enacted: some are still at work, others drinking tea, a third party is entertaining a friendly visitor; in a fourth parents are joking and playing with their children. . . .'

The matter-of-fact Fanny was almost overwhelmed by Sophie's effulgent sentimentality on the occasion of their first meeting, but soon had worse troubles, for she heartily disliked her life at Court. 'I was averse to the union and I endeavoured to escape it,' she wrote 'but my friends interfered—they prevailed—and the knot is tied.' Poor Fanny, having already published *Evelina* and *Cecilia*, had been fêted and honoured as a brilliant young novelist and had become intimate with Dr Johnson and the amusing literary circle of Mrs Thrale's drawing-room. Although the Queen was amiable, well-read and particularly fond of the theatre, Fanny was bored by the dreary etiquette and formality of the Court and sadly missed the sparkling conversation to which she was accustomed in her own family circle and among her literary friends.

In 1791 Fanny was allowed to retire because of ill-health, though the Queen showed a good deal of resentment at first. However, after several months of discussion Fanny was free. Joyfully she laid aside 'her saque, court hoop and long ruffles' and became 'no more dressed than other people'; and two years later she married General D'Arblay, a French emigré.

Mrs Backmeister took her place at Court and one of the assistants was Mrs Papandiek, who in her reminiscences described the history of her first satin gown. It was made in 1782 of puce colour, trimmed with white satin, with a petticoat of the same colour, to match the trimming. The following year the 'puce satin was new trimmed with white', as her bridal gown. Two years later, in 1785, it was 'trimmed with a row of flat steel down each front, the white being taken off, cap and petticoat being trimmed to match, and steel buckles on black satin shoes'. In 1788 it was worn at a dance, 'with the trimmed sleeves and gauze handkerchief as before, the edge of it being fastened in front by three white satin broad straps, buckled with steel buckles'. In 1789 the puce satin was again given white satin trimmings with gauze. By 1792 Mrs Papendiek sadly reported that the puce satin was at its last gasp. So, unfortunately, was she, for her diary ends abruptly in this year, so no one will ever know the real end of the puce satin dress.

It must have been woefully out of fashion by this time, for with the French Revolution women's fashions changed as drastically in England as in France. The bouffants and rumps which had followed the hoops and panniers disappeared. Women discarded their corsets and braved the weather in the most inexplicable manner by wearing thin, transparent muslin gowns over the flimsiest of petticoats. Breasts were often exposed, though not many Englishwomen went to the extreme of the French by wearing nothing but flesh-pink tights underneath their clothes and even dampening their dresses to help them fall into the folds of classical drapery.

The headdress was a turban of muslin surmounted by two or three ostrich feathers, the indefatigable Duchess of Devonshire managing to find one that was three feet long.

It was about this time that men adopted their high hats and a few leaders of fashion took to zebra-striped coats, which they wore with huge cravats.

Women's dresses were very high-waisted and made of English cottons and muslins, so it was now the turn of the East India Company to complain of loss of business, but this time the English manufacturers won. By 1794 waists were so high that they disappeared, thereby inspiring the following lament:

> Shepherds, I have lost my waist,
> Have you seen my body?
>
> For fashion I that part forsook
> Where sages place the belly;

> Never shall I see it more,
> Till common sense returning,
> My body to my legs restore,
> Then I shall cease from mourning.
>
> Folly and fashion do prevail
> To such extremes among the fair,
> A woman's only top and tail,
> The body's banish'd God knows where!

In a caricature of 1796, entitled *The Fashionable Mamma or the Convenience of Modern Dress*, Gillray suggests that if pocket holes are placed high enough a lady of rank and fashion 'could perform the duties of a mother, while her carriage waited at the door, without any derangement of her garments'.

The severe winter of 1799 is said to have ended the craze for transparent dresses. It was the end of the naked bosom and, by the early years of the nineteenth century, though dresses remained high-waisted and of flimsy material, nearly always white, for at least another decade, they were more complicated. An overdress with puffed sleeves was fashionable. Stays came back and the poke bonnet appeared, together with plaid scarves and shawls, ankle boots, furs and heavier cloaks. It was about this time that long, tight-fitting, lace-trimmed drawers were designed and quickly gained favour. By 1830 they were worn almost universally and from this date the long years of prudery in English women's dress began.

The royal Princes and Princesses were a handsome, intelligent and lively family, the Prince of Wales being particularly charming, witty and talented. Unfortunately the dislike of the reigning monarch for his heir, so characteristic of the Hanoverians, appeared strongly in the relationship of George III and his eldest son. During their childhood and adolescent years, the family passed their time mainly between Windsor and Kew. Their régime was strict, formal and frugal. The boys studied with their tutors. They worked on their model farms. Occasionally they played cricket together. In the evenings they danced with their sisters or played card games. And once a week the whole family promenaded in a crocodile, to show themselves to the public.

At sixteen the Prince of Wales fell in love and proposed marriage to the twenty-three-year-old Mary Hamilton, one of his sisters' ladies-in-waiting, but she handled the situation tactfully and he soon transferred his affections to Mary Robinson, the actress, whom he had first seen as Perdita in *A Winter's Tale*. He settled her in a house in Berkeley Square, but after his angry father had had to pay £5,000 to recover some of his son's indiscreet letters, the Prince's ardour cooled.

The Royal family made much of their birthdays. The King always held a Court ball and the Queen a Drawing-room, while for the children there was some special party or entertainment, and for these occasions all the members of the household, servants and family alike, had to have new clothes. On the Prince of Wales's eighteenth birthday he made his formal entrance into society, and at his first grand ball, in 1780, 'his coat was of pink silk, with white cuffs, his waistcoat white silk, embroidered with various-coloured foil, and adorned with a profusion of French paste. And his hat was ornamented with two rows of steels beads, five thousand in number, with a button and a loop of the same material, and cocked in a new military style'.

The Prince was now anxious for his own establishment but the King insisted on his living at Buckingham House and gave him only a small annuity. Here for the next three years he spent a gay and wildly extravagant time and, to the King's fury, his most intimate friend was the Whig, Charles James Fox. Yet the King refused to allow the Prince to have any hand in affairs of state or even to learn the duties of statecraft.

By 1783 the Prince owed £29,000 to tradesmen alone and after much discussion his allowance was raised to £62,000 a year and he was granted Carlton House. This house had been bought by George II from the Earl of Burlington in 1732. The Prince's grandmother, Princess Augusta, had lived there during her last years, but after her death in 1772 it had stood empty. The Prince, delighted with his freedom, now spent lavishly on the reconstruction and refurnishing of his new establishment.

He entertained in the grand manner, lavishly and brilliantly. The King was appalled at the extravagance but at this time the Queen did her best to keep the peace.

It was in 1784 that the Prince first met Mrs Fitzherbert and fell deeply in love. The following year they were secretly married, but the marriage was illegal, for as heir to the throne he was not allowed to marry a Roman Catholic and under the Royal Marriage Act he should have obtained the consent of the King.

The Prince also bought the farmhouse at Brighton which he commissioned Henry Holland to rebuild as a small, classical villa and which, twenty years later, John Nash was to transform into the Pavilion.

Mrs Fitzherbert was hardly a leader of fashion, but she was always dressed with elegance and good taste. Her portrait painted by Gainsborough in the 1770s, when she was still in her twenties, shows her with her hair dressed high and with long curls hanging down her back, wearing a simple, low-cut dress with elbow-length sleeves. In the miniature by Cosway she wears a wide-brimmed hat tied in a large bow under her chin. In another, highly glamorized portrait, he shows her with her hair dressed in short curls all over her head, with a few hanging down to the nape of her neck, and this time she is dressed in a hooped skirt with a bunched overskirt and a tight, low-cut, long-sleeved bodice finished with a small Medici collar. Romney painted her in a hat with a brim so wide that it drooped at the back on to her shoulders. Her neckerchief is folded high under her chin and puffed out in front, with the end tucked into a high waist, and she wears a shawl draped loosely over her arms. Hoppner showed her with her hair dressed high and encircled by a ribbon in the Empire style, wearing a simple dress with a low, draped neckline, and a high sash.

She always kept a separate establishment from the Prince and lived in considerable style. 'When Mrs. Fitzherbert was living in Pall Mall, within a few doors of Carlton House,' wrote Mary Frampton in 1786, 'we were at one of the Assemblies she gave which was altogether the most splendid I was ever at. Attendants in green and gold besides the usual livery servants, were stationed in the rooms and up the staircase to announce the company and carry about refreshments. The house was new and beautifully furnished. One room was hung with puckered blue satin from which hangings the now common imitations in paper were taken. A whole length portrait of the Prince of Wales was conspicuous in one of the drawing-rooms and his bust and that of the Duke of York ornamented the dining-room. Her own manners ever remained quiet, civil and unperturbed and in the days of her greatest influence she was never accused of using it improperly.'

The Prince of Wales's younger brothers all departed from the family circle as soon as they were old enough. The Duke of York went into the Army, the Duke of Clarence into the Navy, but the Prince of

Wales was not allowed to enter either Service. The Princesses were still kept with their parents, although Princess Charlotte, the Princess Royal, was now twenty and the beautiful Princess Augusta eighteen. They divided their time between reading, needlework, card games and conversation. They met no one outside the Court circle and neither the King nor the Queen would consider the question of their marriages. At one time, when it seemed that the Prince of Wales, the Duke of York and the Duke of Clarence were all going rapidly to the bad, they were not even allowed to write to them, though they were deeply attached to their brothers and remained so all their lives.

As for clothes, they had no personal incomes and had to wear what their mother decreed, bought from the small allowances she gave them. Often their dresses were well behind the current fashion. At a concert at Westminster Abbey in 1784 the three eldest princesses appeared in 'tissue silk frocks with a lace cuff turned over the bottom of the sleeve, and simple caps with no jewels'. Their trains were 'about one yard on the ground' and they were all wearing hoops, but the Queen's hoop was unfashionably small and those of the Princesses 'only large enough to prevent their dresses from clinging'.

When the high-waisted, narrow-skirted Empire dresses came into fashion, the poor Princesses were still forced to wear their hoops, though they were at least five years behind the times, and it was now, long after plumes were out of fashion, that the Queen took a fancy to them and insisted on them for Court wear. 'Their hoop petticoats filled the room,' wrote one young woman who saw them at a Court reception. 'Princess Mary had a large plume of white ostrich feathers, with a small plume of black ones in front, while Princess Elizabeth wore eleven immense yellow ostrich feathers, which you may imagine had not a very good effect.'

There were still no arrangements for their marriages and when the subject was mentioned the King is said to have burst into tears. However, in 1786 Princess Elizabeth, the artist of the family, who was then sixteen, was taken ill and remained in close seclusion for some time at the King's Cottage, Kew Green. The illness was never diagnosed for she was giving birth to a daughter. The father was George Ramus, one of the King's pages. They had probably been secretly married, but she seems never to have seen either him or her daughter again and was soon back in the family circle, her father having apparently had no idea of what had happened.

136

King George had always been eccentric and in 1788, while driving in Windsor Great Park with the Queen, he suddenly stopped the carriage, stepped out, approached one of the trees, doffed his hat, shook one of the lower branches by the hand and addressed it as the King of Prussia. His behaviour became increasingly disturbed and two days later, when the Prince of Wales had joined them for dinner, he suddenly grasped the Prince by the throat and tried to throttle him. For the next three months the King was hopelessly insane. The doctors recommended his removal to Kew and here the Queen and the Princesses spent a sad and gloomy winter. The palace was cold, damp and draughty, and the princesses slept in uncarpeted attics. No music was allowed and with their household of one hundred and fifty the weeks passed in a cheerless, chilling silence.

With the New Year the King rallied and his condition improved so satisfactorily that on 23 April 1789, a thanksgiving service for his recovery was held in St Paul's Cathedral. The King was genuinely popular at this time, and as he drove to St Paul's in his blue Windsor uniform he was warmly cheered. The Queen and the Princesses—all six of them, including the five-year-old Amelia—wore purple with petticoats of Indian gold muslin over white satin. On their white satin bandeaux 'God Save the King' was inscribed in letters of gold. Five of the princes were abroad, but the Prince of Wales and the Duke of York attended the service, though the Queen complained bitterly of their behaviour. She alleged that they were talking together and eating biscuits all the time, and it was many years before she forgave them.

For the next few years the King maintained his improvement. He and the Queen, with the Princesses, took to staying at Weymouth for three months of each year, the other nine months being spent either at Windsor or Kew where, apart from occasional visits to the theatre, the Drawing-rooms, Court balls, receptions and similar State functions, the King passed his time in riding, hunting and looking after his farm.

The Prince of Wales was falling more heavily into debt each year and by 1795 he owed £630,000. The King said he would settle his debts only if he married someone of whom he approved. At last, with matters not going smoothly with Mrs Fitzherbert at this time, he agreed to marry his cousin, the twenty-seven-year-old Caroline of Brunswick. She arrived in England after a miserable journey of six or seven weeks across war-ravaged Europe, knowing not a word of

English. The English ambassador to Brunswick had already noticed that the Princess 'seldom bothered to wash or change her clothes' and had to suggest to her lady-in-waiting that the Prince would expect 'a cleaner wife', but when the Prince saw her for the first time he was appalled. Not only was she grubby in appearance, but despite her attractive fair hair and tolerably good features, he found her coarse, vulgar and altogether unbalanced, a bitter contrast to the immaculate and elegant Mrs Fitzherbert.

At the wedding, which took place at the Chapel Royal on 18 April 1795, he looked 'like Death and full of confusion, as if he wished to hide himself from the looks of the whole world'. The marriage was a disaster from the outset. Nine months after the wedding their daughter Charlotte was born, but after the wedding night he never slept with his wife again, and although she lived at Carlton House for a short time after the birth of Princess Charlotte, they seldom met. 'I would rather see toads and vipers crawling over my victuals than sit at the same table with her,' he once said. He asked her to leave but at first she refused. However, the Queen and the Prince's new mistress, Lady Jersey, made life so impossible for her that she eventually retired to a villa near Blackheath, leaving the infant Princess Charlotte at Carlton House.

Lady Jersey brought him no more contentment than Caroline and he wrote despairingly to Mrs Fitzherbert, begging for a reconciliation. With the approval of her confessor, she forgave him and for the next nine years they lived together again, spending most of the time at Brighton, where Mrs Fitzherbert had a villa close to the Pavilion, overlooking the Steyne. By about 1806, however, their relations were again strained. The Prince had fallen in love with Lady Hertford and Mrs Fitzherbert made a dignified withdrawal.

The Princess Royal was the least contented of the princesses, for she had always been repressed by her mother. As a girl she had been rather gauche and now, at thirty, she longed to escape to an establishment of her own. In 1797 a marriage was arranged with Prince Frederick of Württemberg. There had been considerable doubts about the match at first, for Prince Frederick had already been married to a sister of Caroline, Princess of Wales. While Frederick was in Russia she had run away and given birth to an illegitimate child. For this escapade she was thrown into prison, where she was said to have died, but there were rumours that she had escaped and was living in hiding with her Russian lover. However, risking the chance that the marriage with the Princess Royal might be bigamous, the wedding took place and Queen Charlotte made the Princess's wedding-dress herself, as well as most of the trousseau.

It was customary for the bride of a widower to wear white and gold, but the fact that she was a king's daughter took precedence and her wedding-dress was of the accepted white satin and silver, with a train of fur-trimmed crimson velvet. The Princess was not particularly interested in clothes and was notoriously a bad dresser, but for this occasion her mother superintended everything and she looked beautiful, a worthy match for her portly, forty-year-old bridegroom, resplendent in a suit of 'silk shot with gold and silver richly embroidered, and embellished with gold and silver flaps and cuffs'.

They departed for Württemberg and the Princess was cut off from England for many years by the Napoleonic wars, but the family ties and affection were strong and in 1827, by which time she was a widow and prematurely aged with the dropsy which was eventually to kill her, she paid a last happy visit to her brothers and sisters in London.

No arrangements were made for the marriages of the other princesses and by 1804 it was apparent that the King was once again deteriorating mentally, while the Queen, ill with dropsy, was becoming increasingly irritable and difficult.

By 1800, when Princess Augusta was thirty-two, she was deeply in love with one of the royal equerries, the forty-year-old Major-General Sir Brent Spencer, and through all their long separations when he was on foreign service they remained devoted to each other until his death in 1828, a sad but romantic love affair which gave her much quiet happiness.

Princess Amelia, the youngest of the sisters, developed tuberculosis when she was fifteen, from which she never recovered. When she was seventeen she fell desperately in love with another of the King's equerries, General the Honourable Sir Charles Fitzroy, who was twenty-seven years older, but she died when she was twenty-seven and it was the shock of her death which was thought to have sent the King into his final bout of madness. The Prince of Wales was made Regent the following year, 1811.

Princess Sophia's story is the most extraordinary of all. In 1788, when she was only eleven, Thomas Garth, then forty-four, was appointed a royal equerry. She was always fond of him and in 1799 she retired from Court for a while, suffering from an undiagnosed illness. She was delivered of a son by Garth, though presumably without the King's knowledge, for Garth remained at Court and was always particularly popular with the King, though he was far from handsome. In fact Greville described him as a 'hideous old Devil, old enough to be her father and with a great claret mark on his face'.

With the passing years the affair seems to have cooled and she took her place once more in attendance on her parents, though she occasionally saw her son in secret, and years later, after the King's death, when she had apartments in Kensington Palace, along with the Duchess of Kent, he sometimes visited her. He joined the army but never rose above the rank of Captain and was, according to Greville, 'an idiot as well as a rogue'. Old General Garth died in 1829, 'a fine gentleman of the old school, in powder and pigtail', but after his death Captain Garth tried to blackmail the Royal family into giving him an annuity of £3,000 a year in exchange for documents proving that he was the son of Princess Sophia.

They refused and the old scandal was revived, but Captain Garth disappeared and was never heard of again. Sophie lived on at Kensington Palace until 1838, when she went blind. Then she moved to York House, where she died in 1848.

Princess Mary, the beauty of the family, though perhaps the least romantically inclined, had decided when she was quite young that she would ultimately marry her cousin, the Duke of Gloucester, but the affair dragged on for twenty years and the marriage did not take place until 1816, when she was forty. It was held at Buckingham Palace, the bride, still beautiful, wearing silver tissue, with a diamond necklace and tiara.

Princess Mary always declared that she was perfectly happy with her husband, but after the first few years he became aggressively jealous of her devotion to her sick parents and was thought to have ill-treated her.

The mad old King lingered on at Windsor, spending his days clad in a purple velvet dressing-gown and ermine night-cap, singing hymns, playing his flute and his harpsichord, dreaming in a misty world of his own and remembering nothing of his family. The Queen's health was also deteriorating and she spent most of her time at Kew, with Elizabeth, Augusta and Mary in constant attendance, while Sophia stayed at Windsor with the King.

Early in 1818 the Queen gave her last Drawing-room, insisting still on hoops and plumes. 'It was amazing to see the whole room of nodding plumes—blue, red, violet, green but mostly white like tufts of snow,' wrote the American ambassador, 'with diamonds sparkling round them—and a thousand ladies in hoops.'

Princess Elizabeth was now forty-seven and when she received an offer of marriage from Frederick of Hesse-Homburg, a bachelor of forty-nine, she accepted, to the intense annoyance of the Queen, who had come to depend on her and proceeded to make things as difficult as possible. In the eyes of the Court Prince Frederick could do nothing right. They complained that he smoked, a habit that no gentleman at that time ever practised in England. They disliked his large whiskers. 'An uglier hound with a snout buried in hair, I never saw,' wrote one critic. At a royal levée before the marriage, while bending down to retrieve the Queen's fan, he split his tight trousers so disastrously that the Royal dukes had to gather round quickly while he retired to borrow another pair from the Duke of York, a mishap which lost nothing in the telling amongst the Court gossips.

Nevertheless the trousseau and the wedding-dress, of silver tissue with flounces of Brussels lace, were made, the wedding took place and Princess Elizabeth departed to Homburg with her husband, where she attained great happiness and contentment for the last twenty-two years of her life.

Queen Charlotte died in 1818 and George III in January 1820, when the Regent became George IV. Both as Regent and as King, he was bitterly lampooned by Gillray and Cruikshank for his extravagance, his ill-treatment of his wife and his various love affairs. Yet he maintained a Court which was the most brilliant since the days of Charles II. It was the centre of fashion and culture and he was a generous patron of the arts, albeit at the expense of the nation. Painters, architects and furniture designers all benefited. John Nash transformed the Pavilion at Brighton into a fabulous Eastern palace with its minarets, domes and pinnacles, and added the magnificent banqueting-room and music-room.

Fashion followed the Prince Regent and the King to Brighton and the town became both prosperous and elegant, for it was about this time that many of the beautiful terraces and crescents were built, as, for example, Sussex Square and Lewes Crescent. After the death of George III, Carlton House was pulled down and Nash designed Carlton House Terrace on the site and also transformed Buckingham House into Buckingham Palace for the new King.

These were the years of the great cabinet-makers, who now worked in mahogany. Chippendale had opened his workshop in St Martin's Lane in 1753 and a few years later, with the awakening interest in China and the East, was introducing the motifs characteristic of the Chinese-Chippendale style.

Hepplewhite opened his business in Cripplegate a few years afterwards. By 1780 Robert Adam was at the height of his achievement and in 1790 Sheraton arrived in London from the north of England.

To upholster all this beautiful furniture, women did ever more needlework, following the example of Queen Charlotte and the Princesses.

In the early years of the nineteenth century a new generation of dandies or beaux arose, the most famous being Beau Brummell who, for a time, was a friend of the Prince Regent. After he left Eton he spent much of his time at Brighton or Carlton House. His clothes were always beautifully tailored and the fashionable London tailors vied with each other to secure his patronage. His impeccable coats, snuff-boxes and canes were the talk of the town. It was he who first thought of starching the cravat, and the *Mirror* of 7 May 1825, reporting this latest fashion, said that at the sight of it 'dandies were struck dumb with envy and washerwomen miscarried'.

Brummell fell out with the Prince one day and was never invited to his presence again. He spent all his money at the gaming tables and had to flee the country, ending up at Caen, where he obtained the poorly paid post of British consul and died, in 1840, in near penury.

Mrs Fitzherbert's famous contemporary, Lady Hamilton, was living in Naples in 1786. When she was Emma Hart, her lover, the Hon. Charles Greville, finding himself short of money, had sent her there to stay with his widowed uncle, Sir William Hamilton, the English Ambassador.

He was in his late fifties and she was just twenty-one. He was a cultured aristocrat, already famous for his collection of Greek and Roman antiquities. She was the daughter of a blacksmith, uneducated, speaking all her life with a broad Lancashire accent, brash, in many ways uncouth, yet possessed of a voluptuous beauty, an exuberant vitality and a generous heart which were to ensnare both Sir William and Lord Nelson.

In 1787, when Sir William was away on a hunting-party for a week or two, Emma wrote to him about a portrait for which she was sitting: 'It shall not be two naked, for it would not be so interesting . . . and those beautys that only you can see shall not be exposed to the common eyes of all, and wile you can even more than see the originals, others may gess at them, for the are sacred to all but you, and I wish the wos better for your sake. . . .'

A day or two later she described her meeting with Beatrice Acquaviva, who 'admired my dress, said I looked like an angel, for I was in clear white dimity with a blue sash'.

On another occasion she and Sir William called on the Countess Mahoney at Ischia, who 'came down to the sea-shore to meet ous. . . . She took ous to her house where there was a full conversazione and tho I was in a undress, onely having a muslin chemise very thin, yet the admiration I met with was surprising.'

In 1791 she was writing to Greville about a party she and Sir William gave: 'Sir Wm dressed me in wite sattin, no collar about me but my hair & cheeks. I was with out powder as it was the first great assembly we had given publickly. All the ladies strove to out do one another in dress and jewels, but Sir William said I was the finest jewel amongst them.'

Later that year they were back in London, where Sir William obtained the royal consent to marry Emma. The wedding took place early in the morning and by eleven o'clock Emma was in Romney's studio sitting for the portrait which he called 'The Ambassadress'. She was still in her bridal clothes, wearing a large hat with an upright feather at the side, the hat being held by a scarf tied under her chin, a long-sleeved dress with a deep collar and very full skirt. Later that day they set off for Naples again, passing through Paris, where they met the King and Queen, by now virtually prisoners. Marie Antoinette gave Emma a letter for her sister, Maria Carolina, the Queen of Naples.

Back in Naples, Emma, the new Lady Hamilton, was received by the Queen and they became close friends, Emma little realizing that the Queen saw Sir William as her life-line with England. She was overwhelmed by her new honours and gradually her pretty head grew ever more swollen.

The Comtesse de Boigne, who heartily disliked her, wrote at this time that 'in conformity with her husband's taste, she was generally dressed in a white tunic, with a belt round her waist, her hair down her back or turned up by a comb', but she followed the fashion in this regard and in 1794 was writing to Greville for 'an English riding hat, very fashionable, but I desire you to put it to Sir Wms account'.

It was in September 1793 that Captain Nelson first arrived in Naples with dispatches for Sir William Hamilton. By 1798 he was an admiral and after his brilliant victory at Aboukir Bay, Emma was writing to him: 'My dress from head to foot is alla Nelson. . . . Even my shawl is in Blue with gold anchors all over. My earrings are Nelsons anchors; in short, we are be-Nelsoned all over.'

By the late summer of 1800 Nelson had set off for London in company with the Hamiltons and on Emma's insistence they travelled overland, by way of Vienna. Already Nelson's behaviour with Emma was causing widespread gossip and consternation, though Sir William, now over seventy and in failing health, and with a sincere liking for Nelson, seems to have turned a blind eye on the affair. Emma's mother, who never left her side during all her travels and fifteen years in Naples, was as complaisant as always.

However, Emma was not received at Court, and London society, for the most part, shunned her. After Nelson had broken with his wife and established a *ménage à trois* at Merton with Emma and Sir William, her troubles came quickly. Sir William died in 1803, Nelson in 1805 and her mother in 1810. Both Sir William and Nelson had left her money, but she was recklessly extravagant and had taken to drink; her financial affairs were woefully mismanaged. By 1812 she was hopelessly in debt and together with Horatia, her small daughter by Nelson, was arrested and taken to 12, Temple Place, a 'sponging house' of the King's Bench prison. By July of 1814 friends had organized her money sufficiently to obtain her release and she and Horatia, almost penniless, crossed to Calais to escape further writs, where, six months later, she died in a shabby rooming-house.

CHAPTER ELEVEN

PRELUDE TO VICTORIA

Princess Charlotte, the only child of the future George IV and Queen Caroline, married Leopold of Saxe-Coburg-Gotha who, in 1831, was to be offered the Crown of Belgium, but in 1817 the Princess died in childbirth and also her baby. As her father, still Prince Regent, was fifty-seven and irrevocably separated from the Queen, it was unlikely that he would have a legal heir and the question of the succession arose.

The Duke of York was married but had no children. In 1809 he had been in grave trouble when the scandal broke concerning his mistress, Mary Ann Clarke, who had been using her influence to sell army commissions. At the trial he had been exonerated from direct guilt but had been removed from his position as Commander-in-Chief of the army, although he was restored two years later.

Prince William, who was to become the Duke of Clarence, had enjoyed his early life in the Navy and had been a close friend and fervent admirer of Nelson, but his father had refused to allow him to continue his naval career. He was given rooms in St James's Palace and a country house at Richmond and ordered to remain ashore. However he soon picked up the bad habits of his brothers, before long falling in love with Dorothy Jordan, the comedy actress at Drury Lane, who was so much more fun than her contemporary, the haughty and austere Mrs Siddons.

Dorothy Jordan was by no means inexperienced. In Dublin she had had an illegitimate daughter, and she had had four more children by Richard Ford, with whom she was living when she met the Duke. By 1790 the Duke had wooed her from Ford, who had made it quite clear that he had no intention of marrying her, and they had settled down at Richmond. Here, for the next twenty years, during which they had ten children, they lived in 'blameless irregularity', with Mrs Jordan's previous five children lodged close by, for her maternal instincts were highly developed.

In between childbearing she managed to continue her successful stage career and the money she earned was very useful, for the Duke was always hard-pressed and they had a very large household to maintain.

The Duke was a simple soul and apart from occasional bickerings with Dorothy over money troubles he lived in domestic felicity and had little contact with the world of fashion, which mostly ignored him.

Mrs Jordan was an attractive woman; her portrait by Romney shows her wearing a white dress with a full skirt, tied with a sash at the natural waistline, a plain bodice, demurely cut, with elbow-length sleeves. Her hair was simply dressed, hanging in long curls down to her shoulders. The Prince Regent was tolerant about Mrs Jordan, as well he might be for he had long been unfaithful to Mrs Fitzherbert, but Queen Charlotte heartily disapproved of her.

By 1810 the Duke was heavily in debt and ill with asthma and gout. He went to Windsor to be with his mother and she urged him to give up Mrs Jordan and find himself a suitable wife. It was just about the time of the public scandal of the Duke of York and Mrs Clarke. Perhaps to comfort his mother, who was certainly beset with troubles, or perhaps because he was quarrelling too often with Mrs Jordan over money, he agreed.

It was a cruel business, after so many years, but he treated Mrs Jordan financially as well as he could. The establishment at Petersham was closed, and he took full responsibility for his ten children, the Fitzclarences. Mrs Jordan was sad but philosophical about the break and although she ultimately died in France in obscure poverty, this was more through the neglect of her children, who were all well endowed, and the mismanagement of those responsible for paying her annuity, than through any fault of the Duke's.

So, at the age of forty-five, Prince William, Duke of Clarence, returned to London and entered the world of fashion again. He found many changes from the eighteenth-century London of his youth. The beautiful Duchess of Devonshire, Pitt, Fox and Nelson were all dead. The capital was spreading rapidly and its population was already well over a million. In 1807 gas-lighting had been introduced and before long there was to be the first experimental street lighting by gas. The days of the Grand Tour were over, for England was at war with Napoleon. Young men of fashion now passed from Eton to Cambridge and thence either to the Army or the Navy, to their family seats to enjoy country pursuits or to London to savour the delights of the town.

During the Regency there was no Court over which a royal lady presided and Almack's, the club in King Street, St James's, with its magnificent ballroom, became so exclusive that it was almost a substitute. Walpole called Almack's 'the Ladies' Club of both sexes' for it was controlled by six 'lady patronesses' who, in 1813, were Lady Castlereagh, Lady Jersey, Lady Cowper, Lady Sefton, Mrs Drummond Burrell (afterwards Lady Willoughby de Eresby), the Princess Esterhazy and the Princess Lieven. They decreed who might be admitted and the social prestige of entrance to Almack's ranked with presentation at Court.

They also laid down what the men should wear. No gentleman 'should appear at the assemblies without being dressed in knee-breeches, white cravat and chapeau-bras', and once, when the poor Duke of Wellington arrived in black trousers and was politely but firmly informed that 'Your Grace cannot be admitted in trousers', he meekly retired.

Lady Jersey introduced the quadrille at Almack's and Princess Lieven the waltz. 'No event ever produced so great a sensation in English society as the introduction of the German waltz in 1813,' wrote T. Raikes. 'Up to that time the English country dance, Scotch steps and an occasional Highland reel formed the school of the dancing-master, and the evening recreation of the British youth, even in the first circles. . . . In London, fashion . . . was everything. Old and young returned to school, and the mornings which had been dedicated to lounging in the Park, were now absorbed at home in practising the figures of the French quadrille or whirling a chair round the room, to learn the step and measure of the German waltz. Lame and impotent were the first efforts, but the inspiring effect of the music, and the not less inspiring airs of the foreigners, soon rendered the English ladies enthusiastic performers. What scenes have we witnessed in those days at Almack's. . . .'

When the Duke of Clarence returned to London, in the middle of the Napoleonic Wars, it was at the peak of its social prestige. How else did society pass its day in London? Fashionable young women took music and drawing lessons. During the season they left cards on their friends.

> A thousand cards a day at doors to leave,
> And in return a thousand cards receive.

Shopping was a never-failing delight. Fortnum and Mason's was already established in Piccadilly and so was Swan and Edgar. Dickins and Smith, later to become Dickins and Jones, was at its first home in Oxford Street. Peel the fashionable bootmaker and Clark and Debenham's, later to be Debenham and Freebody, were in Wigmore Street and Style and Mantle in Leicester Square. Women were still wearing their high-waisted frocks with short puffed sleeves, or long ones with *berthe* collars, and straight skimpy skirts. Caps were worn indoors and all manner of hats and bonnets for driving and walking, but the enveloping poke bonnet was growing increasingly popular. More underclothes were being worn. The corset grew more like an instrument of torture every year and everyone who aspired to high fashion wore drawers, including Princess Charlotte who on one occasion 'was sitting with her legs stretched out and showed her drawers which, it seems, most young women now wear.'

French silks and lace were not obtainable unless they were smuggled, and English cottons, muslins and lace were mostly worn, with a certain amount of Indian muslins. White was still very popular, but towards the end of the war colours became more usual and also patterned materials.

With the end of the war in 1815 there was once more an exchange of visitors and fashions between London and Paris. By 1817 Prince William was still not married and was spending most of his time accompanying the Prince Regent to the balls and theatres in London and the similar delights which were being offered at Brighton, where parading on the Steyne was as fashionable as driving in Hyde Park.

The Duke of Kent was also becoming concerned about his matrimonial future. Shortly after the death of Princess Charlotte he was in Brussels and sought the advice of Thomas Creevey, in a conversation of which Creevey made a careful note on 11 December 1817.

The Duke began by observing that 'the death of the Princess had caused a derangement of the succession of the throne and he felt it was time that the unmarried Princes became married, if the crown was to be kept in the family'. He did not think the Regent would try for a divorce, because the adultery of the Queen 'must be proved in an English court of justice, and if found guilty she must be executed for high treason.

'As for the Duke of York, at his time of life and that of the Duchess, all issue, of course, is out of the question. The Duke of Clarence, I have no doubt, will marry if he can.'

Martha, Countess of Elgin, wears a muff against her beribboned bodice, and a black Spanish lace shawl swathes the upper part of her charming flounced sleeves

The Duchess of Argyll (then Lady Lorne) softens the severity of her coiffure with a sprig of small roses, and pretty bows adorn her sleeves, her bodice and her gathered ribbon collar

The little Princess Mary (c. 1815) wears a romantic picture hat of straw and silk tulle and a small shawl with her young girl's dress

Mrs Perdita (Mary Ann) Robinson, with whom the Prince of Wales was once infatuated, favours a fetching bonnet of muslin and ruched ribbon, with a rosette worn on the centre of her brow

Charles X, King of France, who succeeded his brother Louis XXIII, in a uniform of dark blue laced with silver and carrying a plumed hat, wears the Garter above his left boot

In war and peace, uniforms of this calibre were generally worn. Charles, Archduke of Austria, wears the Golden Fleece, and the ribbon and star of the Order of Maria-Theresa

Les beaux militaires are exemplified here in the dashing person of Alexander Ivanovitch, Prince Chernichev. He, and other high-ranking officers, were painted in 1818 for George IV by Sir Thomas Lawrence while in Vienna, where the Prince was in attendance upon the Tsar

A slightly romanticized picture of George IV when Prince of Wales. He is squeezed into a smart uniform, topped off by an especially visible and magnificent hat, which is further heightened by egret plumes rising from a jewelled mount

Her Royal Highness the Princess Sophia, sister of George IV, seated comfortably in ample folds of lustrous velvet, wears in the shoulder of her square-cut décolletage a miniature of her brother the King; an eye-glass is tucked into her high waistband

An early portrait of the little Princess Victoria, *c.* 1821, in a pretty baby-girl dress, with her mother, the Duchess of Kent. The Duchess displays an interesting sleeve of transparent flowered material spiralled with narrow black satin ribbon

Queen Adelaide, wife of William IV particularly requested the artist, Sir Martin Archer-Shee, not to flatter her in this painting. With a feathered hat, she wears a crimson velvet pelisse trimmed with ermine

Almost like a wreath of flowers themselves, this famous and entrancing picture by Winterhalter of the Empress Eugénie and her ladies portrays the romantic beauty of the exquisite crinolines designed by Worth, the English couturier to the Court of France

The difficulties and dangers of wearing the crinoline are wittily displayed in these delicate sketches. Such skittish misadventures must have been regrettable indeed during that Victorian period of prudery

L.434

Queen Victoria did not dictate fashion but was resigned to wearing the voluminous crinoline of her day. This photograph of Her Majesty alongside her husband the Prince Consort was taken in 1861, a few months before Prince Albert's death. His fanciful waistcoat, then regarded as normal wear, went out of fashion when he died and after that coloured waistcoats were déclassé for about ninety years

The personal beauty and true elegance of Queen Alexandra inevitably made her a royal leader of fashion, her favourite colours being lilac and violet. This fitted, full-backed jacket releases the fullness of an ample bustle, wherefrom the rich material falls in a graceful line on to the grass

After the decline of the crinoline the bustle became increasingly accentuated. Here a gathered or ruffled basque at the foot of the bodice back complements the tiered skirt with its eight flounces

Queen Mary ignored the frivolous fashions of the Edwardian era and later instituted her own regal rigidity of style. Here she is gowned in black satin and black moiré, embroidered with jet

Strange flowers that resemble tiger-lilies and hollyhocks, expressed in satin appliqué and studded with jewels, climb up the flowing skirt worn by Edna May, amidst a shower of dew-drop diamonds. She was a popular actress famed as the leading lady in *The Belle of New York*, and usually wore lovely dresses

Queen Mary was strongly influenced by the wishes of her husband King George V. Her individual style remained basically unchanged throughout her life. The dress of pastel-coloured cloth has a short-sleeved lace bodice; her hat is a confection of clustered flowers beneath a veil of spotted net, speared with an upstanding osprey

This is a genteel version of the hobble skirt. Worn with a short coat, slashed with patterned silk and weighted with Russian sables, it is balanced by a large dish hat surmounted by the body of a bird with feathers and tendrils included

Miss Camille Clifford, a stage celebrity, was a setter of Edwardian fashions. Her dresses were notable and usually in dramatic black, clinging closely to her hour-glass silhouette

This Edwardian dress, of indisputable impact, inspired Cecil Beaton for one of his black and white dresses in the famous Ascot scene in *My Fair Lady*

But William, as heir to the throne, was demanding from the government payment of all his debts 'which are very great, and a handsome provision for each of his ten natural children. Should the Duke of Clarence not marry, the next prince in succession is myself; and altho' I trust I shall be at all times ready to obey any claim my country may make upon me, God only knows the sacrifice it will be to make, whenever I shall think it my duty to become a married man. It is now seven and twenty years that Madame St Laurent and I have lived together; and you may well imagine, Mr. Creevey, the pang it will occasion me to part with her. I put it to your own feeling —in the event of any separation between you and Mrs. Creevey. . . . My brother, the Duke of Clarence, is the elder brother, and has certainly the right to marry if he chooses, and I would not interfere with him on any account. If he wishes to be king—to be married and have children, poor man—God help him! let him do so. For myself— I am a man of no ambition and wish only to remain as I am. . . .'

But like so many people who seek advice, the Duke had already made up his mind and had his eye on the Princess of Saxe-Coburg. He decided that if Prince William were not married by the following Easter he must go to London and discuss the matter in more detail.

The Duke of Kent did his duty and parted with his much loved Julie de St Laurent who, though now fifty-eight, was still beautiful. She retired to Paris, where Louis XVIII created her the Comtesse de Montgenêt, and he duly married the Princess of Coburg, sister of Leopold, who had been married to Princess Charlotte. She was a widow with one daughter, the Princess Feodore of Leiningen, for whom the Prince Regent had a great fancy for a time.

It must have been mortifying for Madame de St Laurent when she heard that the occasion was a double wedding, for the Queen Mother had at last found a bride for the Duke of Clarence, whose bachelorhood had been the main cause of the parting. Willy Clarence's bride was Amelia Adelaide, daughter of the late Duke of Saxe-Meiningen. She was twenty-five, virtuous and serious-minded, if not particularly beautiful, her bridegroom fifty-three.

In the same year the Duke of Cambridge married a Princess of Hesse and the forty-seven-year-old Princess Elizabeth was married to the Prince of Hesse Homburg. 'They immersed him several times in a warm bath to make him a little clean,' wrote Lady Jerningham, 'and they kept him three days without smoking, which, as he smoked five pipes a day, was great forbearance.'

The following year there was a satisfactory crop of royal babies. The Duchess of Cambridge had a son, the Duchess of Clarence a daughter, who died within a few minutes of birth, however, and the Duchess of Kent a daughter, who was called Victoria.

Less than two years later, however, the Duke of Kent was dead and the Duchess, left alone at Kensington Palace, brought up her small daughter in strict seclusion, for she had no great opinion of the rest of the royal family, except for Adelaide, the Duchess of Clarence, who was unfailingly kind to her.

The Prince Regent had deserted Mrs Fitzherbert for Lady Hertford by this time and had become extremely unpopular, particularly after the trial of Queen Caroline.

By the time he became George IV he was fifty-eight and during the last ten years of his life he paid little attention to affairs of State, living luxuriously in his immediate circle of friends and mistresses and growing steadily more bad-tempered and blind. The Duke and Duchess of Clarence lived quietly at Bushey, contented with each other though sad at the death of their second and last child. The Duke of York died in 1827 and as the King's health declined they knew that it would not be long before they were on the throne. And when Sir Henry Halford carried the news of the King's death to William at Bushey, very early on a June morning of 1830, he found him already abroad 'in his old green coat and white beaver hat'.

There were few to mourn George IV and although people knew little about William IV, he soon became very popular, particularly as he was quite unashamedly in love with his wife.

Among the rich and the rising middle classes, the manufacturers, industrialists and contractors, who had made their fortunes during the war, life was prosperous enough and London was gay and enticing, with Nash's new, colonnaded Regent Street, the new mansions and terraces surrounding Regent's Park and Carlton House Terrace. Shoolbred's furniture emporium had moved from the City to Tottenham Court Road. The new Burlington Arcade was full of intriguing little shops. Henry Hall, the hatter, was established in Oxford Street, Thomas Wallis at Holborn Circus, and during the 1830s Lilley and Skinner were to open business in Paddington Green, Peter Robinson in Oxford Street and Marshall and Wilson, later to be Marshall and Snelgrove, in Vere Street.

The Lancashire cotton industry was increasing steadily and by

1830 the import of raw cotton from America was four times that of 1800. The woollen factories of central Yorkshire were busy and the riots of the Luddites of 1811 and 1812, who resented the introduction of machinery, had been suppressed by the expedient of changing the penalty for machine-smashing and factory-burning from transportation to death by hanging.

The Spitalfields silk-weaving industry was flourishing and by 1832 there were 50,000 people in Spitalfields dependent on the industry and 15,000 looms at work, weaving thousands of yards of expensive velvet and silk, still by hand.

Lace was still a cottage industry, employing many cottagers in the villages around Honiton, and also in Bedfordshire and Buckinghamshire, where the important lace market was at Newport Pagnell.

Yet by 1830 foreign imports had affected many branches of the textile trades in England. Cheap hosiery was coming in from Saxony, gloves from Germany and France, as well as French lace, dress fabrics and innumerable accessories. Pay and conditions of labour in England were appalling, both in the factories and amongst the home workers, and to add to the workers' miseries unemployment was spreading.

King William and Queen Adelaide gave a private dinner party at St James's shortly after their accession, and among the guests were Colonel and Mrs Clitherow and Miss Clitherow. Miss Clitherow later recorded that 'the Queen had on a particularly elegant white dress, and all English manufacture. She made us observe that her blond was as handsome as Lady Mayo's French blond. "I hope all the ladies will patronise the English blend of silk," she said.'

Queen Adelaide went further than this by announcing that in future only English clothes might be worn at Court. In April 1831 she appeared in a 'very handsome white and silver brocade dress of Spitalfields produce' which the weavers had presented to her, but nothing that Queen Adelaide or anyone else could do could prevent Englishwomen from buying French accessories, trimmings and lingerie whenever possible, from using the French paper patterns which were now coming into the country or from copying French fashions.

With the restoration of Louis XVIII in 1815, Frenchwomen copied English fashion for a few years, taking to straw bonnets and velvet spencers and long cloaks. Then, with a general revival of trade and the increasing splendour of the Court, came a craving for costly and luxurious clothes. Dresses became more complicated. Waists dropped. Corsets became more rigid and leg-of-mutton sleeves grew so big that they made women as wide as in the old days of panniers. They could not pass through an ordinary doorway easily and the sleeves had to be kept in shape with whalebone or pads stuffed with down.

Underclothes were delicately embroidered and trimmed with lace. Drawers became more elegant and secure. In the early days they had consisted of two legs attached precariously with a tape and Dr Cunnington records the sad story of the English lady who in 1820 complained: 'They are the ugliest things I ever saw; I will never put them on again . . . I lost one leg and did not deem it proper to pick it up again and so walked off leaving it in the street. . . .' The next week she saw her neighbour 'wearing it as a tucker—the bold thing'.[1]

As skirts became fuller to balance the large sleeves, corsets grew tighter, despite all the protests from doctors and many other critics, including the new king, Charles X. 'Formerly it was not uncommon to see Dianas, Venuses or Niobes in France; but now we see nothing but wasps,' he said.

'The limbs should be free beneath the garments covering them; nothing should interfere with their action, nothing should fit too closely to the body; there should be no ligatures,' declared Rousseau, but Frenchwomen laughed at him and added steel busks to their expensive stays, even though the famous Dr Pelleton warned that busks 'attracted electricity to the chest, and might occasion internal irritation in that region'.

Corsets were padded at the back to make a small bustle and the fashion became as extreme in England as in France, spreading to all classes. To quote Dr Cunnington again: at the end of the 1820s a tradesman described in a letter what happened when his daughter ventured to stoop down in her new corsets. 'Her stays gave way with a tremendous explosion and she fell to the ground. I thought she had snapped in two.'

One advertiser of corsets advised a mother 'to make her daughter lie face down on the floor in order that she might then place a foot in the small of the back to obtain the necessary purchase on the laces.'[2]

In France, with the revolution of 1830 and the accession of Louis Philippe, fashion did not change a great deal. It remained elegant

[1] C. Willett Cunnington, *The Perfect Lady*, Max Parrish, 1948.
[2] James Laver, *A Concise History of Costume*, Thames & Hudson, 1969.

and attractive, with its fuller skirts, natural waistline, modified leg-of-mutton sleeves, long, fur-lined cloaks and large, rather flat hats, which gradually gave way to poke bonnets.

If French fashions tempted Englishwomen, English tailoring attracted Frenchmen, for it had remained unsurpassed since the days when Beau Brummell had helped to establish it as the finest in Europe.

The Dandies of the Regency were all growing elderly by now but a new generation had arisen during the 1830s who were still taking immense pains with their appearance. Men's coats were darker and black was becoming usual for professional and businessmen, but they still blossomed forth in cloth coats of green, blue or brown for social and sporting occasions. Coats were shapely and elegant and of two main types: one, worn out of doors and for riding, was close-buttoned, with high, wide revers and a long, full skirt. Later in the century this coat developed into the conventional morning coat. The other had a long tail but was cut away in front to reveal a wide expanse of fancy waistcoat and high neckcloth. This, within a few generations, was the accepted style for men's evening dress.

Breeches had almost disappeared, though occasionally old men wore black breeches with a high-buttoning tail coat and top hat, and countrymen and farmers still wore them on Sundays. However, men of fashion wore trousers which were lighter in colour than the coat and tight enough to display their neat waists and shapely curves. They were made of all manner of materials and colours; checks, shepherd's plaids and Scottish tweeds were popular for a while, but mainly they were of fine English cloth or cashmere.

Waistcoats were of a third colour and cut very short, giving a high-waisted effect which emphasized the length of the leg. It was the last chance for a long time that men had of displaying their legs, for a generation later these were regarded as objects which should, as far as possible, be ignored, and certainly never emphasized in any way. Nevertheless, the fashion for coat, waistcoat and trousers to be of three different materials and colours lasted well into the 1870s. It was permissible for waistcoats to be very odd indeed, occasionally even being made of sealskin.

The tall hat was almost universal and taller and shinier than ever, and winter overcoats were thigh-length, waisted and high-buttoning, with wide revers.

Hair was worn rather long, with curls in the nape of the neck, and it was sometimes brushed forward at the sides to curl over the ears. Moustaches were coming in and the first side-whiskers appearing.

Count D'Orsay, who was living in London during the first half of the nineteenth century, was known as the 'grand master of the dandies'. He was 'one of the padded men who wear the stays', but Disraeli, as a young man, was equally famous for his colourful clothes. Early in the 1830s he appeared at a dinner party wearing a coat of black velvet, poppy-coloured trousers embroidered with gold, a scarlet waistcoat and a profusion of rings worn over white kid gloves; and for his maiden speech in the House of Commons he wore a bottle-green coat, a white waistcoat and an enormous black cravat.

There was no regulation black evening dress for men as yet, but they would wear tail-coats, waistcoats and trousers in a startling assortment of contrasting colours as, for example, an olive-green coat with a floral waistcoat and jade-green trousers, or a bright blue coat with violet trousers. Nevertheless, Disraeli was still able to cause a stir when he appeared in green velvet trousers and a canary-yellow waistcoat, with lace ruffles on his shirt and silver-buckled shoes.

In 1834 Jane and Thomas Carlyle came from Scotland to live in Chelsea and one of their visitors in the early days was the elegant Count D'Orsay. He arrived in a blue and silver coach, with prancing horses and attendant flunkeys, wearing, according to Jane, a 'skye-blue cravat . . . with white French gloves, light drab surcoat, lined with velvet of the same colour, invisible inexpressibles, skin-coloured and fitting like a glove.' He also sported 'two glorious breast-pins attached by a chain and length enough of gold watch-guard to have hanged himself in'.

Very soon after their arrival in Chelsea, Jane and Thomas also saw King William and Queen Adelaide, who were paying a visit to Chelsea Hospital. The Queen had not, after all, made herself very popular in England, though she was well-meaning and kindly. At the time that Jane and Thomas saw her she was extremely nervous, convinced that a revolution was about to break out in England at any minute. 'Poor Queen, after all!' wrote Jane. 'She looked so frost-bitten and anxious! curtsied, with such cowering hurriedness, to the veriest rabble that was ever seen. I was wae to look at her. . . .' King William, being more democratic than his queen, was better liked. 'Poor old fellow,' said Carlyle. 'He looked fresh and decent; clear as from spring water.'

He had not much longer. In 1837 he became very ill and Queen Adelaide watched devotedly by his bedside to the end. Very early on that same June morning the eighteen-year-old Princess Victoria was roused from sleep to be told that her Uncle William was dead and that she was now Queen of England.

CHAPTER TWELVE

CRINOLINE

Even at eighteen, with all the freshness of youth, Queen Victoria was no beauty. Despite her clear pink and white complexion, she was short and already rather plump, with prominent pale blue eyes, a receding chin and slightly protruding teeth.

Within a month of her accession she had moved from Kensington Palace to Buckingham Palace, making it clear that she was now for ever free from maternal domination. Yet she was not as ruthless with her mother as has so often been suggested, and the Duchess was given rooms at Buckingham Palace, even though they were a long way from the royal apartments. One of the reasons for the Duchess of Kent's close guardianship of her daughter was a real fear that she might be assassinated or poisoned, for there had been a strong rumour in Court circles that the Princess Charlotte had been poisoned, and years later an old woman dying in an almshouse wrote to Queen Victoria saying that her mother, who had been a servant to Princess Charlotte, knew that poison had been put in her 'brew' before she died.

Englishwomen's dress when Queen Victoria came to the throne was relatively simple and very charming. Women were increasingly warmly clad and skirts, after being ankle-length in the early 1830s, were down to the ground again and full. Sleeves were long, sometimes full above the elbow, sometimes below, but invariably confined at the wrist by a neat cuff. Bodices were long-waisted and close-fitting, daytime dresses often finished with a neat, flat collar. Evening dresses were cut low on the shoulders, with short puffed sleeves, and heart-shaped necklines were very popular.

Silk stockings were very delicate, but usually worn over a pair of flesh-coloured cashmere stockings. Shoes were low-heeled with square toes, and black satin was usual for the evening. Materials included velvet, silk, satin, crêpe and poplin, with gauze and organdie for young girls' evening dresses in the ever-popular white, as well as pink, blue, parma violet and yellow.

Hair was dressed rather low, often parted in the middle, with ringlets falling on the cheeks.

Nearly every woman wore the poke bonnet as well as a shawl. In summer the shawl might be of the flimsiest material—even lace—but something of the kind had to be worn when out of doors, in order to be properly dressed. In winter-time it was more often than not the Paisley shawl, for the factory at Paisley was now producing shawls copied from the expensive products of Kashmir, and the Queen herself lent some of her valuable originals to the Paisley designers for them to reproduce.

For those who rode, cloth riding-habits had voluminous skirts and masculine jackets. The poor, of course, wore the cheapest material obtainable. This was usually cotton, both summer and winter, for wool was too expensive.

For the first few months of her reign the Queen was in mourning for King William, but when the mourning was over she emerged into a spell of gaiety and pretty dresses, bonnets and shawls, many of which came from Paris, which was still regarded as the centre of women's fashion, even though the court of Louis Philippe was so dull and uninspired. Louis Philippe, the Citizen King, was no dresser and aroused the scorn of the French nobility by appearing with an umbrella, the symbol of middle-class mediocrity, for it implied that the user had no carriage. Both Queen Marie Amélie and the King's sister, Madame Adelaide, were middle-aged and dowdy, the worthy Princesses were thrifty and simple in their tastes, and the Princes had married German princesses who were more interested in intellectual pursuits than clothes. The young Queen Victoria was therefore regarded as the leader of Royal fashion in Europe, but although she liked clothes and had a great many, she did not have a constructive attitude to fashion. Her dresses were beautifully made but all too often were very similar, giving the impression that she was wearing the same dress over and over again. She found fittings tedious and sometimes had several dresses made at the same time, to a stock pattern, quite content that the fashion should remain unchanged.

Only two years after her accession she was married to Prince Albert, wearing a beautiful white satin wedding dress on which the Honiton lace trimming alone cost £1,000. After the first few troublesome months, when the Prince complained that 'the difficulty of filling my place with proper dignity is that I am only the husband

and not the master of the house', the marriage settled down to great happiness.

Although the Prince was an essentially cultured man, the centres of fashion and culture in England during the late 1830s and throughout the 1840s were to be found not so much at the Court as in the London mansions, such as Lady Blessington's Gore House, in Holland House and Devonshire House, and in the great country seats where the English aristocracy tended to spend an increasing amount of their time when Parliament was not in session, such as Belvoir Castle, Chatsworth, Hatfield, Panshanger, Knole and Ashridge, all of which were maintained in almost regal splendour on the accumulated wealth of the eighteenth century, and staffed with anything from a hundred to a hundred and fifty servants.

During the year of the Queen's accession, a twelve-year-old boy, Charles Worth, arrived in London by coach from his native Lincolnshire to be apprenticed to Swan and Edgar and learn the drapery trade. For the next eight years he lived amongst silks and muslins, merinos, poplins and velvets, bonnets and shawls. He had all the artist's perception for line and colour and was fascinated by women's clothes. Having practically no money, for apprentices were paid little or nothing, one of his greatest pleasures was to study the paintings in the National Gallery and the other national collections. He gloried in the elaborate costumes of the Renaissance queens and princesses, the Stuart beauties and the great ladies of the eighteenth century and was puzzled and depressed by the garb of the Victorian women he saw, day after day, in their eternal bonnets and shawls. Fashion both in England and France seemed to be unchanging. Changes were, in fact, taking place, but they were almost imperceptible. Skirts were growing wider, fuller and heavier. They were worn over at least two white cambric or long cloth petticoats and two of flannel, and then came a petticoat made of a stiff material woven from horse-hair, called crinoline. This was sometimes reinforced with lines of solid cord piped into the material, which helped to keep the skirt extended. Bustles stuffed with horsehair were fixed at the back and the sides of the waist. The corset was longer, extending from the top of the bust to the abdomen, and more tightly laced than ever, causing an untold number of internal injuries. Over the corset went a camisole and under it a chemise, while drawers reached below the knees.

In 1843 Queen Victoria and Prince Albert paid a state visit to the French Court. As they embarked for the crossing in the royal yacht, the *Illustrated London News* reported that 'the Queen was dressed in a claret-coloured silk dress, over which she wore a Paisley shawl worked with green; she had a straw bonnet with green feathers and ribands'. On her arrival at Dieppe she appeared in a purple satin dress and bonnet trimmed with yellow feathers, and that night at dinner at the Chateau d'Eu, she wore crimson silk. The Press, both in London and Paris, applauded the Queen's appearance as being the height of elegance.

Queen Marie Amélie and Madame Adelaide were just as brightly clad, appearing in black and purple stripes, yellow shawls, cloaks of green, lilac and crimson, with bonnets decked with flowers, feathers and streamers of gaily coloured ribbons, on all of which the *Illustrated London News* dutifully reported that 'the dress of the ladies showed a most exquisite distinction'.

Eighteen forty-three was also the year that Tom Hood published his *Song of the Shirt* in the Christmas number of *Punch*, a passionate plea for the conditions of work of the sempstresses who made all this finery.

> With fingers weary and worn,
>   With eyelids heavy and red,
> A Woman sat, in unwomanly rags,
>   Plying her needle and thread—
>   Stitch! stitch! stitch!
> In poverty, hunger and dirt,
>   And still with a voice of dolorous pitch
> She sang the "Song of the Shirt!"
>
>   Work! work! work!
> While the cock is crowing aloof!
>   And work-work-work,
> Till the stars shine through the roof!
> It's O! to be a slave
>   Along with the barbarous Turk,
> Where woman has never a soul to save,
>   If this be Christian work!

The poem carried two cartoons—'Needle Money' and 'Pin Money', showing a thin and lonely sempstress, stitching an elaborate piece of Victorian clothing by candlelight in a squalid attic, and by contrast a young woman seated at her flounced dressing-table, choosing the jewellery she would wear for the evening, while a lady's maid dresses her hair.

The conditions of the linen drapers' apprentices like young Worth were bad enough, but those of the dressmakers infinitely worse, for the dresses with their flounces and linings, their tucks and frills, involved endless stitching which was still done by hand. In 1843 there were fifteen thousand dressmakers working at their employers' places of business in London and Westminster, in conditions which all too often produced tuberculosis, various internal complaints and serious eye trouble. The girls were apprenticed at fourteen for two or three years, after which they became improvers for another one or two years and finally journeywomen, when they received a small wage. If they lived in, they had to pay a premium of £30 to £60 and were lodged by their employers. Otherwise they paid no premium but had to provide their own board and lodging.

In the best establishments the hours of work were half-past eight in the morning till eleven o'clock at night in the winter and eight in the morning till midnight or later in the summer, but one girl is recorded to have worked twenty hours a day for three months on end.

The girls usually had ten minutes off for breakfast, fifteen to twenty minutes for dinner and fifteen for tea, and if the establishment were generous enough to provide supper, this was taken in the workroom. The girls never stood the strain for long. Those who did not marry or find other work soon broke down and the system was maintained only by a constant supply of fresh young girls from the country.

It was not until 1850 that Singer patented his first sewing-machine in America and it gradually came into general use. It was not the first machine to be invented, but the first that was practical and popular, and with it came the beginning of ready-made clothing and clothing factories, though here again ready-made and partly ready-made clothes had already made their appearance in some stores.

As early as 1830 a New Bond Street store was advertising 'Muslin Bodices exceedingly useful for the country trade. The dresses can be completed for wearing in a few hours' notice': and within the next ten or fifteen years other stores offered ready-made cloaks and skirts, which had been designed and stitched in their own workrooms. Elias Moses and Son were probably the first ready-made clothing business when they opened their shop in New Oxford Street in the 1850s, and Swan and Edgar followed, with ready-made skirts, though bodices were made to measure.

But back in the 1840s, Charles Worth had no thought for this kind of mass production. He wanted to design beautiful clothes for elegant and beautiful women and had a growing desire to go to Paris. To the penniless young salesman it seemed at times nothing more than an impossible dream, but at last some rich relations of his mother rather grudgingly provided the fare, and in 1845 he left Swan and Edgar and crossed to France to seek his fortune. He was twenty. He had no introductions and could not speak a word of French; and when he arrived in the charming old lamplit Paris of Louis Philippe he had just five pounds in his pocket and his worldly possessions consisted of a small trunk of clothes.

There was as much poverty and destitution in Paris as in London and a great deal of unemployment, but Worth had courage and a beguiling charm of manner, an exhilarating enthusiasm and a sound knowledge of his trade. After weeks of bitter disappointment, during which he faced near starvation and desperation, he obtained work in a small draper's shop, La Ville de Paris. Here he arrived early each morning to sweep the floor and dust the shelves, before changing into his smart black jacket to serve customers until eight o'clock at night. The pay was poor and he lived frugally, spending his few leisure hours studying French, which he could soon speak fluently, and learning all he could about fabrics and fashion.

Within a year or two he found work in one of the most fashionable Paris fashion shops, Gagelin and Opigez, in the rue de Richelieu. They were famous for their materials, particularly hand-woven silks, and they sold cashmere shawls and a little ready-made clothing, mainly cloaks and mantles.

Worth was now in the heart of Paris fashion, for in the same street were the King's tailor, Mme Delatour, the Queen's dressmaker and the establishment of the Court jeweller. The dressmakers were all women, the most fashionable being Delatour, Camille, from whom Queen Victoria ordered many of her clothes and accessories, Palmyra, Vignart, Debaisieux and Roger, all of them producing variations of the same type of dress, made laboriously with the cheap hand labour of the girls and women who arrived each morning in their workrooms. Worth found the Paris fashions rather dull. Only the very rich and the wealthy courtesans went to the couturier dressmakers; other women of fashion still used their own private dressmakers. There were no large shop window displays from which to gain inspiration, although there were several fashion magazines by this time. Throughout the 1840s they had little new to report. This has been described as the most static decade in fashion during the whole of the nineteenth century and there was no one in Paris to compare with Marie Antoinette's Rose Bertin or the Empress Josephine's Leroy.

Worth was disappointed. Even the exclusive Gagelin and Opigez were producing the same mantle and cloak they had been making for years, as an alternative to the eternal shawl, and Worth found them as tedious as the everlasting bonnets. Materials were beautiful and trimmings attractive, but women seemed to shrink into their clothes instead of displaying them with style and grace.

In 1848 came a violent change. There was revolution in France, brought about by the Bonapartists, and after several days of terrible street-fighting and bloodshed in Paris, Louis Philippe and his family were forced to flee the country. The Second Republic was declared and Louis Napoleon, Napoleon's nephew, was elected President.

For the next three unsettled years in France trade declined, the fashion business being one of the first to suffer. Hundreds of people were thrown out of work and the rest were afraid to spend their money, least of all on clothes. Gagelin and Opigez weathered the storm, however, and Worth, through his unfailing taste and knowledge of his business, rose to a position of importance in the firm. In 1851 he married the beautiful Marie Varnet, a colleague who had begun in the business as a *demoiselle de magasin*. It was an ideally happy marriage. Marie continued to work in the shop and she inspired Worth to make sketches of dresses which he thought would suit her.

By this time trade was beginning to improve and Louis Napoleon's position in France growing stronger each month. This was the year of the Great Exhibition in Hyde Park, to which many French exhibits were sent and in which Louis Napoleon was intensely interested.

Every kind of criticism had been hurled at the Prince Consort and Paxton's glass palace as the plans for the Exhibition developed. Extremists in the Church thought the idea was arrogant and would be damned by the wrath of Heaven. Doctors foretold an outbreak of plague and said that the arrival of hordes of foreign visitors in London would mean the spread of venereal disease. *The Times*, which disapproved of the site, reported months before the Exhibition opened that aliens were leasing houses nearby which were to be used as brothels.

Prince Albert listened to it all and went ahead with his plans un-daunted, so that on 1 May 1851 Queen Victoria walked happily into the Crystal Palace beside the Prince, with their two eldest children, the Princess Royal and the Prince of Wales, for the opening ceremony.

For the occasion the Queen wore a dress of pink watered silk, embroidered with silver and diamonds, and a bejewelled, sparkling, feathered headdress.

The Exhibition was an unqualified success and when it closed nearly six months later the Royal Commissioners were able to announce a profit of £186,000, which was used for the establishment of the South Kensington museums.

The days of the cage crinoline had not yet arrived, but skirts were fuller than during the 1840s and made heavier with tiers of flounces, of fringe or gathered lace. The bodice was sometimes opened to the waist to reveal a white underbodice. Sleeves were wide and three-quarter length, with a long undersleeve gathered in at the wrist. Shawls were still worn but small jackets were fashionable, cut in at the waist and flaring out over the hips. The poke bonnet was con-siderably smaller and the peak had slipped back, to make a horizontal line across the top of the head.

There was a magnificent display of English silks at the Exhibition. Keith, the firm of Spitalfields silk weavers, exhibited 'rich tissues, brocades, diaphanes and every variety of silks required for up-holstery', and Samuel Courtauld's company showed 'specimens of crape and aerophane', while Swan and Edgar exhibited 'gros de Naples, Ducape, gros de tour, glace, satin, barrathea, Balmoral, paraphanton, watered silk, velvet, armozine, gros royal, radzimore, Berlin, Orleans, vest satin and antique watered silk'.

Plush, brocade, bombazeen, moiré, taffeta, tabinet, lutestring, poplin, sarsenet, gossamer and gauze were all on display. There was fine lace from Honiton and exquisite needlework, quilting and embroidery, some of which was displayed by Heal's.

Among the articles of clothing were bonnets of crape, horsehair and straw, boots and bootees, stays of silk and rubber, gloves of fine kid from Woodstock, of cashmere and velvet from Yeovil, mittens, muffs, comforters, boas, capes, tippets and shawls.

For men there were silk hats by the hundred as well as a com-prehensive range of headgear for every contingency, from smoking caps to 'railroad' caps, which acted as crash helmets and were intended to remove any danger of concussion if involved in a railway accident.

Victorian prudery was at its most rigid by now. Not only were male legs less obvious than they had been in the days of the Dandies, but women were not supposed to possess them at all, nor in fact any part of the human anatomy between the neck and the feet. A fashion adviser of this time informed ladies that 'check materials are not worn by ladies, being entirely given up to the nether integuments of the sterner sex'.

Dr Willett Cunnington, in his book *The Art of English Costume*, makes the interesting point that: 'The Victorian prudery, once well established, served as a kind of regulator by which a constant but safe emotional pressure could be maintained; its practical value in the general improvement of behaviour has not received the credit it deserved now that we no longer, we think, require this ingenious refinement of sex-appeal.'

At the close of 1851 Louis Napoleon staged a *coup d'État* and by the end of 1852 he was proclaimed Emperor Napoleon III. The Second Republic had come to an end and now began the glittering days of the French Second Empire, which were to last until 1870.

Elsewhere in Europe there may have been misgivings, but in the fashion world of Paris, where the memory of the glories of the First Empire still lingered, there was excitement at the prospect of a new Court. The Tuileries was restored and refurnished and plans were announced for a more modern and glorious France and the rebuilding of much of the picturesque seventeenth-century Paris on the lines of the new London.

The Emperor was forty-four, a fine figure of a man, with a neat pointed beard and wide moustaches. His uniforms were immaculately cut, he was spruce and alert and gave an impression of immense energy and power, enhanced by his sense of the dramatic and his love of pomp and display. His appearance had a rapid effect on men's fashions and women, too, began looking to their appearance, casting aside the plain, cheap dresses they had worn during the lean years of the Second Republic.

Worth knew that his day was coming. He had some of the dresses he had designed for Marie made up in the workrooms and she wore them when she was serving customers. They were soon admiring them and inquiring who had made them, and before long Worth's employers allowed him to design dresses for their customers. He prepared muslin models and they were able to choose from among the vast stocks of materials available in the shop.

The next excitement in the Paris fashion world was the news of the Emperor's forthcoming marriage to the beautiful twenty-six-year-old Eugénie Montijo. It was a very quick courtship. He had met her while she and her mother were on holiday in France from their native Spain, and the wedding took place at the end of January 1853, only a fortnight after the Emperor's proposal. It left little time for the preparation of the trousseau of fifty-four dresses. Worth had no hand in them, although the couturières came to him for their materials, and the dresses were made so quickly that they were on public display before the wedding. Worth found them all too elaborate for his taste and, indeed, they came in for a good deal of criticism from other members of the fashion business.

The trousseau included a scarlet velvet dress covered with the Napoleonic symbols of eagles and bees embroidered in gold thread; a pink watered silk with a basque bodice, trimmed with fringe, lace and curling white feathers; a green silk with feather-trimmed flounces; a mauve silk trimmed with Brussels lace and at least three identical afternoon dresses, in white, pink and blue. There was no new line and no inspiration. The dresses were beautifully made, of exquisite materials, but in the final analysis their style suggested no fresh fashion development.

For the ceremony at Notre-Dame, Eugénie wore a dress of white velvet, with a long train, the bodice embroidered with diamonds and sapphires and trimmed with orange blossom. The skirt was draped with 'point d'Angleterre' to match the veil, and on her lovely reddish-gold hair rested the coronet of sapphires and diamonds which Josephine had worn for her coronation.

It was the policy of Napoleon III to establish a Court as magnificent as that of Louis XIV, and the beautiful new Empress, with her flair for clothes, quickly became the natural leader of fashion in Paris and throughout the whole of Europe. Everything she wore was noted, described in the fashion papers and the Press and, as far as possible, copied by other women, particularly Parisiennes.

There was quickly a demand for fine clothes in Paris and Worth's employers allowed him to organize a large dressmaking department. He was not able to introduce any drastically new fashion yet, but his skirts grew ever wider and his cloaks more voluminous. When he thought of a new variation of this style, he persuaded Marie to wear it first, to arouse the interest of the customers, and thus introduced to the trade the first idea of models, who were to be called mannequins.

Worth's dresses were very expensive, but those who could afford them considered the money well spent and he began to make a name for himself.

In 1855, despite the Crimean War which had broken out the year before, came the Paris Exhibition, on the lines of the Hyde Park Exhibition four years earlier. It was even wider in scope, designed to advertise the glories of the new Imperial régime. Amongst the pictures in the Palais de Beaux Arts appeared Winterhalter's picture of Eugénie with her matrons of honour, and although she was not to meet Worth until 1860, the dress she is wearing in the picture, a filmy white gauze over white silk, with blue ribbons to match her eyes, was in fact made by Worth, probably having been ordered by one of her ladies-in-waiting.

Worth made many mantles and dresses for Gagelin and Opigez to exhibit on their stands at the Exhibition and his new bonnets soon became the rage both in Paris and London. They were very small, for he was determined to see the end of them before long, and were worn far back on the head, daringly displaying the nape of the neck, which some people thought positively indecent at first, but they were very fetching affairs of silk, straw, ribbons and feathers.

Worth now organized showrooms where foreign buyers could see his models and, with the use of the new sewing-machines, copies of Paris dresses were soon on sale in cities all over Europe.

Another famous name was now established amongst the Paris fashion houses. During a visit of Eugénie and Napoleon III to Queen Victoria and Prince Albert, in 1854, the Queen had recommended her tailor, Charles Creed, to the Empress, and she was so pleased with his work that she persuaded him to open a branch in Paris.

The following year, when Victoria and Albert paid a visit to the Paris Exhibition, Victoria's clothes were considered hopelessly old-fashioned, her bonnets too large, her shoes too flat and her dresses too short, but Victoria was too happy to mind. The Paris of the Second Empire, of Waldteufel, Offenbach and Strauss, of balls at the Tuileries and nights at the Opera, where more and more women were wearing Worth's luxurious dresses, was gayer and more alluring than it had ever been, but Victoria and Albert had discovered Deeside and 1855 was the year that they moved into the newly built Balmoral Castle.

They had first fallen in love with the Highlands in 1848, enchanted by the simplicity of the crofters, their 'but and ben' crofts, their box beds, peat fires and cruises, and the old women in their tartan shawls, who still wore the 'mutch', a high white muslin cap, fastened under the chin, and went to church each Sunday with a Bible wrapped in a clean white handkerchief.

The Queen also took a long lease of Abergeldie Castle, some two miles from Balmoral, and throughout the 1850s this was the summer residence of the Duchess of Kent. Every August she gave a birthday ball to the servants and tenants of the estate. 'On these occasions the Duchess always wore white, and, though at the time she must have been approaching seventy, it was still becoming to her,' wrote Patricia Lindsay. 'On her head was always a cap of lace and ribbons, a genuine cap of the old-fashioned type. . . . At these dances we girls and the younger ladies in attendance on the Duchess always wore silk or satin tartan scarves, fixed on the shoulder, Highland fashion, over our white or black dresses.'

In the world of fashion, skirts were still growing wider each season, held out by an ever-increasing number of starched petticoats, horsehair underskirts and pads. Who first introduced the cage which came to be known as the crinoline is not quite certain, but most of the evidence points to Worth himself. The story goes that the cage was invented by an Englishman who took it to Worth, and Worth promised to launch it. It first appeared in 1856, being described as 'a skeleton petticoat made of steel springs fastened with tape'. The crinoline was made of metal or whalebone hoops held together by curved ribs, and over it the skirt hung in a smooth bell-shape.

Eighteen fifty-six was also the year of a simple but interesting English country wedding, when Samuel Beeton married Isabella at Epsom. The bride wore a white silk dress, each flounce of which had been embroidered by a different sister. Two small bridesmaids attended her, wearing white muslin, and six older bridesmaids, three in pale green silk and three in pale mauve.

In 1852 Samuel Beeton had published the first magazine which catered especially for women's interests, the *Englishwomen's Domestic Magazine*, which cost twopence and offered articles on household management, recipes, the toilette, dressmaking, gardening, household pets, literary criticism and fiction and Bella wrote cookery and fashion notes for the magazine. In 1859 her great book of Household Management began to appear, in twenty-four monthly parts costing

167

threepence each, and in 1861 the complete volume was published, with a quotation from Milton on the title page which epitomized the Victorian ideal of womanhood:

> For nothing lovelier can be found
> In woman, than to study household good.

In 1860 Sam and Bella visited Paris and arranged for the hand-coloured fashion engravings which had been so popular in France for some years to be introduced in the *Englishwoman's Domestic Magazine*, replacing their black and white engravings. At the same time, they arranged for the import of paper patterns for the French fashion plates they showed.

'The full-sized paper patterns, tacked together and trimmed, may be had by enclosing 42 stamps' ran the advertisement, and a member of the staff who handled this service was Mr Weldon, who was ultimately to found his own fashion papers and pattern service.

Worth had made a fortune for Gagelin and Opigez by the late 1850s, but not a great deal of money for himself, and in 1858 he left the firm and went into partnership with a young Swede, Otto Bobergh. They took rooms in the rue de la Paix, the Worths also having living quarters there. They engaged a staff of twenty, announced themselves in the Paris trade directory and waited for customers. Business was slow at first. Customers who had followed Worth from Gagelin and Opigez expected him to make cheaply for them, now that he was in business on his own, and this he had no intention of doing.

The crinoline was still high fashion. Inevitably it had been ridiculed when it first appeared, but very soon it was being worn by every woman in Europe with any pretension to elegance. The Empress Eugénie delighted in it and it was worn by day as well as for evening. The great advantage of the cage was that it relieved women from the burden of so many petticoats and, compared with the immense weight they had been carrying, it seemed extremely comfortable and light.

Nevertheless, it was an extraordinary fashion to be introduced in the early years of the railway age. It was even worn in the factories and cotton mills and by servants while they were scrubbing and cleaning. In 1864 Jane Carlyle was away from home for a few days while the house in Chelsea was redecorated, and she wrote anxiously to Thomas: 'When the rooms are done, pray charge the maids not to rub on the clean paper with their abominable large crinolines.'

Another disadvantage of the cage, according to the moralists if not to the wearers, was that the least pressure caused the skirts to sway provocatively from side to side, thereby revealing the ankles, which for so long had been hidden, but the only result of that was the introduction of neat little ankle-boots. The theory that crinolines made women unapproachable was certainly not borne out in practice and manufacturers claimed that their crinolines would 'bear a good squeeze without getting out of order'.

In 1862, an inquisitive small girl of twelve, who was to become the novelist 'Gyp', was taken to Longchamps by her uncle. She disliked the crinoline and though she thought the Empress superbly beautiful she considered her blue dress was ugly. Neither did she have much opinion of her white bonnet, 'from the back of which fell an enormous cascade of fair curls reaching to the waist and covering her back completely. Her sunshade, green as usual, was trimmed with fringe'.

While the women watched the races, Gyp watched the women. As a race began 'all the women jumped on their chairs,' she wrote. 'There was an ocean of cages balanced just above me, showing legs which seemed to me to be short and heavy. . . . When the race was nearing a finish all the women suddenly leaned forward, and the pressure of the cages against the backs of the chairs made them shoot up behind like a lot of fans. And then I could see everyone's underwear right up to the waist, and found that now I had plenty of variety before me. Some of the interiors were frothy, a foam of lace and muslin, some were cold and severe, others had a casual air or were frankly ludicrous. The weather was extremely hot, and most of the women had not put on a *petit jupon*, that is to say a skirt between their knickers and the cage, and I noticed to my surprise a thing I had not seen before, small ends of material which hung down here and there.' She asked her uncle what they were and as he turned his binoculars from the race to the women, he replied, casually but knowledgeably, 'chemises'.

It was astonishing how agile women were in their crinolines, even to undertaking alpine climbing, but there were sometimes disasters, one of the saddest stories being that of the elegant Duchess of Manchester, who caught her hoops while climbing over a stile and landed upside down, displaying for all to see a pair of scarlet knickers. 'C' etait diabolique,' said the Duc de Malakoff.

In London it was not long before the crinoline, hopelessly inconvenient in narrow city streets, was worn at ankle-length, to reveal a simple underskirt and the now universal ankle-boots. Alternatively women took to a device known as the 'cage americain', by which the crinoline could be pulled up when necessary, by a system of interior laces.

In Paris life was gay and extravagant and during the late 1850s the seaside resorts of Dieppe, Trouville and Biarritz became very fashionable. For seaside holidays, women wore the costliest and most unsuitable clothes imaginable. 'Ladies walked by the sea splendidly attired in silk gowns, brocaded, or shot with gold or silver. One would have imagined one's self present at a ball at the Tuileries, or some ministerial reception, rather than at a seaside place of resort,' wrote Augustin Challamel in his *History of Fashion in France*. 'On fine days ladies wore satin spring-side boots, with or without patent leather tops, but invariably black; blue and chestnut-brown boots being no longer in fashion. In the heat of summer, however, grey boots were admissible. High heels were worn, and have since that time become higher still, until one wonders how women will at last contrive to keep their balance.'

By 1860 Napoleon III had become the most important man in Europe. The Crimean war had come to an end in 1856 and although at the time a Frenchman aptly remarked that 'there was no indication as to which was the victor and which the vanquished', Napoleon assumed the role of a conquering hero. His son, the Prince Imperial, was four years old and bid fair to be as handsome and dashing as his father. With the Empress Eugénie leading the way, fashionable Parisiennes were gay, obsessed with fashion and wildly extravagant.

For the middle classes there were as many temptations as for the rich, for the Bon Marché and the Magasins du Louvre had both been opened, where women could wander round at will, choosing at leisure from among the cheap, attractive ready-made clothes for sale.

A year or two after Worth had moved to the rue de la Paix, he and Marie caught a glimpse of the plain but supremely elegant Princess de Metternich, wife of the Austrian ambassador, driving to the Tuileries for an important reception. It was for women like this that Worth wanted to make clothes and a few days later Marie, summoning all her courage, called on the Princess, taking with her an album of Worth's dress designs, and asked her if she would consent to becoming one of his clients. The Princess liked the designs and agreed to allow Worth to make two dresses for her, one an evening dress which she promised to wear at the next official ball at the Tuileries. Hundreds of people were invited to these balls, many of them on the outermost fringe of society, who were asked in order to court their support for the régime and who came mainly to stare at the Royal family and their entourage, with their magnificent clothes and jewels.

Compared with the over-elaborate dresses which most Parisiennes were wearing at this time, the dress which Worth made for the Princess was refreshingly and elegantly simple, of white tulle and silver lamé, trimmed with marguerites.

The Empress noticed it at once, inquired who had made it and asked the Princess to arrange for Worth to call on her at the Tuileries the following morning. From that moment Worth's fortune was made, and he always remained deeply grateful to the Princess for the opportunity she had given him.

The Empress ordered some clothes from Worth and was so pleased with his work that she was soon ordering a great many more and recommending him to her ladies-in-waiting. Within months he became the most fashionable dressmaker in Paris and fortune and fame came to the firm of Worth and Bobergh. Worth had been in Paris for fifteen years and now, in the year 1860, though he was still only thirty-five, he became the dictator of fashion to the ladies of the French Empire.

He and Bobergh extended their premises, took on more staff and furnished their showrooms like resplendent drawing-rooms. Worth attended the Empress at the Tuileries, but all his other clients, however highborn, were expected to come to the showrooms for consultations and fittings.

In March 1861 the Duchess of Kent died and the following December the Prince Consort. Perhaps no woman in history has conveyed so vividly and poignantly as Queen Victoria the happiness of her marriage and the desolation of her widowhood.

Of the Prince, who had come in for a great deal of unjustified adverse criticism during his lifetime, Dr Norman Macleod said, very wisely, at the time of his death: 'The next generation will know and appreciate the Prince better than the present one ever did or can do.'

The Queen went into deep mourning for the remaining forty years of her life and for the next twenty-five years she lived in seclusion, seldom showing herself to the people.

After 1861 the influence of the Court on the arts and fashion disappeared entirely, although the Queen never spared herself in her attention to her manifold State duties, and when she partially emerged from her seclusion during the 1880s, to show herself to her people, they gave her a heart-warming welcome and her popularity was greater than it had ever been.

However, during the 1860s, with the British Court in deep mourning, the world of fashion inevitably turned to Paris. Within a year or two Marlborough House, where the Prince of Wales held court with his beautiful Danish bride, Princess Alexandra, was gay enough, but Alexandra was distressingly deaf, and although she always dressed beautifully she had not the personality to become a leader of fashion.

In Paris the dressmakers and tailors grew rich, and none more than Worth and Bobergh, though Bobergh kept in the background and it was Worth who interviewed the rich clients, decreeing what they should wear and never failing to please them, for his taste was impeccable.

At this time he began to grow tired of the crinoline. He had intended it for only a season or two, and then women refused to give it up. The Princess disliked it as much as he did, but when Worth suggested to his clients that it was growing old-fashioned they held firm. Throughout the 1860s the question was discussed anxiously in the fashion papers, but those in favour of keeping it seemed to win the day with the argument that 'as women now walk so badly in their high heels, crinolines are necessary, and must be retained, because they sustain the weight of the skirts'.

Worth designed a shortened crinoline for walking and outdoor activities, which the Princess agreed to wear. Not long afterwards, the Empress, the Princess de Metternich and two other ladies of the Court were to be seen skating on the lake in the Bois de Boulogne.

As they glided smoothly in a row, they held out before them in their eight neatly gloved hands a rod covered in velvet. They were wearing extremely short crinolines, so short that they barely covered their knees, and billowed up high in the breeze. Beneath were wide velvet knickers, fastened under the knee. Their legs were gaitered, and their flashing, silver skates were strapped on to high-heeled pointed boots. They wore short jackets, drawn in tightly at the waist and trimmed with sable and chinchilla; and small velvet toques were perched on the front of their heads.'[1]

[1] Edith Saunders, *The Age of Worth*, Longmans, 1954.

The Empress held her position as the most beautiful and fashionable woman in Europe. Mrs Moulton, a wealthy young American, described her at a ball at the Tuileries, when the Prince and Princess of Wales were present. The Empress, she said, outshone everyone. 'She wore a white tulle dress trimmed with red velvet bows and gold fringe; her crown of diamonds and pearls and her necklace were magnificent.'

Yet Eugénie was not happy. Napoleon was an unfaithful husband and only two years after the marriage the Archduke Maximilian of Austria had remarked that 'the Emperor's assiduity with all the pretty women is unpleasantly conspicuous'. In 1860 her sister had died and in private Eugénie dressed in mourning for a time and then very simply. The glitter and superficiality of the Court wearied her, though she still wore her magnificent Worth ball gowns and evening dresses for important public occasions.

By the middle 1860s, during the American Civil War, she was preoccupied with the fatal Mexican campaign, which was launched, with the backing of French troops, to establish the Archduke Maximilian as a Catholic Emperor of Mexico.

At first things went well and there were celebrations in Paris which meant more work and prosperity for the couturiers. The rue de la Paix had become the most fashionable street in Europe.

Worth had a wonderful collection of materials in his showrooms, all of them made in France, and the Lyons silk industry revived and flourished during these years. The number of looms in operation more than doubled and the fortunes of the Spitalfield weavers in London began their steady decline, until by the beginning of the twentieth century only a few elderly Flemish weavers were left, making silk cloth for neckties and Jewish praying shawls on their complicated hand-looms, though they could still remember the days when thousands of yards of valuable velvet and silk were being sent all over the world from Spitalfields and there were five hundred master weavers living in Spital Square.

Life in Paris seemed gayer and more frivolous than ever and the question of the crinoline more important than the obvious decline in the Emperor's health, the changing face of Europe and the plans of Bismarck.

The Boulevard Haussman was completed, the Magasins des Printemps had opened and Paris was now lit by gas. Worth had more than a thousand employees and had opened several new showrooms. He had built himself a sumptuous Gothic villa on a small estate in the suburbs of Paris and drove to the rue de la Paix in an impressive carriage.

In 1866 Prussia launched a quick seven-week war against Austria, in order to gain control of northern Germany. As a precaution French troops were recalled from Mexico, leaving Maximilian in grave danger. A few months later the Empress Charlotte arrived in Paris to beg help for her husband, but Napoleon, unwilling, and perhaps by now incapable, of realizing the true situation out there, did nothing. Charlotte, only twenty-six, overwrought and terrified for her husband, went suddenly and incurably insane.

The parties went on. An invitation from the Emperor and Empress to spend a week at Compiègne involved the purchase of twenty new dresses, including seven ball gowns, for guests were not expected to appear in the same dress twice.

In 1867 came the second Paris Exhibition, to display the new Paris to the world, with all its attractions, including its superb dressmaking industry, for which Worth had been largely responsible. The Empress wore his clothes and nearly all the queens and princesses of Europe became his customers.

In the midst of the Exhibition festivities came the news that Maximilian had been defeated and captured and in Paris there was an attempt on the life of the Czar as he was returning from Longchamps. A few weeks later Maximilian was tried and shot and the festivities of that brilliant summer of 1867 ended abruptly, as the Court went into mourning.

Paris was never to be the same again. Worth's new, severer fashions seemed to precede the new mood of France. In 1868 he designed a crinoline with the fullness all at the back, ending in a short train and giving the female form the shape of a truncated centaur, and by the following year the Empress was appearing in his entirely new dress, which was straight and narrow and suited her admirably. It was the end of the crinoline, after a reign of nearly fifteen years.

In the following year the Empress ordered a large collection from Worth for her trip to Egypt for the opening ceremonies of the Suez canal. For the occasion Ismail Pasha plunged himself more deeply than ever into debt by building Ismailia, with its hotels and palaces to accommodate the vast concourse of European monarchs and Eastern potentates who assembled for the ceremonial procession along the hundred-mile canal and the four days of balls, banquets and receptions which followed.

But back in Paris the people were growing hostile to the Court, with all its extravagance and ostentation. Bismarck's intentions were becoming all too clear, moreover. In 1870, war broke out between France and Prussia. Napoleon III was a sick man, but he left Paris with his army, taking the young Prince Imperial with him. Just six weeks later, in September 1870, half the French army, including Napoleon himself, were forced to surrender to the Prussians. Two days later, the disillusioned French declared the Third Republic. The Second Empire had collapsed and the Empress Eugénie, with a single lady-in-waiting, had to flee from a back door of the Tuileries, while an angry mob surged round the gates at the front of the palace. Eventually they reached the residence of the Empress's American dentist, who accompanied them to exile in England.

The Prussians pressed on to Paris and the city was besieged. For the next five months the people of Paris endured the most appalling privations. Worth's palatial showrooms became hospital wards and all normal life came to a standstill. At last starvation forced the people of Paris to surrender and their gracious new city was occupied by the Prussians.

By the terms of the peace treaty, France had to relinquish Alsace and Lorraine and, as a final indignity, on 18 July 1871, William I, King of Prussia, was proclaimed Emperor William I of the German Empire in Louis XIV's palace at Versailles.

In England, Eugénie was living at Chislehurst and here Napoleon III and the Prince Imperial joined her, but in 1873 Napoleon died and only six years later the Prince Imperial, who had joined the English campaign of 1879 in Zululand, was killed by Zulu assegais. He had been the last hope of the Bonapartists, planning for a revival of the Empire. With his death, the Third Republic was firmly established. The Empress Eugénie lived on in England for many years, dying in Spain, in 1920, at the age of ninety-four.

In 1902, by which time the Empress was in her mid-seventies, Lady Airlie, a granddaughter of the Lady Cowper who had been one of the famous 'lady patronesses' of Almack's, happened to be in the neighbourhood and was invited to call on her.

'When I arrived at the house I was arrested at the sight of Winterhalter's famous painting of the Empress, and her ladies which was hanging in the hall facing me,' wrote Lady Airlie. 'The Empress's superb beauty, outshining even the galaxy around her, took my breath away. It little prepared me for what I was to see.

'I was conducted to a small door under the staircase, and shown into a conservatory. Behind a magnificent tea table, with fine silver, sat an old woman. There were still traces of the great beauty she had once possessed in the delicately chiselled nose and the slightly slanting eyes, but her skin was wrinkled and uncared for, her figure heavy and shapeless. What most struck me was the way in which the Empress had let herself go—like any old French peasant woman. She wore an old black gown, a dingy woollen mantelet trimmed with a little black jet, and a shabby big black garden hat. Her bushy eyebrows had become white, like her hair, and her sole concession to the past was to blacken them—but only half the arc. Her voice, like many Spanish women's, was rough.

'There were some other English guests at tea, but when the Empress told—in English—an impossibly indelicate story about two swans they were so shocked that they rose hastily and took their leave. She then turned to me and we talked in French. She gave me the impression of being easily bored, and I was not sorry when the entourage came in and we all went for a walk in the garden.

'I felt dismissed, and falling behind suggested to the Dame de Compagnie that I should go. I asked her whether I ought to kiss the Empress's hand, and was told that she liked it and always took leave in the room containing the Emperor's portrait. Sometimes she stood beneath it.

'I waited alone in a rather untidy room until the Empress came in, leaning on her stick, for she was a little lame. She looked more majestic than before, but did not station herself beneath the portrait as I kissed her hand.

'As I left I glanced at that dazzling Winterhalter picture. I could hardly believe that I had seen the same woman.'[1]

[1] *Thatched with Gold: The Memoirs of Mabell, Countess of Airlie*, London, 1963.

CHAPTER THIRTEEN

INTO THE TWENTIETH CENTURY

In Paris during the 1870s life gradually settled down under the new régime, with Adolphe Thiers and then Marshal MacMahon as President. A new privileged class arose in the Presidential circles who were wealthy and became the leaders of fashion, and Worth, though heartbroken at the fall of the Empire and always sad when he passed the burnt-out shell of the Tuileries, was soon busy designing clothes for a new generation of clients, for although there were by now many distinguished and successful rivals in the business, his prestige as the world's supreme fashion dictator was unimpaired. And by this time Worth's two sons, Jean and Gaston, were growing up and taking their place in the business, Jean as a designer and Gaston as the man of business.

It was in 1871 that an English journalist, writing for *Blackwood's Magazine*, called on Worth to discuss his theory that the design of women's dress bore a close psychological relationship to war or the threat of war and also to the character of the wearer, but Worth was completely at sea. Such thoughts had never entered his head and he was extremely dubious of the erudite theories put forward by the young journalist, a further proof that critics often read into an artist's creations motives and designs of which he was not even faintly aware while he was at work. Nevertheless, with hindsight, it is obvious that there was a good deal to be said for the writer's point of view. All he gained from his interview with Worth was facts and figures about women's spending habits on dress. Frenchwomen were habitually thrifty and Englishwomen did not, generally speaking, spend lavishly, while Germans seemed hardly interested at all in clothes. Worth's most valuable customers at this time were Russians and Americans, some of whom were spending up to £4,000 a year in his salons.

Otto Bobergh retired from the firm, with a fortune, after the Franco-Prussian war, but Worth, utterly absorbed in the business of fashion, continued. Yet although Frenchwomen were soon as interested as they had ever been in dress and the house of Worth continued to dress most of the Courts of Europe, the fashion world was never the same for him after the end of the Empire. His most valuable customers were usually visitors or birds of passage and the personal touch was gone, for he was seldom able to see his dresses being worn at the functions for which they had been designed. He was growing old and his health was failing, but he went on working, though he never betrayed his loyalty to the old régime.

The straight dress which Worth had designed for the Empress during the last years of her reign did not become universally worn, but as the crinoline disappeared, the fullness at the back of the skirt was caught up in a horse-hair bustle. The Paris Exhibition of 1878 marked no startling new fashion, except an even larger bustle, which gave women what must surely have been the oddest shape they had ever adopted since fashion began.

In England, after the Prince Consort's death, colours remained subdued for a few years after the usual mourning period, in deference to the Queen's long-continued mourning, but late in the 1860s came the discovery of chemical dyes and suddenly bright colours became the rage. Although pastel colours in silk or velvet were much admired for evening dresses, except yellow, which was considered at this time as unladylike as orange, for day wear colours were brilliant. The first aniline dyes to be marketed were reds and blues, producing brilliant purple and the magenta and solferino blue which became so popular after Napoleon III had won the battles of Magenta and Solferino, during the brief war with Austria in the 1860s.

In 1889 there was another Exhibition in Paris, its most lasting feature being the Eiffel Tower. In the dresses shown by Worth he finally dispensed with the bustle, and though complaining that all the elegance had now gone from women's clothes, he showed some dresses which were as attractive as any he had ever designed.

Six years later he died suddenly, after only two days' illness, having remained almost to the last at the work he loved so much.

Jean and Gaston Worth continued the business and in 1900 opened their London branch in Grosvenor Street. Gaston, more acutely aware of the changing world and all its implications in regard to dress than the romantic Jean, was anxious to break away from the

Second Empire traditions of tiaras and trains, so dear to Jean, and engaged the brilliant Paul Poiret as an additional designer, to make the more practical clothes which women were now wearing, but his clever, plain clothes were a constant source of irritation to Jean.

Gaston was right. Many of the Courts of Europe, which for so long had been arbiters of fashion, were about to disappear or undergo a change as radical as the altered functions of the surviving crowned sovereigns.

In Paris, after the rising of the Commune in March 1871, following the capture of Napoleon III, the flight of Eugénie and the departure of Bismarck, powder trains were laid in the Tuileries and the rooms were daubed with liquid tar and turpentine. As the trains were fired and the Palace collapsed in flames, the commander of this operation sent a message to the Hôtel de Ville: 'The last vestiges of Royalty have just disappeared.'

The end of the Tuileries was symbolic, for never since has a European queen led her Court and country in fashion in the way that the Empress Eugénie had.

Queen Victoria died in January 1901, by which time the peak of Britain's imperial power had already been reached. For the coronation of Edward VII and Queen Alexandra the Worth brothers received many important orders from the English nobility for Court trains and robes, and for weeks beforehand their rooms were filled with yards of magnificent hand-woven crimson velvet and ermine skins. Jean was in his element but Paul Poiret was astonished and dismayed at the solemnity with which these ancient appurtenances of power and sovereignty were regarded. To him, a republican of the twentieth century, they seemed utterly incongruous, and he and Jean became so entirely out of sympathy that, despite Gaston's high regard for his work, Paul Poiret resigned from the firm and set up in business on his own.

Jean was no great admirer of Queen Alexandra's style of dress, however, and when as a young man of twenty-three he saw her at a ball during the Paris Exhibition of 1878, he said that her gown 'was laboriously elaborate, with a great flounce of lace on the skirt and a court train. She looked for all the world like a maid decked out in her mistress's cast-off finery on her afternoon off'.

Those were hard words, for she was a beautiful woman, tall and graceful, and looked magnificent in Court dress, but there is no doubt that her daytime clothes were often over-elaborate. Cecil Beaton, in his *The Glass of Fashion*, says:

Queen Alexandra probably started the modern tradition that British royalty can wear anything. During her husband King Edward's reign she would wear spangled or jewelled and bead-embroidered coats in the daytime, an innovation which has now become an accepted royal habit. Or she might wear half-length jackets covered with purple or mauve sequins and garnished with a Toby frill collar of tulle. These were clothes which most women would have worn at night, but the fact that she wore them during the day removed her from reality and only helped to increase the aura of distance that one associates with the court.

The Edwardian Court was gay and brilliant, but women's fashions were influenced by styles seen on the stage or in fashion magazines as much as by those worn at Court by the Queen.

In spite of the death of Edward VII in 1910 and the accession of George V and Queen Mary, there was little change in the social scene until 1914.

Queen Mary adopted very early in her life an individual style of dress which bore no close relation to the fashions promoted by the English and French couture houses for the women of society, and by the time she came to the throne royalty was no longer the arbiter of fashion in any democratic country. Nevertheless, she established a tradition of wearing clothes which could be easily distinguished in a crowd and which looked well from a distance, and for this reason invariably wore pastel colours and a toque, which enabled people to have a clear view of her face.

Like the Empress Eugénie, her clothes for the day were first put on a dressmaker's dummy, made to her exact measurements, so that she and her dressers could decide which jewellery and accessories should be worn with them.

For the last forty years of her life, Queen Mary wore the same style of beaded evening dress and tailored coat and skirt, with strapped, flat-heeled, long-toed shoes, a rolled parasol and a toque.

Lady Airlie, her lady-in-waiting, says in her book *Thatched with Gold*, that Queen Mary's style of dressing was dictated by the King. 'She never even wore a colour which the King did not like. Her style of dressing was dictated by his conservative prejudices; she was much more interested in fashion than most people imagined, and sometimes I think longed in secret to get away from the hats and dresses which were always associated with her.'

As a result of the First World War the great empires of Imperial Germany, Austria-Hungary and Russia, which had dominated Europe, all collapsed and their Court life ended. The ancient Turkish empire also disintegrated.

During the half-century since these social and political revolutions, the Royal Courts of Spain, Italy, Rumania, Bulgaria and Greece have also all vanished.

Gaston Worth died in 1922 and Jean in 1926, but Gaston's sons and later his grandsons continued the business, maintaining the firm's impeccable standards of couture. Throughout the 1920s dozens more dress designers, both in London and Paris, entered the couture field, designing dresses for royalty and the Courts, and for the wealthy of all classes.

Since the end of the Second World War, the role of the couturiers has become even more influential, for today, besides designing for the few remaining Courts, the wealthy women of the aristocracy, the business and commercial worlds and the higher-paid professions, they design for the vast, modern wholesale clothing industry, which caters for the female population of the entire world.

It is they who are the dictators of that mysterious, illogical and elusive thing called Fashion—and fashion will always be with us, for as Colley Cibber said nearly three hundred years ago, 'one has as good be out of the world as out of fashion'.

BOOKS CONSULTED

ADBURGHAM, ALISON   *Shops and Shopping, 1800–1914.* Allen & Unwin, 1964.

— *View of Fashion.* Allen & Unwin, 1966.

BEATON, CECIL   *The Glass of Fashion.* Weidenfeld & Nicholson, 1954.

BROOKE, IRIS   *English Costume of the Seventeenth Century.* A. & C. Black, 1934.

BROOKE, IRIS, and LAVER, JAMES   *English Costume of the Eighteenth Century.* A. & C. Black, 1964.

— *English Costume of the Nineteenth Century.* A. & C. Black, 1964.

BURNEY, FANNY   *Early Diaries—1768–1778.* George Bell & Sons, 1907.

CHALLAMEL, J. B. M. AUGUSTIN   *History of Fashion in France.* Sampson Low, 1882.

COLE, HUBERT   *First Gentleman of the Bedchamber.* Heinemann, 1965.

CONNELL, NEVILLE   *Anne, the Last Stuart Monarch.* Thornton Butterworth, 1937.

CREEVEY, THOMAS   *The Creevey Papers, 1793–1838.* Batsford, 1963.

CUNNINGTON, C. W.   *The Art of English Costume.* Collins, 1948.

— *The Perfect Lady.* Max Parrish, 1948.

DUTTON, R. *English Court Life from Henry VII to George II.* Batsford, 1963.

ELAND, G. (ED.)   *Purefoy Letters—1735 to 1753.* Sidgwick & Jackson, 1931.

ERLANGER, PHILIPPE   *The Age of Courts and Kings.* Weidenfeld & Nicholson, 1967.

FIENNES, CELIA   *Through England on a Side-Saddle in the Time of William and Mary.* Simpkin Marshall, 1888.

GERNSHEIM, ALISON   *Fashion and Reality.* Faber, 1963.

HARTNELL, NORMAN   *Silver and Gold.* Evans Bros., 1955.

HOLME, THEA   *The Carlyles at Home.* O.U.P., 1965.

HERVEY, LORD (ED. ROMNEY SEDGWICK)   *Lord Hervey's Memoirs.* Batsford, 1952.

JOLSON, ANNETTE   *Heirs to the Throne.* Heinemann, 1966.

KELLY, F. M., and SCHWABE, R.   *Historic Costume: Fashion in Western Europe, 1490–1790.* Batsford, 1925.

LAMAR, VIRGINIA A. *English Dress in the Age of Shakespeare.* Folger Shakespeare Library, Amherst College, Washington, 1958.

LAVER, JAMES *A Concise History of Costume.* Thames & Hudson, 1969.

LESLIE, SHANE *Mrs. Fitzherbert.* Burns & Oates, 1939.

LINDSAY, PATRICIA *Recollections of a Royal Parish.* John Murray, 1902.

MARGETSON, STELLA *Leisure and Pleasure in the Nineteenth Century.* Cassell, 1969.

MARPLES, MORRIS *Six Royal Sisters.* Michael Joseph, 1969.

MELVILLE, LOUIS *The First George in Hanover and England.* Pitman & Son, 1908.

MITFORD, NANCY *The Sun King.* Hamish Hamilton, 1966.

MOSSIKER, FRANCES *Napoleon and Josephine: The Biography of a Marriage.* Gollancz, 1965.

PARRY, E. A. *The Overbury Mystery.* Fisher Unwin, 1925.

PEPYS, SAMUEL *Diary.*

REICH, EMIL *Women Through the Ages.* Methuen, 1908.

ROBIDA, ALBERT *'Yesteryear': Ten Centuries of Toilette.* Sampson Low, 1892.

SAUNDERS, EDITH *The Age of Worth.* Longmans, 1954.

STUBBES, PHILIP *The Anatomie of Abuses.* 1836.

THOMPSON, GRACE *The Patriot King, Life of William IV.* Hutchinson, 1932.

THOMSON, A. T. *Memoirs of Sarah, Duchess of Marlborough and of the Court of Anne.* Henry Colburn, 1839.

THOMSON, GLADYS SCOTT *The Russells in Bloomsbury, 1669–1771.* Jonathan Cape, 1940.

TOURS, HUGH *The Life and Letters of Emma Hamilton.* Victor Gollancz, 1965.

WALPOLE, HORACE (ED. MATTHEW HODGART) *Memoirs and Portraits.* Batsford, 1963.

WATERSON, N. M. *Mary II, Queen of England 1689–94.* Duke University Press, 1928.

WILLIAMS, CLARE (translator) *Sophie in London—1786* (Diary of Sophie v. La Roche). Jonathan Cape, 1933.

WRIGHT, THOMAS *England Under the House of Hanover.* Bentley, 1848.

INDEX